BEING BLACK, BEING MALE
ON CAMPUS

BEING BLACK, BEING MALE ON CAMPUS

Understanding and Confronting Black Male Collegiate Experiences

DERRICK R. BROOMS

Cover image from shutterstock

Published by State University of New York Press, Albany

© 2017 State University of New York

All rights reserved

Printed in the United States of America

For information, contact State University of New York Press, Albany, NY
www.sunypress.edu

Production, Diane Ganeles
Marketing, Anne M. Valentine

Library of Congress Cataloging-in-Publication Data

Names: Brooms, Derrick R., author.
Title: Being Black, being male on campus : understanding and confronting
  Black male collegiate experiences / by Derrick R. Brooms.
Description: Albany : State University of New York Press, [2017] | Includes
  bibliographical references and index.
Identifiers: LCCN 2016031488 (print) | LCCN 2016033936 (ebook) | ISBN
  9781438463995 (hardcover : alk. paper) | ISBN 9781438464008 (pbk. : alk.
  paper) | ISBN 9781438464015 (e-book)
Subjects: LCSH: African American male college students. | African American
  men—Education (Higher) | African American men—Social conditions. |
  African American men—Social life and customs.
Classification: LCC LC2781.B757 2017 (print) | LCC LC2781 (ebook) | DDC
  378.1/982996073—dc23
LC record available at https://lccn.loc.gov/2016031488

10 9 8 7 6 5 4 3 2 1

This Book Is Dedicated to the Memory of
Rufus Brooms Jr.
Beloved Father

Contents

ACKNOWLEDGMENTS   ix

PREFACE   xiii

CHAPTER 1
Introduction: Making Space to Hear Black Men   1

CHAPTER 2
College Aspirations, Expectations, and Concerns:
Thinking about and Preparing for College   25

CHAPTER 3
College as a Learning Experience: Transitioning to College
and College Life   55

CHAPTER 4
Being Black, Being Male on Campus: Experiencing the
College Environment   89

CHAPTER 5
Black Men Emerging: Experiencing Self in College and
Engaging Resiliency   119

CHAPTER 6
Brotherhood and Bonding: Shared Experiences in
Black Male Initiative Programs   149

Contents

CHAPTER 7
Black Men in College: (Re)Envisioning the Trajectory   181

APPENDIX   197

NOTES   203

REFERENCES   233

INDEX   249

Acknowledgments

First and foremost, I give thanks and praise to my grandmother, Ms. Vivian Covington. Thank you for teaching me how to believe, even in times when the path was not in sight and the valleys seemed too low to continue. Also, thank you for your steadfast example of prayer and service. Each of these has played a critical role in helping me get to this day . . . whole and intact . . . and with a righteous indignation to stay true to myself, always. There are so many reasons why I should not be here, or at least where I am, today. However, I know, without doubt, that the prayers you offered on my behalf and the belief you invested in me are part of my foundation. I am an embodiment of the possibilities that you saw and envisioned.

Second, I thank the men who shared with me during this research project. They trusted me with their experiences, and some of their life stories; they endured my inquiries and allowed me space to listen and learn with and from them. I truly believe in their possibilities and hope that they secure the educational and personal successes that they desire. I hope this work contributes to all of us better appreciating who we are and who we can be.

I cannot separate my yesterday from today. Thus, long before this book was ever conceived, I developed relationships and connected with people who helped me find my place and helped put me on a trajectory to contribute meaningfully. As iron sharpens iron, so one man sharpens another . . . I give a profound thanks to Joseph McCoy, a brother-friend-mentor, confidant, partner, teammate, and one of my success models . . . if I shine, we shine. . . .

In the course of developing the research that for this book, I was strengthened by a community that sustained me throughout the entire process. I benefitted greatly from scholarly and friendly help and support

from Bianca Baldridge and Earl Wright II. Earl, thank you for supporting
this idea from the very beginning and helping me to shape my ideas into
a book project. Bianca, a sincere thank you for reading multiple drafts,
asking critical questions throughout, and pushing me to help sharpen my
analyses. Thanks to Darryl Brice and Yoshiko Harden who both listened
to every idea I shared and encouraged me with each of our interactions.
Also, Darryl offered his critical eye, willingly read and reread chapters,
and provided thoughtful comments. Individually and collectively, your
willingness to listen, read, and offer feedback and critiques were invaluable. Additionally, at various stages of my budding intellectual curiosities
and development in my student and professional career, I was nurtured
and supported by Edgar G. Epps, Ayana Karanja, Daniel Black, Sandra
Taylor, Regina Dixon-Reeves, Mary Pattillo, Reuben May, and Andre
Phillips. Also, many thanks to Armon Perry, Siobhan Smith, Gwendolyn
Purifoye, Felix Kumah-Abiwu, and Joe Goodman who all provided support as well.

I believe in collectivity and acknowledge that this is not a solo
project. I was strengthened by the knowledge that my family, scholarly,
and personal communities wanted to see me complete this project. I give
thanks to my brothers: Mario, Andre, and Dee, my sister Reisha, and
my Brotherhood community: Arthur Davis, Reggie McClain, Matthew
Smith, and Matthew McCoy. I give gratitude to my scholar community:
Chezare Warren, Alford Young, Jr., Bryan Hotchkins, David Ikard, Billy
Jeffries, Marvin Lynn, Odis Johnson, James Moore III, Deadric Williams,
Linn Posey-Maddox, Lori Wiebold, Zandria Robinson, Sandra Barnes,
BarBara Scott, and Theresa Rajack-Talley. In addition, a larger com-
munity supported me on my path: Bob Green, Bannon Stroud, Tanya
Robinson, Kenneth Hutchinson, O. T. Mahone, Ana Vazquez, Eric
Smith, Leon Gordon, Stanley Muhammad, Bro. Dr. Corey Jordan, Rashad
Norris, David Ferguson, Juan Carlos Rivera, Eric Boria, Hank Rich, Kyle
French, Carol Ben-Davies, Adrienne Baytops Paul, Matt Wonzier, Nofi
Mojidi, Kyle Cepeda, James Snowden, Arlen Wiley, Michael Turner,
Booker Whitt, Nicaya Rapier, Lori Tanaka, Ben Potts, Donna Edwards,
Phillip Coleman, Broderick Hawkins, Curtis Miller, Poochie, Lee, and
Tommie Levinston. My Get UP community: Darion Blalock, Jamil
Boldian, Rayvaughn Hines, Marlon Marshall, Anthony Ponder, Byron
Caulton, Eric Charles, Anthony Hubbard, Cameron Barnes, Tyler Beck,
Dontaye Polk, Smith Francois, Robert Henderson, James Reed, and

Rafael Wordlaw. My coaches who helped me find my place at various points: Neal Bailey El, Greg Quick, Mike Orechia, Andrew Thomas, Mr. Bush, and Dick Maloney. And, a community of teachers as well: Dr. Adrian Beverly, Ms. Thomas, Ms. Bell, Ms. Pauline Lee, Ms. Jones, Ms. Williams, Ms. Nettles-Bey, Dr. Harold E. Whitfield, and Mr. Green.

A special thanks to many members of my professional communities at the Association of Black Sociologists, especially our Executive Committee, the Scholars Network on Black Masculinity, and the International Colloquium on Black Males in Education. In these spaces, I attended conferences and fellowshipped with many of the individuals named above; my engagement in events, gatherings, meetings, and annual conferences helped me stay on my path.

Thanks to an incredible group of students with whom I have formed community as well: Student community: Craig Alexander, Brandy Woods, Addison Jackson, Dwayne Morrow, Tamika Hill, Raven Nance, JB, MJ, Kenneth Manns, Daniel Cockrell, Nick McLeod, Jelisa Clark, Brandon McReynolds, Kent Pugh, Imani Beard, Trey Maddox, Cynthia Doyle, Bryson McGuire, Dominique Dishman, Kala Brown, Eric Jordan, Lisa Covington, Tele Kagaba, Dejon Day, Millan Abinader, Corey Farmer, Kirk Monroe, David Hall, Jared Coleman, Gabe Draper, Chad Caldwell, Galen Demus, and Augusta Hillman. And, several colleagues as well, specifically Robin Hognas, Ryan Schroeder, and Debbie Warnock. These communities have helped sustain, encourage, and support me in various ways. A collective thanks to you all. . . .

Thanks to family: Christine Brooms, Jerry and Helen Brooms, BJ and Eddie McCoy, Dedrick Brooms, Jermaine Brooms, Jeff, J. J., Jerome, Boonie, Andrease, Mike, DJ, Deanna, Ryan, Leslie, and Vincent. A sincere thanks to Helen Grain Faulk, Ann Richardson, Rufus Brooms, Sr., Wendy Fuller, Rebecca Edmond, and Wilma Bell; in addition, much gratitude to Jah Breeze, Camy Burrowes, Diane Thomas, Grandma Gummer, Aisha-Becker Burrowes, and Katilyn Thomas. To my Aunt Wilma, a profound thanks and gratitude for your othermothering; thank you for always standing by my side, encouraging my goals and aspirations, and providing holistic support and care.

I give thanks to Natasha Burrowes for your support, encouragement, and patience; thank you for your willingness to listen to a range of thoughts as they developed, helping me process ideas and analysis during data collection and analysis, and offering valuable insights as well.

Finally, to Rufus Brooms Jr., my father . . . I remain blessed in every opportunity to carry your name with me. And to Danielle, Camille, and Gabrielle, you continue to inspire and amaze me. The world will know your brilliance and gifts in the very near future; your time is on the horizon. Thank you for supporting me . . . even in ways that you do not know.

Preface

I am blessed and privileged to work with young men who continue to invite me into multiple facets of their lives—and their interiorities. You, beautiful, brilliant Black men, who are continuing to become who you are, bring a wealth of talents, skills, caring concerns, and ambitions with you into our educational spaces. Your trials and triumphs, missteps and best steps, and shortcomings and successes challenge us to do, be, and give more. I am writing this book for you, those men who have shared their stories with me here and others who have shared elsewhere. I am writing for men who have found their places on college campuses and carved out many of their dreams and goals. I am writing for those men who continue to persist—even unconventionally. I am writing for the next wave of students who will enter college seeking to build their own legacies. We desperately need you and we need to hear your voices so that we can learn from your experiences and (re)affirm commitments, intentions, and actions in supporting your efforts, advocating on your behalf, and harnessing your successes. And, finally, I am writing this book for those men who fell short of or had little to no opportunities to find their place in college.

reaching up
for Black young men
by D. Brooms

reaching up
for young Black men
not singing sin
or thinning gin
pressing freedom on pages
writing for that god w/in
this poem is for hearing hearts
and for seeing souls
watching elders die young while deferred dreams grow old
this poem is for young, gifted and Black
the real descriptions you match
overstand coded languages
and celebrate your Black
we breaking beats
like those abandoned houses
on our inner-city streets
let nobody turn you around
bring your angels down
use your voice-story as a weapon
let your trumpets sound
not being defined by their sign
their imposed scripted attempted invisibilities
can never dull your shine
see your beauty in body, soul and mind
this poem is for Black boys flyin'
breathing life into these lines
wanting to Malcolm your possibilities
you are the fire this time . . .

holla if you hear me

CHAPTER 1

Introduction

Making Space to Hear Black Men

I had some teachers, I think everybody has that one teacher that tells them that they're not going to make it. Mines was different. My teacher was a professor; I'm not going to say that she don't like Black folks because that's too extreme. She had a bad experience with a Black male in her class before and that sorta put a wall up . . . She was a White teacher, she told me "You know Jordan, many African Americans don't pass my class."

—Jordan[1]

I'm still trying to fit in; I'm still trying to figure out what's my niche at the school so that I'll be the best at who I am.

—Byron

It's been a little back and forth. Like I said, I met some great people networking wise; I made some good connections regarding career wise—switching my major. But with me being in my fraternity and the stereotypes that they have there's been a little bump with that. I've really been trying to get my grades up and get my fraternity back active on campus. People have the stereotypes of fraternities but our fraternity has the highest GPA on campus across all the fraternities and sororities. It just astonishes me how people can place a label on someone without knowing them. That's more of an insulting thing and a baffling thing. So, it's a little back and forth.

—Bannon

> I thought I was going to be alone. I didn't think I was going to succeed; I just thought I was going to try [college] and see how it went. I didn't really expect to make it as far as I am now. I probably expected to live on campus all four years and I didn't expect to be part of any organizations or things like that.

—Donald

These are the words of Black[2] men about their time in college, from their concerns and expectations to their general and specific experiences on campus. The men were full-time college students who were involved in campus life and had experienced varying degrees of "success." In many ways, they are statistics; the retention and completion rates of Black men have been tracked closely for the past two decades and their success (and "lack" of it) has been fodder for ongoing conversations, debates, and discussions (e.g., see Cuyjet, 2006; Garibaldi, 2007; Harper, 2014; Wood & Palmer, 2015).[3] Predictably, Black male success in higher education—like all students—is about statistics, primarily tracked by retention and graduation data with the latter given much more weight within public and institutional discourse. To be sure, the men in this study do share graduating from college as a common goal. Yet, in many ways, how they envision their college experiences and successes, navigate college from the time of their initial enrollment, and make sense of their time on campus are critical to better understanding what the data reveal—and hide. Jordan, a fourth-year political science major, expressed conflictions about his college experiences. He was highly motivated to attend college but he was not accepted to the flagship university in his home state, which was his top choice while in high school. He had early difficulties in college because he wanted to go home; being in college was his first time away. He leaned on his spiritual beliefs in "trusting God" whenever he was faced with challenges. Jordan initially began school at a local community college, a decision he made so that he could be closer to his ailing aunt. He recounted his ability to balance the emotional and spiritual demands of his aunt's poor health with his college requirements as evidence of his potential. As he related his time on campus thus far, he focused on a particular in-class interaction with a White female professor that challenged his identity and academic ability. Without ever evaluating any of Jordan's work, or seeming to have the most basic insight into who he is, the professor essentialized his racial identity and clearly expressed a denigrated expectation because of his social identities.

Byron, a third-year business major, has seen his progression through his college years. He, too, attended a community college prior to his current four-year university. His decision to attend community college was twofold. First, school was not stressed in his family and he shared that no one in his home communicated to him the importance of school or a higher education degree. Also, he felt that his high school did not prepare him for college, so he did not have a strong foundation or belief in college success. His experiences at the community college highlighted the academic areas that he needed to strengthen, exposed him to a variety of fields, and helped him mature as both a student and person. Even though he has made great strides, Byron stresses the importance of belonging on campus; he shared that he is still trying to find his place in college "so that I'll be the best at who I am." He believes that finding his place, or establishing a sense of belonging, is the key to his self-actualization.

Bannon, a third-year student, is an applied engineering major and is highly involved on campus. He is a member of the Omega Psi Phi fraternity and is engaged in several African-American student organizations on campus as well, such as the Black Student Union and the National Association for the Advancement of Colored People. Bannon shared that he was a high school football player and chose his current university because he could continue his football participation; additionally, he cited family dynamics, costs, and proximity to home to be factors as well. He noted that his college experience has had both its high and low points. The people that he has met while in college along with the networking connections have contributed positively to his college career. The stereotyping and profiling he has experienced due to his fraternity affiliation, however, have dulled these positive experiences. Expressing surprise to the stereotyping of his fraternity, Bannon felt insulted that people would think lowly of his fraternal organization—even though they perform well academically. Thus, for Bannon, his sense of belonging has shifted based on the social spaces and contexts that he navigates, yielding both positive and negative outcomes.

Donald, a junior political science major and executive board member of his campus's Black Male Initiative program, approached entering college with ambivalence; he thought he would give it a try and see what results he could muster. He expressed concern about being alone or mattering in college and chose his current institution primarily because it was located in the same city as his home. He held no expectations of being involved on campus prior to arriving and did not envision himself making it to his third year. Like many students, he was unsure of his major and also unsure of his future plans regarding employment and career. Although he performed well in high school, he felt unprepared for college and had not given significant consideration to the college experience—or succeeding in college.

Confronting the Narrative

Much has been written about educating Black males across the K-20 pipeline. In fact, current research has noted once again that the under-achievement of Black men in education is directly correlated with their lack of inclusion within American society. Over and over, we are pro-mulgated with data and stories of Black male failures, the widening achievement gap, and what education scholar Pedro Noguera has identi-fied as "the trouble with Black boys."[4] En masse, Black men have been viewed in pathological ways within educational arenas and wider society. The stories told within public media often focus on their presumed defi-ciencies and the "trouble" that entraps their lives. Additionally, within educational contexts, Black males often are perceived and defined by those within the group who perform less well. The negative framing of Black males and constant focus on their punishment, expulsion, or engagement with the criminal justice system have led to a deficit rheto-ric that predominates views and discussions of the entire group. These sweeping judgments and primary focus on retention and graduation data mean that in many instances the actual experiences of Black males in educational settings often are unheard. In specifically examining their experiences in higher education, data from previous research left two fundamental questions: Where are the Black men and why are so few on our college campuses? By extension, a related question permeates: Does higher education matter to Black men? Without a more nuanced exploration into their experiences and their own perceptions, the men cited above would seem to reflect the status quo of the seemingly disin-terested, disengaged Black male that many education professionals and researchers have written off. Men such as Jordan, Byron, Bannon, and Donald, along with many of their peers, offer insights that complicate the generalities often offered about Black male collegians and confront the deficit framing of Black men. These men often critically reflect on their experiences, social identities, and college careers. Unfortunately, their efforts and thoughts—and how they make sense of their educational experiences—have been overlooked and overshadowed too often in wider discussions.

Studies on Black male educational experiences have often posed them as the problem. Conceptions of their presumed deficiencies and opposition to learning and education have been used often to justify their achievement indices. For instance, Signithia Fordham and John Ogbu (1986) suggested that due to past discriminatory practices and limited educational resources, some Black students develop an "oppositional" culture to academic achievement. These types of theorizations led to focusing on the presumed values and norms adopted by the students within their schooling experience, giving primacy to their behaviors and actions while less attention was paid to their own conceptions, narratives, and understandings of their experiences and neglected to investigate institutional cultures and structures. A focus on Black male behaviors and expressions have allowed for discussions of their "difference" in educational settings and within the research arena as well. In institutional settings, this difference often has meant that efforts needed to be taken to get Black males to behave "correctly" or act "right" as well as demonstrating the values and norms outlined by mainstream society.[5] Said differently, the primal focus has resulted in a rhetoric of how Black males ought to act in schools and across campuses and has not given enough attention to how Black males see and experience how institutions act upon them. Even as efforts focused on Black male success have increased in the past two decades, much more attention has been given to why Black male collegians do not achieve as opposed to examining reasons why *they* believe they are and can be successful, how they experience college, and their achievement efforts.

A second arena of inquiry that is ripe for investigation is examining their experiences in student-centered programming, such as Black Male Initiative programs. In response to the data and reports on Black male (under)achievement, institutions have bolstered their programming efforts to include initiatives to strategically target the Black male population. Institutions such as Jackson College (Men of Merit), Parkland College (Brothers United Network), and Prairie State College (Protégé) are just a few examples of the institutional work related to addressing earlier shortcomings at the community college level. Several colleges and universities have committed institutional space (via cultural or research centers), created initiatives, and established holistic programs to increase the retention and academic achievement of these students (for instance, Ohio State University created the Bell Resource Center and UCLA created the Black Male Institute). Additionally, student-led organizations have been created at multiple campuses including Arizona State University (African American Men of Arizona State University) and Rutgers University (Black Men's Collective); and collegiate chapters of 100 Black Men of America and the Student African American Brotherhood (200+ campuses) are national organizational models that focus on Black male success and peer support as well. Some stakeholders have created system-based models such as the University System of Georgia's African American Male Initiative (26 institutions) and the Arkansas African American Male Initiative (17 institutions) to name a few. Finally, some institutions have created conferences to convene stakeholders around the theme of Black male success such as the annual Black Male Summit hosted by the University of Akron. While these programs have been profiled and discussed—for instance, nine chapters of Michael Cuyjet's (2006) edited volume profile such programs—very few efforts have been reported on how Black males experience their time engaged in these programs. Thus, increasing Black male retention, graduation, and achievement requires that we examine their experiences in campus-based activities specifically designed to achieve these goals. Taken collectively, more work is needed that adds depth to the experiential realities of Black males on college campuses.[6]

This book explores how Black male college students manage and negotiate their college years, working to find their place on campus, experiencing the social milieu, engaging in Black male student-centered activities, and persisting toward graduation. The book addresses the following questions: How do Black men articulate and make meaning of their experiences in college? In terms of their identities, how do Black males experience their race and gender on campus? What strategies do they employ in order to persist toward graduation? And, finally, how does participating in a Black Male Initiative program matter in their college experience?

To understand their experiences and tease out the nuances of various campus spaces, I conducted in-depth interviews with 40 Black male students at two different institutions and complemented these interviews with participant observation in some of their student-centered programs. Thirty-seven of the men in this study participated in the Black Male Initiative program on their campus. I spent some time attending meetings, attending events on and off campus, collaborating with program coordinators, and assisting the men in some of their programming efforts. The first institution, Lincoln State University, is a rural, medium-sized, historically White institution[7]; among the 10,000 students on campus, White students account for just over 70 percent of the population while Black students account for about 15 percent of the students. The school is located in Jefferson, which has a population of just over 20,000 residents and can be considered a college town. The median age in the city is 23 as compared to the state median of 42. Within the city, Whites account for 87 percent of the population while Blacks (7%), Hispanics (3%), and Asians (1.5%) account for the other major racial groups. Lincoln State is a master's level granting institution. The second institution, Monroe State University, is a large, public, research-focused institution, located in a metropolitan urban city. White students account for about 85 percent while Blacks account for 7 percent of the more than 20,000 students in the school's population. Monroe State is located in a city of over 600,000 people. The median age in the city is 37, which reflects the median of the state (38). Whites and Blacks account for the overwhelming majority of city residents; Whites make up 70 percent of the population while Blacks are just over 20 percent. Hispanics and Asians make up a small percentage of the city population as they account for 4 and 2 percent, respectively. Lincoln State and Monroe State report strong trends in student retention; over the past decade, Lincoln State has retained about 80 percent of its students annually while Monroe State's retention is similar at about 77 percent. Additionally, Lincoln State has graduated about 60 percent of its students steadily over a 6-year period and Monroe State, in response to targeted efforts, has steadily increased its graduation rate, which now stands near 55 percent.

As both institutions revere their (increasing) racial and ethnic diversity on campus, celebrated through student programming and various cultural events, they also have made strategic plans to improve the experiences of their diverse populations. More specifically, the Black male student population is a group that both institutions have targeted for increased retention and graduation rates. In an effort to achieve these goals, both of the institutions have an active Black Male Initiative (BMI) program on campus. Lincoln State University's program, Mighty

Men Mentoring, is organized through the Student Affairs office. The program is not a registered student organization, which means that they do not receive funding through student government. Three staff members, all Black males during the years that I observed, coordinated the weekly meetings while Mighty Men members initiated and developed the majority of the program's events and activities. In the fall, Mighty Men hosts a welcome event for Black male students and during the spring the men are engaged in a program retreat that focuses on the men's health and well-being. They also conduct programing for Black History Month as well and collaborate with other organizations on campus when possible.

According to Monroe State University's recently developed Diversity Plan, several initiatives are included to focus on particular student groups, one of which is Black males. The Brothers & Scholars program, established within the past few years and coordinated by one Black male staff member, is charged with researching and implementing strategies to improve the retention and graduation of undergraduate Black males. In attempting to achieve its goals, Brothers & Scholars sponsors activities and events that directly address the needs of their Black male student population. Students are engaged in monthly meetings, social outings, community service, academic study tables, and various other activities as well. Both Mighty Men and Brothers & Scholars are academic and social cohesion programs that focus on peer group development while serving to help students transition to the university and support them throughout their collegiate careers. These efforts, both individually and collectively, are aimed at building a microcommunity for Black male students that provides an academic, social, and personal support network. I report my findings in the context of both campuses.

Most of Being Black, Being Male on Campus focuses on how the men narrate and make meaning from their college experiences. Although the campuses are distinct in their location and size, students from both universities characterize much of their on-campus experiences with race and gender similarly. The stories shared in this book examine their academic aspirations and early college experiences, the strategies they have employed to persevere academically and socially, and the beneficence they assign to engaging in a Black Male Initiative program.

Examining Black male collegiate experiences opens a broad canvas to investigate the intersections of race and gender and how they matter in higher education. The study attends to compounding and intersecting discrimination (Crenshaw, 1991; Feagin, 1992), racial microaggressions

(Harper, 2009; Solórzano, Ceja, & Yosso, 2000; Sue et al., 2007), and racial battle fatigue (Smith, Allen, & Danley, 2007; Smith, Hung, & Franklin, 2011) as prevalent issues that the men face on campus.[8] Additionally, the book also offers insight into how many of these Black male collegians have navigated college successfully to press forward toward graduation. While improving retention for Black males is a key issue for all educational stakeholders, what can we learn from Black males who continuously enroll in courses each semester, who earn enough credits to matriculate toward graduation, who continue to beat the odds, and sometimes surpass their own expectations? In *Being Black, Being Male on Campus*, I examine how Black men perceive, experience, and navigate the academic and social arenas on campus and how they engage resilience, social and cultural capital, and craft coping strategies to persevere in college. Additionally, a key collegiate experience articulated by the vast majority of the men was to fulfill their sense of belonging on campus. In order to better understand this, I probe their participation in their campus's Black Male Initiative Program. Given the need for engaging Black male students both academically and socially (Barker & Avery, 2012; Harper, 2012; Strayhorn, 2008a; Zell, 2011), helping students define and redefine their self-concepts (Harper, 2014; Dancy, 2012), and creating community in college (Brooms, 2016a; Harper & Kuykendall, 2012), investigating their experiences in BMI-type programs could offer important insight into ways to increase engagement, persistence, and degree completion for this student population. These stories and experiences of Black college men are important because they provide counter-narratives to Black male mediocrity and academic disengagement and/or disinterest (see Harper, 2009; Warde, 2008). Additionally, as a range of researchers attest, there is a critical need to address and increase Black men's access, retention, and persistence in higher education (Palmer et al., 2014; Williams, 2013; Wood & Palmer, 2015).

The main title of the book, *Being Black, Being Male on Campus*, speaks to four findings of the study. First, as college students on campus the place that Black males seek reflects how these students engage in a continuous search for belonging throughout their educational experiences. Many of the students reveal that their experiences have abounded in paradoxes; on the one hand, many students share that they did not feel prepared for college based on their secondary school experiences, yet many of these men still maintained high educational aspirations. Thus, how they fit and how their aspirations align with their place are not always harmonious. The men also discuss how they experience campus and the ways that they are perceived. These viewpoints and understandings matter in how the men make sense of their experiences. Additionally, they express high motivations to succeed academically with many preparing to attend graduate schools, they continue to build meaningful relationships among faculty, staff, and peers, and they desire to achieve regardless of their circumstances. The Black Male Initiative programs not only offer the students a unique space to counterbalance some of the hostility and discrimination they face on campus but it also offers them access to a support group where they are engaged personally, academically, socially, and professionally. Their hopes, aspirations, engagements, and successes seem to run against the current from the narratives that are shared often regarding Black men and education. *Being Black, Being Male on Campus* thus attends to how Black male collegians move from a status of limbo and highlights the strategies they developed and employed to persevere. Finally, the voices of the men in this study are viewed as a counter-narrative that aims to disrupt simplified variations of Black male underachievement and gives voice to how their racialized *and* gendered identities impact their collegiate experiences.

Talking *with* Black Men to Hear Their Voices and Experiences

One of the hallmarks of this study is centered on talking *with* Black men about their schooling and college-related experiences. In listening to Black men share their stories, experiences, and perspectives, we have a unique opportunity to *hear them through their own words*. All too often, the narratives and rhetoric about Black men do two things that require our immediate attention. First, the dominant discourse leaves them out of the conversation as contributors about their own experiences. For instance, sociologist Alford Young (2004, p. 209) asserted that the common practice of *talking at* Black men leads "to a societal misrecognition of who these people are, and what their capacities might be." In educational research, two studies are noteworthy. Education scholars have made similar points as well. For instance, in his research on 32 high-achieving Black male students, Shaun Harper (2009) commented that many of the students shared that it was the first time that anyone had discussed their academic experiences with them. Similarly, Tyrone Howard (2008), in his study of 55 Black male secondary school students, also noted that the students offered that they had not been engaged in serious conversations about their schooling experiences. A number of men in the current study echoed these sentiments by asserting that outside of a small number of people, who they developed relationships with through student affairs and engagement on campus, there were very few instances where people engaged them in conversations about their educational experiences. Second, the dominant discourse continues to marginalize Black men to the extent that it is pervasive and institutionalized. Education scholar Michael Cuyjet (1997) argued that one of the first things in need of addressing is to recognize "the broad acceptance and institutionalization of these negative perceptions of black men as threatening, unfriendly, and less intelligent than any other distinguishable segment of the American population" (p. 8). Almost as a direct response, Harper (2009) asserted the need for counter-narratives that problematize the ways that this student population is "niggered" by deficit rhetoric. Similarly, the title and use of counter-stories in Howard's (2008) study is just as scathing as he examines the experiences of Black male students and poignantly asks, "Who really cares?"

Thus, the need for Black men to tell their own stories, and reflect on their own experiences, is critical for all educational stakeholders including the Black male students themselves. Education scholar James Earl Davis (1999) contended that the voices of Black males on college campuses often are not heard, misunderstood, or simply ignored. Without talking *with* Black males, there is no way to appreciate their situated standpoints and understandings and, in effect, we continue to silence and diminish the cultural wealth and cultural knowledge that they bring with them. As we endeavor to build community on campus—and other education-based spaces—it is imperative that we no longer relegate Black men to the sidelines. Black men have a wealth of gifts and talents to offer us, which ultimately will benefit us all. Their ways of knowing and their ways of being can be explicated only by inviting them into conversations, discussions, and decisions. In addition, we must intentionally provide space to hear what they want to share along with some of the things that we need to hear. Providing space for both helps to build community. Additionally, as Black men are given more space to share their experiences, we create space for critical self-reflection and opportunities to tap into their cultural wealth and knowledge. As a result, our communities (and new communities) can be enhanced through their voices, experiences, and sharing.

I echo the sentiments of Black feminist scholar Audre Lorde, and amplify her rejoinder in the case of Black men, in acknowledging that if we do not allow Black men to define themselves for themselves then they will [continue to] be crushed by other people's fantasies as their images, abilities, possibilities, and bodies are eaten alive.[9] Thus, our educational, scholarly, and practice efforts must be humanizing for all students and especially for Black males. I join a throng of educators, researchers, and practitioners who call for (re)enhancing, (re)imagining, and (re)engaging Black males in education. These points also align with the sentiments expressed by Baldridge, Hill, and Davis (2011, p. 133), as they noted:

> Through their stories, we are better able to understand the complex social, cultural, and economic forces that obstruct their pathways to educational success. Such insights not only serve as powerful rejoinders to the current post-racial discourse, but also prompt us to locate innovative solutions to the current educational crisis of Black males.[10]

Without doubt, the stories of Black men are powerful tools to help us see through different lenses, hear with heightened sensibilities, and, hopefully, (re)commit us to effecting change for their betterment. Centering their voices is at the heart of the analysis presented in this book.

Understanding Black Male College Experiences

Three theoretical concepts are central to understanding how Black male students think about their identities and college experiences: Critical Race Theory, Blackmaleness, and sense of belonging. Each of these concepts helps to understand and confront being Black and male on campus.

Critical Race Theory

Dating back to the groundbreaking work of preeminent scholar and Black sociologist W. E. B. DuBois (1903/2005), who sought to uplift the voices and experiences of Blacks in the United States, Critical Race Theory (CRT) is useful to undergird and theoretically frame research on Communities of Color. In his critically important works, critical race theorist Derrick Bell (1987, 1992, 1996, 2004) theorized the role of race and racism in the U.S. society. Bell argued that racism is a permanent, indestructible component within society and for those who "bear the burdens of racial subordination, any truth—no matter how dire—is uplifting."[11] According to Richard Delgado, CRT evolved out of legal studies during the 1980s as a movement that sought to account for the persistent role of race and racism in the United States. Initially, CRT scholars critiqued the ongoing societal racism in Black and White binary terms.[12] Bell, along with other Critical Race Scholars, advanced the framework to examine a full realm of communities to include Black Americans, Asian Americans, Pacific Islanders, Chicanas/os, and Latinas/os and their experiences with racism and various forms of oppression along with their responses and resistances (Yosso, Smith, Ceja, & Solórzano, 2009, p. 662).

Although originally used in legal studies, CRT extends from and draws on a broad literature base in law, sociology, history, ethnic studies, and women's studies. Scholars extended the tenets of CRT to investigate race and racism in education (Delgado Bernal, 2002; Harper, 2009; Ladson-Billings, 1995; Solórzano & Villalpando, 1998; Solórzano et al., 2000). Solórzano and colleagues (2000) were some of the early scholars to use CRT to analyze campus racial climate. Situating their work along other scholars, they contended that CRT was critical in offering "insights, perspectives, methods, and pedagogies that guide our efforts to identify, analyze and transform the structural and cultural aspects of education that maintain subordinate and dominant racial positions in and out of the classroom" (p. 63). In general, scholars also identified five elements shared by CRT scholarship that can be useful in educational research. These elements have been used by a number of scholars in the past two decades to unravel the racialized experiences of Blacks, Chicanas/os, Latinas/os, and other Students of Color at both the secondary and postsecondary levels. The tenets of critical race theory are: (1) the centrality of race and racism; (2) the challenge to dominant ideology (and the status quo); (3) a commitment to social justice; (4) the centrality of experiential knowledge; and (5) an interdisciplinary perspective.[13] Solórzano and colleagues (2000) distinguish the CRT framework for education from other CRT frameworks by noting its simultaneous foregrounding of race and racism in the research as well as challenging the traditional separation of race, gender, and class by showing how these social constructs intersect to impact on communities of color. Additionally, CRT offers a liberating and transformative method for examining racial, gender, and class discrimination by clearly articulating how Communities of Color are racialized, gendered, and classed. The knowledge and methodology are both multidisciplinary, spanning from legal studies and history to women's studies, sociology, and ethnic studies, which creates a platform for better understanding the various forms of discrimination and oppression. According to critical race scholars, these tenets present a "unique approach to existing modes of scholarship in higher education because they explicitly focus on how the social construct of race shapes university structures, practices, and discourses from the perspectives of those injured by and fighting against institutional racism."[14]

Most importantly, as mentioned above, CRT intentionally provides space for those who are marginalized, oppressed, and problematized to have their voices heard through counter-stories and counter-narratives (Aguirre, 2010; Delgado, 1989; Harper, 2009; Solórzano & Yosso, 2001; Solórzano & Yosso, 2002). Solórzano and Yosso (2002) identify counter-narratives as a critical tool for stories from people who are often marginalized in literature (and wider society) and as a means to examine, critique, and counter master narratives composed about People of Color. Master narratives are dominant accounts that often are generally accepted as universal truths about particular groups (i.e., Black males don't care about education)—these scripts, while readily available and easily consumable, caricature these groups in negative ways. Similarly, Aguirre (2010) also asserts the importance of counter-narratives to give voice to People of Color. The lived experiences of People of Color challenge the dominant social reality, revealing their agency and the importance of self-reflexivity. CRT is critical to expose how People of Color are minoritzied by silences and distorts their experiences through deficit rhetoric and deficit-informed reports and research. CRT was used as a conceptual lens for understanding the experiences of the men in the current study and helped to refine the initial study questions to incorporate race, gender, resilience, and narratives as useful methods of inquiry. As scholars suggests, these counter-stories and counter-narratives are vital to knowing more about the psychological resistance, sociopolitical strategies, and creative ingenuity employed by those who "consciously decide to defy racist stereotypes, exceed expectations, and offer more affirming views of their individual selves and the Black male collective" (Harper, 2009, p. 669).

Within the current study, being resilient in college is not simply about persisting toward graduation for many of the men, it is also about resisting the deficit rhetoric, negative framing, and stereotypes and hostilities aimed at their entire racialized and gendered group. Thus, CRT empowers Black men, and other members of marginalized communities, by allowing space where they, along with their stories and experiences, matter. Additionally, these groups have opportunities to hear the stories of others and learn how to improve their efforts to cope, resist, build coalitions, and persevere. As sociologist Patricia Hill Collins acknowledges the power and empowering nature of new knowledge about one's own experience, she further contends that, "revealing new ways of knowing that allow subordinate groups to define their own reality has far greater implications."[15] Throughout this book, I use the main tenets of CRT outlined above to explore the narratives of Black men to better understand and appreciate how they experience their race and gender on campus, the strategies they employ to persist, and their participation in BMI programs. Even more importantly, the book is aimed at allowing the men to define and make meaning from their own experiences on campus.

Blackmaleness: Double Consciousness, Invisibility, and Black Misandry

As a connection and compliment to CRT, examining how Black men experience the intersections of their race and gender require an interdisciplinary perspective. This perspective is particularly useful to study Black males in U.S. society broadly, and in college more specifically, as their experiences on college campuses and public spaces help to tease out and reveal several competing narratives of race and gender. As mentioned previously, Black men continue to be identified as "troubled" which has social, personal, and academic consequences. I situate the convergences of Black male identity within Athna Mutua's (2006) Blackmaleness framework to highlight some of the forces in operation against Black men and to which Black men carve out identities and coping strategies. In the current study, Blackmaleness is used to highlight and investigate the combined impact of Black men's racialized and gendered identities. In theorizing Black masculinities, Mutua argued that Black men routinely faced suspicion, which narrowed their life opportunities as they are "oppressed because they are both Black and men; that is, Black men are oppressed by gendered racism" (p. 6). As the participants in the current study attested, being Black and male on campus leaves them open to an array of challenges and their activities, location, and forms of expression are insignificant in how they often are imagined and projected. Thus, in some ways, they were relegated among the "faces at the bottom of the well" (see Bell, 1992). Their Blackmaleness leaves them subject to prejudices, assumptions, and predispositions of the White gaze—a gaze that constantly surveils their movements and automatically (re)positions them as persons whose presence must be scrutinized.

James and Lewis (2014) defined Blackmaleness as the "individually unique, yet collective development needs and processes experienced by Black male learners within the American inopportunity-opportunity structures."[16] They identified Blackmaleness as both a personal journey and a social reality that ultimately impacted the life chances of Black males across ideological, institutional, and individual inopportunity. Additionally, Blackmaleness also is important in unraveling and understanding Black men's masculine identities and manhood constructs. Ideal (hegemonic) masculinity embodies socially valued traits that typically include strength, aggression, dominance, competition, and control. Manhood is informed by intersecting social identities (i.e., race, gender, class, etc.) and is a multilayered concept referring to the self-expectations, relationships and responsibilities to family and other significant relationships, and worldviews that men accept or acknowledge.[17] As Davis (1999) argued, gender is a significant factor in Black males' social and academic experiences in college. In this study, I investigate the effects of social support on the men's sense of self and the coping strategies they deploy in navigating the campus climate and environment. In particular, I explore the social support they receive from other Black male collegians and through their engagement in an institutionalized Black male program. Academic achievement is related to student satisfaction with general college life. Students' pre-college preparation, support, identity, academic efforts, and engagement on campus all matter in how they experience college. Thus, grounding Black men's experiences within Blackmaleness also allows space to better see their situated standpoints and how their race and gender matter in how they belong (and try to belong) on campus.

BLACK MEN VEILED: A DUBOISIAN FRAME

> Between me and the other world there is ever an unasked question: unasked by some through feelings of delicacy; by others through the difficulty of rightly framing it. All, nevertheless, flutter around it . . . How does it feel to be a problem? DuBois (1903/2005, p. 1)

In opening his classic literary work *The Souls of Black Folk*, esteemed sociologist W. E. B. DuBois (2005) deemed that there existed two different and distinct worlds within the United States: one Black, to which he belonged, and one White, "the other world." The main chasm between these two worlds was their inability to relate to each other; yet, as DuBois relates, the presence and existence of the Black world was a problem. In pondering the meaning of Blackness at the dawn of the century, he offered that being a problem is "a strange experience." DuBois theorizes that Blacks are "born with a veil" and live in a world that denies Black self-consciousness; he writes of the internal struggle of being both an American and a Negro, which he posits as two souls with two unreconciled strivings. Thus, the Black existence in the United States is a history of the strivings for consciousness and wholeness. DuBois' veil gives Blacks a "second sight" to see the world from a particular standpoint and through a particular lens—much different from whites; however, segregation rendered the Black world invisible.

I argue that DuBois's double consciousness and veil concepts also extend to the experiences of Black males at historically White institutions.[18] As significant social institutions within the United States, colleges and universities play a key role in introducing students to different cultures (or further extending their experiences) and orienting them to the larger social structures. Many of the men in this study reveal how being Black and male in college is "a strange experience," which often pulls at both their raced and gendered identities and entraps them in a constant battle. On historically White campuses, Black male students, like other Students of Color, are a numerical minority and must learn to navigate the majority culture of their institution—this includes social and academic campus spaces, students, faculty and staff, and even the surrounding community. At the same time, Black male students also must think about managing their responses to being problematized and attaining their college degree. Thus, they are engaged in various pressures, struggles, and battles to negotiate self against being otherized.

BLACK MALE INVISIBILITY

Critical writers such as Ralph Ellison and James Baldwin, in addition to researchers, provide important insights for understanding Black male positionality and the perceptual lenses levied against them. Ellison's (1952/1995) work suggests that Black men face a unique struggle for visibility in U.S. society. He articulates various contradictions and complexities that invisibility renders on Black men; on the one hand, many people remain aloof of/to his presence while, on the other hand, they treat him within an inferior frame (as if he lacks humanity) when they do "see" him. This imposed invisibility of Ellison's unnamed protagonist extends DuBois's veil concept. Similarly, Baldwin (1961) uses a "fly in buttermilk" analysis to unpack Black male invisibility in both social and institutional predominantly White spaces. Almost as a response to DuBois's burgeoning question, Baldwin exposes the complicity of racial reasoning and demonstrates that the "Negro problem" is, in fact, a White problem.

When they are "visible" in various social and public spaces, Black males are relegated to what sociologist Elijah Anderson terms a "master status"—a stigmatizing effect of "negative" status-determining characteristics that applies to them as a group.[19] The trappings of master status and stereotyping render their individual identities and personas invisible. Ellison's (1995) theory suggests that African-American men have to cope with the simultaneity of being both present and unseen, which ultimately impacts the ways that they are able to engage in various settings. Anderson's (1990, 2004, 2011) application of "master status" offers added understanding about the ways in which Black males experience interracial interactions in public spaces and exposes the realities of race and racism in the United States.

Franklin and Boyd-Franklin (2000) conceptualized the "invisibility syndrome" to identify the struggles that individuals endure with inner feelings and beliefs that personal talents, abilities, and character are not acknowledged or valued by others, nor by the larger society, because of racial prejudice.[20] Several researchers have applied Ellison's invisibility concept to the experiences of Black students in historically and predominantly white institutions (and institutional spaces). Davis and colleagues (2004) found invisibility and hypervisibility as key experiences in students being noticed or not being noticed in school wholly as a result of being Black. Students identified experiencing discomfort and loneliness and being deliberately ignored in their feelings of invisibility. However, many also described being hypervisible in feeling out of place on campus. Similarly, in Harper et al.'s (2011) study, students felt that all eyes were often on them primarily because they stood out racially from the majority. Thus, investigating *how* Black male students feel, experience, and make sense of their experiences in college provides opportunities to better understand their sense of belonging on campus.

BLACK MISANDRY AND RACIAL BATTLE FATIGUE

Given the ways that Black men are racialized, simultaneously invisible and hypervisible, and problematized in U.S. society, researchers have conceptualized racial battle fatigue (or Black male misandry) to identify the racial microaggressions, hostilities, and discrimination that problematize Black men (Smith, 2004, 2010; Smith et al., 2007; Smith, Hung, & Franklin, 2011). For instance, Smith and colleagues (2007) assert that the intersecting identities of Black men are a double burden due to race (i.e., anti-Black racism) and gender (i.e., Black misandry or anti-Black male attitudes and oppression). They surmise that the ongoing and persistent exposure to race-related stressors at the societal, institutional, interpersonal, and individual levels and the interpretations and coping responses employed by Blacks can lead to the traumatic and physiological stress conditions of racial battle fatigue. Furthermore, the authors note that Black males not only face racial microaggressions (in the form of mini-assaults) but they also experience racial macroaggressiosn—large-scale, systems-related stressors that are widespread, that sometimes are highly publicized, race-related, traumatic events.

Thus, considering Black male experiences within Blackmaleness is quite helpful for the current study. In particular, Blackmaleness helps to better appreciate the concomitant pushes and pulls that Black males experience within wider society in general and how various components of being Black and men often are enacted on them during their college years. Many of the men describe their overall college experiences in positive terms; they point directly to their peer relationships, engagement on campus, and various activities and opportunities they have pursued to support their assertions. However, the point of Blackmaleness is to identify more clearly the intertwining of race and gender and the ways that Black men are problematized and always already the subject (and object) of surveillance and scrutiny.[21] As the men specifically discuss the campus racial climate, race relations, and what it means to be a Black male on campus, they narrate and reaffirm these challenges. Thus, Blackmaleness accentuates the micro- and macroaggressions as a constant presence that can and do act upon the men and reveals how the men attempt to negotiate their identities on campus.

The Black men in this study are not passive in how they experience being racialized and gendered. In formulating their academic aspirations and experiencing college, their persistence requires awareness, interpretations, and coping responses to the college milieu. Examining how their social identities matter in their college experience, and asking the men to make meaning of these experiences, allows space for them to narrate how they cope on campus. Above their individual efforts though, better understanding their aspirations and experiences highlights the critical need for educational professionals and policymakers to confront these challenges at the institutional and policy levels.

Student Integration and Sense of Belonging

Previous research has highlighted the significant, positive correlation of belonging and integration to retention and persistence (Astin, 1993, 1999). Astin (1999) identified five basic assumptions about involvement. First, he asserted that involvement requires an investment of psychosocial and physical energy toward various objects. Second, involvement occurs along a continuum where the amount of energy invested varies from student to student. Third, involvement has qualitative and quantitative features. Fourth, the quality and quantity of student involvement impacts the amount of student learning and personal development gained. Lastly, academic performance is correlated with the student involvement. This theory provides fertile ground for higher education research and identifies the crucial nature of involvement on student outcomes. Astin (1999) also identified various forms of involvement (such as academic involvement and student-faculty interaction) and noted several areas for further exploration (i.e., the role of peer groups and attribution and locus of control).

In addition to involvement, Tinto's (1997, 1998) model of student persistence provides a useful framework to examine the experiences of Black college men. Tinto identified institutional experiences, involving the educational system, and academic and social integration as central to the college experience. In acknowledging the many pathways to involvement, Tinto (1998) asserted that involvement could take place inside and/or outside the classroom. Students who feel a sense of belonging, who take part in extracurricular activities, and who feel connected with fellow students and teachers, are more inclined to persist in their studies. Without social integration, persistence becomes more difficult, which ultimately affects a student's ability to graduate.

Education scholar Terrell L. Strayhorn (2012) conceptualized a sense of belonging framework that was based in student persistence and student involvement theories along with Maslow's (1943) hierarchy of needs framework. Strayhorn asserted that a sense of belonging is a basic human need located within Maslow's framework, and organizes his discussion of sense of belonging into three categories: "belongingness as a concept, circumstances that engender (or thwart) belonging, and the relation between belonging and other outcomes or behaviors" (p. 11). The concept of belonging becomes the key to a person's sense of self and the feeling that his or her efforts are valued, both of which in turn impact student persistence and success in college. Like Maslow, Strayhorn theorizes that students' fundamental needs and motivations (physiological necessities, safety, belonging, esteem, and self-actualization) depend on social spaces and the college environment, which in turn lead to outcomes that can manifest into either positive or negative experiences. Additionally, Strayhorn relates Astin's (1999) student involvement theory to sense of belonging. He notes that various factors contribute to an individual's feeling of being valued in the academic and social life on campus and thus ultimately contribute to student retention, including the environment, experiences, socialization, and mattering.

Thus, given the primacy on student experiences, the current study is situated within Strayhorn's (2012) sense of belonging framework to analyze the importance of sense of belonging in student persistence decisions. As researchers have contended, by helping some Black males find a sense of belonging in college, we can nurture their academic self-efficacy and effectively raise their degree aspirations, thereby significantly increasing the odds that they will stay in college, earn good grades, and complete their degree within a reasonable time.[22]

Overview of the Book

This book draws on the voices and narratives of the students themselves to provide a rich picture of their experiences, thoughts, and actions. It is my hope that a broad audience of academics, policymakers, and educational professionals, as well as Black male students and other Students of Color (or those marginalized because of their social identities) trying to understand their own situatedness, will better understand how intersecting identities complicate the ways that students experience their education.

Chapter 2 explores the major factors that contributed to collegiate aspirations for Black male students. In investigating these desires, students narrate the impact of their secondary school experiences coupled with expressions of their family, friends, and faith. In an effort to establish a context for their aspirations, I begin by investigating the factors that contributed to the students' decisions to attend college along with their self-reported preparedness, expectations and concerns prior to college attendance. By establishing this context, we can better appreciate their transition to college and their first year experiences. The data revealed aspirational capital as the overarching theme in the students' future trajectory, in that early aspirations (or lack of it) produced motivation; this was revealed through collegiate expectations.

Chapter 3 examines how the students narrated their transitions to college campuses in trying to find their place. Findings revealed academics as the major expectation and concern for Black males; however, their early experiences are impacted highly by their social world. The men learned a great deal from their early collegiate experiences, which included learning and adjusting to the institutional culture while at the same time feeling their way through the academic environment. Within this terrain, the men discuss their in-class experiences, interactions, and relationships with faculty, and how these first years impacted their college outlook and future aspirations.

Chapter 4 explores the students' experiences within the predominantly White milieu on campus. In particular, students discuss the impact of the campus climate on their collegiate experiences. Students narrate that they see and experience a separate and segregated campus that presents unique challenges for Black students in general. These challenges include low Black student population and lack of opportunities to connect. As Black males at historically White institutions students experienced a range of hostilities, which included discrimination, microaggressions, and racism. Additionally, students described experiencing racialized targeting, profiling, and stereotyping. Thus, I demonstrate how the intersections of race and gender are used to create additional pressures that impact students' academic, social, and personal experiences.

In the next two chapters, I turn to the resilience strategies employed by Black college men, focusing on their individual efforts and their engagement in a student-centered program. Chapter 5 establishes a much-needed focus for studies on Black college men: their efforts to persist. Although the students identify myriad challenges inherent on their respective college campuses for Black students in general and Black males in particular, they still maintain their resolve to persevere. This chapter focuses on the Black men's agency on campus and how this is complimented and amplified by the BMI program. Key here are the realities that the men see (as described in the previous chapter) and the strategies they employ as they remain focused on their main goal of college completion. The chapter also provides space for the men to discuss how they navigate and negotiate the stereotypes and low expectations levied against them individually and of their racialized and gendered group. These narratives offer critical insight into the minds of these college men as they rearticulate their own versions of success and triumph.

Chapter 6 focuses on the students' experiences in Black male initiative programs. In discussing their Black Male Initiative (BMI) experiences, the men weaved in narratives that amplified their own individual needs and how they meshed with both BMI and the larger university culture. Students became involved in BMI as a result of contact with a BMI staff member or student members, both of which helped provide a bridge for students' sense of belonging to the university and helped establish a connection to BMI. The great majority of the students' experiences were described in positive ways, as students were introduced to resources and networking opportunities, and were provided with an immediate support system when they became engaged with BMI. Many students developed a sense of brotherhood through their BMI participation in social outings and the weekly/monthly meetings; additionally, BMI provided the students with counter-spaces to buffer some of the cultural nuances of their institution and the campus climate. Through their involvement, many students felt motivated to achieve academically because of what they learned from various BMI activities, their desires to attain future goals, and newly formed connections to their peer group. Finally, students perceived and experienced the crucial role that BMI played in their college careers.

The conclusion summarizes the major outcomes of the study. This chapter provides summative and prescriptive discussion of the intersections of race and gender for the Black male collegians in this study. I close with recommendations for colleges and universities to enhance the experiences of Black male collegians in addition to recommendations for Black male college students as well.

CHAPTER 2

College Aspirations, Expectations and Concerns

Thinking about and Preparing for College

My mother, my big brother, my older cousins and kinda my uncle too. My brother went to college and he graduated. My mother pushed me to go; there wasn't a "no" answer, so that's kinda the main reason why I'm here now. And my older cousin went here and that helped as opposed to going to another campus and not knowing anybody.

—Elijah

I could say coming out of high school over time I could be irresponsible; I was definitely ready for college and to be on my own. Just that and the responsibility, so I can say I was partially prepared for college.

—Dwight

A good portion of research concerning educational aspirations found that there were significant relationships between students' educational aspirations, socioeconomic backgrounds, and intellectual positions (Allen, Bonous-Hammarth, & Suh, 2004; Freeman, 2005; Toldson, 2008). Students' college aspirations along with their perceptions of their preparation and collegiate concerns provide a window to better understand how they experience college—especially in their transition and early college experiences. Examining these factors is important in creating and sustaining [new] ways to enhance their access, retention, and persistence in higher education. In their study of student high school preparation, college choice, and factors contributing to college enrollment for students of color, Allen and colleagues (2004, p. 96) reminded us that "educational achievement is a social process, shaped by human exchanges within definitive sociocultural contexts." For Black male students, they face a number of challenges regarding their college readiness, which ultimately impacts their access to college. For example, according to the Educational Testing Service (2013) report, 30 percent of the 2004 cohort of Black males met the minimum college preparation curriculum and only 1 percent of Black males met the criteria for finishing an advanced curriculum. Additionally, researchers have argued that a gap exists between African-American aspirations to attend college and actual attendance. Still, much of the literature on college aspirations among Black males highlights their high desires for postsecondary attainment.[1] Thus, beginning an investigation about Black males in college with their precollege experiences is both necessary and proves quite useful.

In this study, I begin by investigating how Black male students thought about and aspired to college. Educational aspirations refer to a student's view and perception of his or her intention to pursue or obtain additional formal educational opportunities in the future.[2] The reflection offered by Elijah, a second-year student majoring in Africana Studies, helps to reveal the important role of family on his college aspirations. Not only did he receive strong encouragement from his mother—who he acknowledged did not give him any other option—he also benefitted from having a brother who graduated from college and a cousin attending his college as well. Elijah believed that each of these connections, in addition to other family members, provided him with support and motivation to pursue higher education. Similarly, Dwight, a second-year sports management major, credited his brothers' lack of college success as a major factor that contributed to his college attendance. He noted that their lives now are not what they want them to be and also cited his parents for "definitely pushing us to go to college and get more education than they did." As he reflected on his college readiness, noted at the beginning of this chapter, he asserted that he was only "partially prepared for college" primarily because he needed to increase his level of responsibility. Although he was ready to be on his own, he did not believe he had the requisite skill set to be as prepared as he needed to be. Both Elijah's and Dwight's reflections offer important insight about how Black males conceptualize their aspirations and preparation prior to attending college.

The Black male collegians in this study represent a range of ages, experiences, and performances; additionally, their standing ranged from first-year college student to recent graduates. The common threads across all 40 are their race and gendered identity, their status as college students, and their desire to graduate from college. As a starting point to appreciate what they offer about their college experiences, I engaged the students in conversations about their entry points to college. Three themes best capture the collection of insights offered by the students relative to an inquiry about their college experiences. The first section summarizes the most salient reflections that they shared about their desires to attend college. These reflections provide a window for examining what factors contributed to students' college aspirations. From here, I explore how students perceive and make meaning of their preparation for college and the concerns they held prior to attending college. This chapter lays a foundation for further nuancing the students' collegiate experiences by focusing in on their pre-college thoughts, preparation, and experiences.

College Aspirations

Talking with the students about their college aspirations and orientations toward college helped to reveal how they thought about college, the meanings they ascribed to college, and how they thought about themselves. Previous research has indicated clearly that African-American families value education and, regardless of their achievement levels, there is a high regard for securing a good education. For instance, research has identified a range of themes associated with the precollege stage: family influence, macro perspectives on race, and factors of motivation. They offered that families lay the groundwork for success long before students get to college; family, especially for Black communities, includes extended family and fictive kin.[3] Thus, contrary to narratives about Black male student apathy or their adoption of "oppositional" behaviors, researchers continue to show that Black families—and Black male students—do care about their education.[4] Perspectives on race help young adults understand how to succeed across a variety of educational settings. And, finally, having a role model or serving as a role model has the potential to increase the motivations of students. For the men in the current study, family was a centerpiece for their motivation and support in aspiring to college. The great majority of the men specifically referenced their family as the main source of their aspirations, framed from both positive aspects ("they encouraged me to go") to feeling inspired by their family's history ("nobody else in my family went"). The men asserted that both of these types of sentiments heightened their desires to attend and complete college. As a result, the primacy of families was inscribed into the lexicon of the students' aspirations. Additionally, they aspired to college as a means by which to improve their lives and the lives of their families. Thus, in many ways, the students' gender role identities played a key component as well as they felt and expressed responsibility for continuing the family's college-going legacies, an accountability for the plight of their families, and liable for serving as a model for younger siblings. In effect, the men conceptualized that college could afford them social mobility, future job prospects, and a range of other opportunities.

Family Support: "They Encouraged Me to Go . . ."

The focus of this study is on how Black male students experienced their racialized and gendered identity on campus. In order to investigate this, it is useful to examine how they conceptualized college, what meanings they attached to college, and what expectations they held in attending. For the majority of the men, their college aspirations spawned because of the encouragement and support they received from their family. Researchers continue to note the significance of family on college aspirations for African-American students. For example, researchers have asserted that education has always been a matter of interest for the entire family and community based on the idea that each generation is to have more opportunities than the generation before. Yet, Freeman (2005) argued that many researchers only point out the changing structures of Black families when they discuss education of African-American students. Kory, a third-year journalism major, discussed how his future aspirations changed as a result of his family's support. He recalled:

> Honestly, probably my family. They kinda encouraged me to
> go and see what it's about. I remember talking to my dad

about his school experiences . . . he knew that in the world that we live in now we need a college degree. I was thinking about a simple thing like signing up for the army.

Kory acknowledged that his family was the main source of his college aspirations. Initially, according to him, he was considering joining the military; however, encouragement from his family and conversations with his father helped him decide on college. He credited his father with also helping him see the future utility of a college degree. Kory's approach to and expectations for college were centered on what he had been told prior to attending, that it would help prepare him for the real world. He continued and added:

> I honestly expected it to be that "real world" that they're always telling us about. I just expected responsibilities for myself. In coming to college that summer, I tried to prepare to do more for myself because that was my focus because I didn't want to be that person who had to come home. I feel like my parents raised me to take care of myself because I have a brother and a sister. Let's just get out there and do it.

As can be gleaned by what he shared, Kory's family was a significant source of his preparedness for college and he leaned on the prior experiences of others as his motivation to be self-reliant. Importantly, he inscribed masculine identities into his future self as he shared his college aspirations and expectations. According to Kory, college was important for two primary reasons: to prepare for his future career and to develop his masculine independence. His focus was squared on graduating from college, not simply attending. Thus, he continued to prepare for college even during the summer before his eventual fall enrollment and he envisioned himself as responsible for garnering college success so that his siblings could follow later.

Similarly, D'Angelo, a fifth-year student majoring in management information systems, shared that his college aspirations increased because of encouragement from his mother and how he conceptualized his role within the family. He accounted for his aspirations in the following way:

> My mother's persuasion, obviously; I didn't grow up with a father so that drive of wanting to be better than him. He had

some college and I'm not sure if he graduated or not. So I wanted to be better than him and be in a good position for my family in the future. My financial situation at home and being a role model to my two little brothers. And, at the end of the day, just making money.

In specifically speaking about his mother's persuasion, he explained:

Just encouraging, especially that first semester my senior year. "What are you going to do? At 18, you gotta go somewhere." Her drive in wanting me to do it made me want to do more than just being at home. My peers motivated me as well because the company I keep was very motivated and goal-oriented. So, I tried to match their hustle.

For D'Angelo, college became important as he began to think more concretely about the options available to him at the time. Beyond his mother's direct encouragement, his family played an important role in thinking about college because he conceived of his educational endeavors in relation to his father's absence and considered how his efforts could impact his younger brothers. Almost three-quarters of the students' sense of responsibility to their families and for their families was evident throughout their narratives and often was inscribed through their aspirations and efforts. Similar to D'Angelo, many of the men saw higher education as an opportunity for social mobility, which also impacted their peer group relations as well. Researchers continue to point out the direct economic benefits of higher education. For instance, one study contended that the decision to attend college has increased significantly given the associated educational, economic, and social benefits that accrue to most graduates. Additionally, another study demonstrated the value of a college education and provided correlates between earning a formal education and self-efficacy and improved life chances.[5]

In addition to feeling encouraged, several students discussed how their parents and guardians delimited their options outside of college. For instance, Reggie, a third-year political science major, asserted that attending college—and successfully completing it—was a crucial part of his family's history. As a result, going to college for him was not a choice. He acknowledged:

My parents; they kinda just it wasn't an option, I just had
to go. Both of them had college degrees so that was the
expectation. I have a sister and she said we were both
going. My mother has a masters, she has an MBA, so there
was definitely an expectation. Even my grandparents, my
granddad had his PhD. So he instilled it in my mom and
she instilled it in me. My dad's father didn't go to college
but they taught him about the importance of it. He wants a
better life for me and my sister and the only way he knew
was through education.

According to Randy, college was critical for how his parents—and their
parents—conceived of social mobility and improving their life opportunities. Not only did his parents hold bachelor's degrees, but both held
graduate degrees as well. He exclaimed that there were clear messages
shared from one generation to the next about the importance of college; this message was prioritized whether the elders of the family had
attained higher levels of education or not. A final reflection by Deondre,
a third-year psychology major, is revealing in how focusing on students'
assets has the potential to help them reframe their self-perceptions. He
asserted that his mother helped him better understand and appreciate
that college was where he was "supposed to go." In responding to a
follow-up question about attending college, Deondre explained:

I mean, I used to want to go to the military. My mom and
dad were in the military and my uncles were in the military
and my mom told me that I was too smart for the military
and they probably wouldn't use my smarts.

In the literature on Black males' college aspirations and academic
performances, a range of researchers assert that Black males are in a
constant battle for their intellectual pursuits and integrity.[6] Deondre's
recollection of his conversation is important because his college aspirations were bolstered by the perceived opportunity to use his academic
and intellectual talents in college. Deondre's reflection pulls at the core
of discussions regarding future opportunities in many families of color
and low-income communities that debate the merits of college versus
the military.

Family Connections and Critical Consciousness:
"I Grew Up with that Message"

In discussing their college aspirations, the students identified their family histories as important connections to how they thought about college. These family connections helped many of the men develop critical consciousness about their aspirations for college and their future endeavors. Several of the men reflected on how they felt motivated to attend college through family relations. The comments from Monte, D.J., and Marvin help explicate this phenomenon:

> MONTE: Most of my family members attended college. Like ninety percent of the females attended college and have a degree and most of the males attended college. So I felt an obligation to go to college. So, with a college degree you know where it can take you.

> D.J.: The high school that I went to was basically a college prep school; in the hallways they had banners. They said you need to be thinking about college; I played sports and they wanted me to think about college, so I was preached college. And my dad, he was strong on that too. [DB: *What do you mean that your dad was strong on college?*] He really encouraged me to go to college; I'm the first male in my family to attend college so it's kinda of a big deal.

> MARVIN: It was really demographics and sports. I was playing football at the time and trying to get a scholarship somewhere. I didn't play my junior year and I tried to make it off my senior year. I ended up talking to the coach. My stepfather and my mother got a divorce that summer and I was real shaky about being out of state and leaving my mom so I wanted to be close. [DB: *What did your parents say to you about college?*] College wasn't really something that was expected out of me. Acknowledging that they were there for me when I was gone. My father didn't graduate from college but he had gone. "Call me if you need me."

Monte, like several of his peers, acknowledged a college-going tradition in his family. He specifically "felt an obligation" to go to college because of the many people (mostly women) in his family who successfully completed college. Given the strong pull that he felt toward college, he also began to conceptualize how it would benefit him as well. For D.J., he was informed about college through the high school that he attended and the activities that he participated in. However, it was conversations with his father that helped crystallize his motivation and aspirations. His father's support and encouragement was important for how he conceptualized his college attendance; his father focused on the significance of his status as the first male in his family to attend college. Thus, not only was it important for him to attend, but it was also quite important for him to graduate as well. For D.J., like several of his peers, graduating from college would establish him as a trailblazer in his family and was grounded in his gendered identity. Similarly, Marvin felt his college aspirations were motivated and encouraged by his family. He identified demographics and sports as the main two criteria for his eventual college selection process where he perceived participating in football as a potential avenue to make college even more of a realization. Eventually, though, it was his parents' divorce that ultimately piqued his college interests; in going to college, he wanted to remain within the state to be closer to home and, just as important, college attendance was (re)narrated into his manhood construct.

Finally, Mark's comments about his college aspirations are revealing as well. His motivation stemmed from his family's efforts to support his educational endeavors and the opportunities that he was afforded. He shared his college aspirations with the following statement:

> Ultimately, my parents. The way I was raised they put me in a Baptist private school so it was very morally based and they preached not only on the religious side but also in education. So I grew up with that message and that was the whole goal to go to college. Since it was a Black private school in that area they let us know that you're going to face a lot of trials because of who you are and where you come from. I knew a lot about MLK [Dr. Martin Luther King, Jr.]—that was bashed in my head—and [I] learned a lot of Black history. So, it first started off with my parents putting me in my school and also my parents never going to college—neither one of them graduated from college or even attended college. So that was a big deal for me was not only to make them proud but also for myself and for my family.

Mark credits his parents' early investments in his education as motivation for his college aspirations. The private school he attended helped reaffirm messages of learning history, investing in the future, and enhancing his self-awareness. Thus, he saw that attending the school was critical for his development personally and academically. He summed up his thoughts about his college aspirations by reaffirming his parents' investments and noting that he was motivated even more because they did not attend college. As many of the students attested, attending college was not an individual endeavor but rather one that held deep connections and meanings for themselves and their families.

As researches have noted, the family plays a vital role in students' self-conceptions, aspirations, and motivations. For instance, research by Toldson, Braithwaite, and Rentie (2009) support this finding as they demonstrated that social modeling plays an important role in promoting college aspirations among young Black males. For many of the men in this study, their family served as capital, offering powerful resources that help them confirm or reaffirm their interest in attending college.[7] Thus, many of these Black males entered college holding on to the central importance of family as a significant component of their sense of self, their masculine identities, and their manhood constructs. Just as important was how the men were motivated because of their family's investments in them. The men expressed a sense of feeling encouraged that was rooted in the family's college-going tradition. In each of these ways, the men raised their level of critical consciousness as it related to school, higher education, and academic achievement.

Improve Self: "A Better Life for Myself"

In addition to connecting to family as a source of strength and inspiration, what stood out to a significant number of the students was conceptualizing college as an opportunity to improve themselves and their life trajectories. Some of their responses are multipronged, as they did identify family and other factors; but, ultimately, the main thrust of their response was about self-improvement. The following stories by Cameron, Myron, and Arthur are representative cases of this theme:

> CAMERON: Basically, neither of my parents went so I would've been the first. I just wanted to be successful in my life, better myself, step outside of my comfort zone, and contribute to

my community. Just be a better African American in general, like being responsible and accountable to my family and my community.

MYRON: To attend college? I guess a better education, better life for myself upon completion. I've had different family members who've gone to college and they seem to have done well. So, I'm following in the same footsteps.

ARTHUR: It was honestly the logical next step in the process of education. I just finished high school and I just had an understanding that the way the world is evolving around us is that a high school diploma is not going to get you much in life. So for me to provide for my family then the [next] logical step was going to college and continuing my education.

The students cited here identified college as an opportunity for social mobility and as an investment in their futures. Investigating how students conceive college is important for better understanding their efforts to matriculate college successfully as well. A good number of students believed college was a way for them to improve their lives. For instance, Cameron and Myron specifically noted that they want to succeed and they want to have better lives for themselves. Additionally, Arthur perceived college as a natural educational progression, especially given many job requirements, and as a way for him to provide for his family in the future. As noted across a wide array of research, the lifetime benefits of college are crucial to individuals, families, and communities. Being able to provide for their current and future families was an identity construct that many of the men interwove throughout their college aspirations.

For many of the men in this study, attending college was a means that they envisioned could help change their own trajectory, impact a "new" history of their families—especially as many were the first in their immediate family to attend or the first male to attend—and provide them with ways to contribute to their families as well. Thus, the men's constructions of college were vested heavily in a family-orientation. The men identified college as a way to change their life outcomes. Several of the men acknowledged a lack of enthusiasm for school, yet they believed there were significant outcomes possible with degree attainment. Their sentiments were acknowledged by Fred as he explained, "To be honest, I hate school and I know people don't need school but it's the best opportunity to get a career and improve your life from where I started off with." Fred, much like many of his peers, expressed understanding college within the context of "where [he] started off" and saw it as the "best opportunity" to improve his life.

Black, a second-year majoring in biology, held a particularly clear lens on the multiple factors that enhanced his college aspirations. He noted family, self-improvement, and future career as a combined force that impacted his thoughts. As he reflected on his college aspirations, he shared:

> BLACK: Well, honestly, I've always wanted to go to college because I knew that I wanted to become a doctor. So that's the reason why; I had the drive to have a better life.
>
> DB: What do you mean by better life?
>
> BLACK: I would say, somewhere down the line I'm going to have kids and if I don't have a good job then I wouldn't have the ability to take care of them like I need to. I think about the sacrifices just like my mother did for me, I want my kids to have a good education. I'm just looking ahead to the future.

Clearly, as he pointed out, Black thought about college from his career goal of being a doctor and coupled this by looking ahead to being a future parent. For him, college was connected directly with both of these thoughts. In reflecting on his mother's role in making him want to attend college, he stated:

> She's a single parent; I've always seen her work really hard—working like two or three jobs. Dad's not around and I can't do anything about that; but she really inspired me to do something better. Later on down the line, I know that I want to be there for her and be able to take care of her if she ever needed it.

Black identified his mother as a source of motivation for his college aspirations and pursuits. His mother's work ethic raised his own expectations of himself and inspired him to "do something better." Black's framing of his family experiences runs counter to the deficit approach; feeling inspired and motivated by a single mother who worked multiple jobs opposes the often used projection that family dynamics like his are a hindrance for success. In many ways, Black already is defying the odds and resisting the rhetoric in his college aspirations. In offering his motivations, he also reveals some of his strengths including an ethic of care, family orientation, and resilience.

The encouragement, motivation, and support students received from their families helped to inspire their matriculation to college. Students shared that their families played a critical role in their thoughts about college and thoughts about themselves. This is consistent with two of the themes identified by previous researchers, family influence and factors of motivation, both of which are associated with the precollege stage and are important for students' collegiate success.[8] In addition, students identified school as a space and an opportunity to enhance their futures. Even for students like Fred, who did not correlate a positive experience with school per se, he still perceived its significance on his future opportunities. In the following section, I turn attention to how students perceived their preparation for college.

College Preparation

In talking with students about their preparation for college, their responses primarily fell into two main categories: the role of their secondary school in their preparation and an assessment of their academic, social, and personal skills. As the men shared, self-reflection also emerged as an important theme as well, which helps to reveal how the students thought about themselves.

Secondary School Preparation: "Didn't Really Prepare Me . . ."

Across their secondary school experiences, the men identified a number of deficiencies that undermined their college preparation. Jordan and D'Angelo speak to different experiences that helped them learn about what their high school did not do but that also helped them feel prepared at the same time. The students offered the following reflections about their preparation:

JORDAN: I wish I didn't . . . I was in Upward Bound, so Upward Bound did what the school did not do. I feel like that's the school's job and Upward Bound was supposed to back it up. But Upward Bound did what the school didn't and that really pushed me.

D'ANGELO: Academically, Central I feel like it was poor because I know for a fact that they let people go through as far as to graduation. One class in particular, and I only took it for one semester, and that prepared me more than anything other class over four years of high school. It was Advanced Biology, he taught it like a college class. He didn't hold hands, he gave us a lot of information; it was a lot of work and he just treated it like it was a college class.

Jordan noted that his high school did not prepare him in the ways that he needed for college; however, he benefited from participating in Upward Bound. Instead of building on what he believed was the responsibility of his high school and acting as a supplement, he leaned heavily on the lessons and opportunities afforded through the program. Researchers have indicated that after-school and community-based youth development programs have garnered positive results for students, especially Black males.[9] For instance, youth worker community-based education scholar Bianca Baldridge (2014) found that a critical feature of some community-based educational spaces was "imagining students from an asset-rich perspective and setting high expectations," which is important work that "acknowledges and honors the talents, gifts, and strengths that young people already possess."[10] These acknowledgments and attestations are grounded in positive youth-adult relationships and developing a supportive peer environment. In addition, other research findings speak to the "need to develop educational models that respond to the unique circumstances of Black males in America, which include structural, historical, and cultural explanations."[11] Programs like Upward Bound and other nontraditional educational spaces play a crucial role in supporting Black males in academic achievement, provide necessary alternative educational sites, reframe understandings of Black youth, and provide safe spaces that can protect youth from negative outcomes.[12]

According to D'Angelo, although students graduated from his high school, the school did not do well in preparing students for college. This sentiment was echoed by a significant number of men in the study; they noted how college counselors only worked with a select small group of students in talking with them about options for college while too many others felt that they often were encouraged to consider the military as their best option after high school. Previous research has found that Black students indicated that they lacked college preparation and had less access to information at their school.[13] D'Angelo identified his Advanced Biology class as an important learning opportunity to prepare him for college. Specifically, he cited the amount of information covered in class and the teacher's teaching style as lenses to what college might be like. Researchers continue to note the importance of rigorous academic preparation during the secondary school years.[14] Additionally, many state standards fall short of college readiness standards and, as researchers have indicated, Black students suffer academically from under-resourced schools and underqualified teachers.[15]

Randy and Bryan's experiences are important as well as neither believed their high school did an adequate job in preparing them for college. In particular, Randy perceived racial differences in the types of help and information that students were made privy to at his suburban, diverse high school.[16] The gap in opportunities did not quell his desires for college; in fact, he noted that he leaned more heavily on his drive and determination as he matriculated toward college. Similarly, Bryan felt that his school did not emphasize the importance of college and did not prepare him with skills that would help him be successful. Randy provided the following reflection about his college preparation:

> My high school, I would say, didn't really prepare me as much as they should have because I would see my White peers, because I played soccer with them, they went to Catholic school, and they seemed to be better prepared. I'm not really sure why, maybe it was funding or something like that. I feel like I could've been prepared better, but I was very intellectual and both of my parents had college degrees so they prepared me as well. And, my own drive and own self-motivation to be successful in college, I read books just to broaden my vocabulary so that I wouldn't be going in not knowing anything about school. They did prepare me as well as they could in my high school but there was room for improvement there. But I did feel that I was better prepared than my peers with my parents and I had a sibling who was in college.

Similarly, Bryan shared:

> Education wise, with me getting out of the city environment
> and moving to the suburbs I feel like I was better prepared.
> But my school didn't really do a lot of stressing for college so I
> don't feel like I was that prepared. Like time management and
> then being able to sit down with teachers and getting more
> information. But, that probably had to do with me being an
> athlete and they figured that I'd go to school for football and
> I'd be good. So, time management was a huge thing because
> you really have to manage your time in college.

Although Randy did not believe his high school prepared him well for
college, especially in comparison to his White peers, attending college
was still his main focus. Primarily, he leaned on the educational attainment of his own parents to set the standard for what was expected of
him within his family, and he noted that his parents contributed to his
preparation as well. Additionally, Randy shared that his college readiness also stemmed from his self-motivation, active efforts to improve
his academic skills, and learning from his older sister's experiences in
college. Bryan believed that his family's move to a suburban residence
provided him with a better environment to prepare for college than the
large inner-city school district that they moved from. Still, he noted areas
where the school could do more—such as making college more of a focal
point and providing opportunities for students to work with teachers outside of class time. Although often considered a "promised land," recent
research scholarship highlights the opportunity gaps for Black students
in suburban schools that belie some of the equal opportunity rhetoric.[17]
Also, Bryan's status as a student-athlete, like many Black males who
participate in sports, placed him within a unique category where football was thought of as his "ticket" to college. All too often, Black male
student-athletes' academic aspirations may suffer from an overemphasis
on their athletic identities at the expense of their academic identities.[18]
    Unfortunately, a significant number of men discerned their sec-
ondary schools as places that did not prepare them for college. The
students identified their schools as places where they were not engaged
in serious conversations about college as a possibility for their futures.
Yet, the men still held high college-going aspirations and they were able
to tap into a range of resources to support their goals and efforts. For

instance, students like Jordan felt supported and encouraged through his participation in Upward Bound. Other students identified a particular class and/or teacher that had a significant impact on their college aspirations. These advanced classes exposed students to an accelerated pace and higher-order thinking skills, enhanced their academic skill set, and elevated their self-expectations. Additionally, students relied on their own noncognitive skills such as drive and determination to help bolster their efforts.[19] Students like Randy were able to couple these with the cultural and familial capital they could access from their parents and siblings' college experiences. Finally, through their participation in extracurricular activities (such as sports), students learned important skills such as prioritizing tasks and time management. Consistent across these experiences and reflections were ways that students identified their own strengths, assets, and capital that potentially could help them garner college successes despite the deficits they experienced in secondary school.

Trying to Be Ready for College: "I Didn't Know What to Expect"

In addition to reflecting on their secondary schools as a factor in creating deficiencies in preparing for college, nearly half of the men did not believe that they were prepared for college. This lack of preparation spanned the gamut from being unsure what college was about and lacking mental preparation to more specific deficiencies such as focusing on the social aspects of college and lacking some fundamental skills that could position them for early college success.

Marvin shared that his uncertainty stemmed directly from not being able to engage in critical conversations about college. He exclaimed:

> I didn't know what to expect really. I hadn't had too many people right over me to talk to me about what to expect. There were people in my family that went to college but there weren't any conversations. In my head I was just ready for the new environment just to learn.

Although Marvin had family members who had attended college, he believed that he would have benefited from conversations with them about their college experiences and the cultural wealth they could have offered. Much research shows that first-generation college students in general, and many Black male students in particular, may struggle or feel disconcerted about college specifically because they lack access to college know-how. Stated simply, many of these students lack human, social, and cultural capital that they can use to counterbalance some of the challenges they face in college preparation and how they leverage it in college.[20] For instance, Stanton-Salazar (2011) articulated "institutional agents" as critical resources for academic achievement—especially among low-status students and youth. He identified institutional agents as "high-status, non-kin, agents who occupy relatively high positions in the multiple dimensional stratification system, and who are well positioned to provide key forms of social and institutional support."[21] The key point is that these students need additional resources, and opportunities to deploy their capital, to help buoy them toward academic success.

Elijah and Black also discussed their lack of college readiness. Elijah was more reflexive in his response, as he noted that his struggles during his first year in college were a direct result of not being prepared. He shared the following reflection about his preparation:

> I wasn't ready at all. Because my first semester here I did terribly; I got a 1.5 [grade point average] my first semester. I thought it would be like high school when you come in and turn in some of the assignments and it would be good. I was wrong! I ended up passing like two or three classes that semester. [DB: *Why did you feel like you were not prepared?*] The workload. In high school I didn't really push myself, I just coasted by. Now, I know I have to put in that extra time and do the work.

Elijah entered college with a perception that it would "be like high school." Additionally, he acknowledged that he "coasted by" in high school and did not exert much effort in his schoolwork. The combined effect of Elijah's academic perceptions and efforts resulted in his underpreparation for college and self-admitted first year struggles ("I did terribly"). Similarly, Black also expressed that he was unsure of the skills needed to be successful in college. He noted:

> Honestly, I don't feel like I was prepared for it at all. It's *way* different than high school. I had a hard time adjusting to it. Thanks for my Gen Ed class 202, I learned how to take

notes, learned how to be a student and learned good study habits. I also learned about different fields that I could go into as well . . . I didn't have a clue whatsoever what I was getting into.

As Black recounted his early collegiate experiences, he noted that he struggled because he was unprepared. In particular, he offered that he did not possess strong academic skills such as note taking, time management, and study habits. Black began his higher education endeavors at an in-state community college precisely because of worries such as these and due to his concern that he might not succeed in college. He finished his reflection by concluding that he "didn't have a clue whatsoever" about college and what it might take in order to succeed. Both Elijah and Black identified that their early college struggles were due to their lack of college readiness. In responding to a follow-up question about the college counselors at his high school and discussions about college, Black added, "Basically, only about the FAFSA; that's pretty much it." If students are not engaged in meaningful conversations about college and they lack college-ready skills, then not only are they underprepared but the lack of wherewithal about college also contributes to heightened levels of anxiety and concern, both of which could easily compromise student performances in class and on campus, their mental and emotional fortitude, and their physical health.

In a report by the American College Testing (ACT) program on college readiness and student success, the agency acknowledged:

> Preparing students for college and careers doesn't occur at a single point in time. Instead, readiness is a process that needs to occur over a number of years—a process that must be well under way by the middle school years, if not earlier.[22]

Two key steps in the ACT's action plan for college readiness include a rigorous curriculum and student guidance.[23] The ACT program encourages schools (and school systems) to offer a rigorous core preparatory curriculum for all students and provide student guidance. A rigorous curriculum is important as it provides students with foundational skills that align with readiness for college. Additionally, schools are encouraged to engage students in early college and career awareness, which could help increase students' aspirations. The need for college readiness is even more imperative for students from marginalized communities and minoritized student populations.

As can be gleaned from student comments, and based on their self-reporting, many seemed to be adversely affected by schools that did not have practices that aligned with college readiness action steps. Bruce's comments speak directly to the benefits of rigorous secondary school training. A third-year political science major, he exclaimed that his strong performances in high school and rigorous coursework prepared and propelled him into college. He shared:

> I felt prepared; I did feel prepared. In high school I was always a step up in my writing courses, my English courses excuse me, and my history courses and math courses. Most of my courses here at Monroe State require us to do writing and essays and so because of that I felt prepared. In high school I was on the AP route, so most of the courses that I took were honors and AP and they were designed to prepare me for college.

The student reflections about their college preparation, specifically as it relates to their schooling experiences, provide helpful insights regarding how *they* felt prepared (or not) for college. Bruce believed that he felt prepared for college precisely because of the rigor and academic work that was required of him during secondary school. As he makes quite clear, these courses were "designed to prepare me for college." Paying attention to students' conceptions of their preparedness and readiness for college can be informative, as it can relate to their concerns regarding college and their early college performances as well. Additionally, their insights help identify potential areas of improvement. And, as is the mantra across various schools and institutions, and as is supported by researchers and a number of educational stakeholders, we must do whatever it takes to prepare Black and Latino males for college.[24]

Self-Reflections: "Mentally, I Feel Like I Wasn't Prepared"

In addition to discussing their college readiness with regard to academic preparation, a handful of the students also discussed other factors that contributed to their preparedness for college. What is outlined in this section reaffirms the importance of holistic approaches to education where we pay particular attention to the social-emotional needs of students. For these Black male students, academic preparation was not their main focus in considering their college careers as some of the students identified personal development and growth, family dynamics, and academic identity issues as important caveats to their experiences. What they share helps to complicate and nuance mitigating factors that are critical for student preparation, transition, and success in college. Below I highlight a range of the students' thoughts about their preparation for college that touch on their socioemotional development, preconceived college focus, and focus on academics.

Denzel, a second-year engineering major, experienced two stints where he took time off from college, both of which were due primarily to financial reasons. His mother was enrolled in a doctoral program during his college years, which helped to acclimate him to college campuses at an early age. He noted that he felt comfortable on college campuses because he had "grown up" being on a variety of campuses because of his mother's academic aspirations. Additionally, he shared that a significant source of his motivation to attend college was based on his mother's role-modeling the importance of college and his desire to be an engineer. Denzel's story about college readiness provides a classic example of the importance of paying closer attention to socioemotional intelligence. Although he felt academically prepared for college, he had a range of personal experiences that impacted his emotional preparation for college. In particular, he believed it was important that he had time for critical self-reflection prior to attending so that he could put some of his personal experiences in perspective. Denzel did not have time to take a break between finishing high school and attending college, and because he needed financial support, he felt underprepared as he enrolled in college.

> I feel like I was prepared as far as academic wise, but maybe on an emotional level I had some things I felt like I had to deal with before I got to college. Just some family stuff that happened in the past I felt like I needed some time to do some reflection and time to understand what was going on because I didn't really get a chance to do it when I was a kid. I felt like this was the time to do it because I had been in school for so long . . . I was ready academically but I needed a break; emotionally I needed a break but it wasn't allowed. Not from mom but the system because I wouldn't have had any money.

Denzel's self-awareness is insightful, as it allows him to locate an area of growth important to his holistic development as a student and as a person. Although he felt prepared academically, he believed that he needed more time and space to prepare emotionally for the demands of college.

Similar to what Denzel offered, several students framed their thoughts about preparation around their mental approach to beginning college. Sean's experiences exemplify this phenomenon. A second-year communications major, he recounted confidence in his academic preparation and knowledge about his chosen field of study; however, he felt underprepared mentally. He exclaimed:

> I knew what I wanted to do as far as my major goes but I thought, I knew I wanted to go to parties and stuff like that. I knew I was going to go to parties and then do my homework and should I go to parties and then do homework. I'll get a call from friends and stuff like that. Mentally, I feel like I wasn't prepared.

For some of the students, attending college was a pathway to being away from home and being on their own. College provided them with a level of independence that they looked forward to and desired, as they continued to develop their masculinity and manhood constructs. Sean's reflection accurately sums up those students who identified how their mental preparation and approach to college undermined their academic efforts. He elaborated on his mental approach to college, he noted that "my mind was on the wrong thing; I was thinking about girls and going to parties. I knew I needed to focus on my work but mentally I was focusing on the wrong things." Several researchers identified that Black males value the development of social skills over academic ones.[25]

College Concerns

In talking with students about their concerns in attending college, they offered a range of areas that created some anxiety and unease. Listening to student concerns helped provide a window to better appreciate the interplay of their college aspirations and preparation with their transition to college and early experiences (discussed in chapter 3). Consistent with previous research, the students' primary college concerns centered on academics, finances, and belonging.

Academics: "Just Keeping My Grades Up"

As the students spoke about their academic concerns for college, they mainly focused on their ability to perform well academically—especially given some of their thoughts about lacking college readiness. Kory and Mark's comments are representative of the students' academic concerns prior to college. Their remarks clearly indicate the importance of student services, college programming efforts for first-year and transitioning students, and students' sense of belonging once they are on campus. Kory shared that he chose his current college because it offered a "small, intimate" feel, which he considered much like his secondary school atmosphere. Additionally, he believed that he would be able to fit in on campus precisely because of its size and his ability to navigate the college easily. As he considered his college concerns, he stated the following:

> Just keeping my grades up and keeping my head on straight because at the end of the day that's why I was here. I'm the type of individual that if I have to do something then I'm going to try to do it to the best of my ability not just because I have to do it.

Like other participants, Kory was concerned about his academic work and his ability to perform well. He wanted to keep school as his primary focus and he was determined to do his best. Mark held similar academic concerns, especially given his football participation. He offered:

> Keeping up; keeping up with the course work and the curriculum. Coming from Park West High School, it was always one of those schools that everybody talked down to. If you go to Oakwood then that's a whole different ball game academically and you heard about Yates, so you just knew that your school was at the bottom. So, I knew that it was going to be difficult coming from Park West. I was just concerned about the course work and the curriculum and just keeping up.

Mark's concerns about college stemmed primarily from the high school that he attended and how it might not have helped him be as competitive as students who attended different high schools. He specifically noted that the other schools had a strong academic reputation, so he believed that he needed to be prepared mentally for the challenges that he was sure he would face. Thus, his concerns about the course work and curriculum and his ability to keep up were well warranted. Mark's comments bring to the fore the ways in which many students have precollege experiences that place them at a disadvantage—especially within and along the higher education trajectory. These disadvantages often are shouldered by students, as they are relegated the individual responsibilities to close academic deficits, when in fact they are part of a larger system of educational inequality.[26]

Finances: "Paying for It"

A number of students also were concerned about their financial aid and paying for college. These students examined their own family history and socioeconomic status and saw these as potential barriers to their college matriculation—and success. Monte and Elijah's reflections accentuate this concern:

> MONTE: Paying for it, that was one of my biggest concerns. Coming from a single parent household, I didn't want it to be a burden on my mother—and that's another reason why I really tried for athletics. And, staying focused.

> ELIJAH: How I was gon' pay for it; that was the biggest concern and I'm still worried about it now. Now I have to take out a loan and I didn't have to take out a loan last year. How to fill out the FAFSA; that's one of my concerns too.

As the students in this study affirmed, paying for college was a significant concern that they faced as they prepared for college. For Monte, he situated his college attendance within his family dynamics of not wanting to burden his mother. Additionally, as has been highlighted by other researchers, Monte alluded to the appeal of athletics as "a way out" to help lessen the burden on his family as well.[27] Similarly, paying for school was the central concern for Elijah as he entered college; and, as he noted, it is *still* a concern while he is in college. In particular, his financial aid status changed for the current school year as he had to take out a loan for the year, which was not the case during his first year. In talking with the students about how they are paying for school and their student loans, many of the students estimated that they would have at least $40,000 in loans. Given the rising costs of tuition, this number seems to be on par. However, a troubling concern is that these students attend a public institution of higher education and many of the students have in-state status. According to researchers, nearly two-thirds of Black men who start at public colleges and universities do not graduate within six years, which is the lowest college completion rate among both sexes and all racial groups in higher education.[28]

Belonging: "Not Being as Close to Family"

The third major concern for students as they pondered their collegiate transition was belonging on campus. Students offered a range of reasons about why belonging in college mattered to them and functioned as a major concern. As students discussed this concern, they paid particular attention to their "fit" on campus, the campus environment, potential feelings of isolation, and distance away from their families. According to Strayhorn (2012), a sense of belonging in college refers to students' "perceived social support on campus, a feeling or sensation of connectedness, the experience of mattering or feeling cared about, accepted, respected, valued by, and important to the group and others on campus."[29]

Jordan shared that college attendance and completion was important to him and his family, yet he was still concerned about belonging on campus. Recalling the experiences of other college-bound students, and given his early academic performance in high school, he wondered about being admitted to college and his ability to persist. He submitted:

> Will I drop out? That was the biggest one. I know too many people who've gone to college and after their first semester they drop out and say, "College is not for me." The second concern was who was going to accept me, where was I going to go? I didn't do too well my first two years of high school. I had a lot of stuff going on at home and with my mother; we'd have an argument the night before and I'm in school thinking about that argument. There was so much pressure put on me; neither one of my parents went to college and I was pressured because I was the oldest.

Complicating Jordan's concern about belonging on campus was the pressure of being a first-generation college student. Recall, he began his college career at a community college because of his ailing aunt. Although he held onto a range of concerns, Jordan relied on spiritual guidance to help alleviate some of his concerns. In reflecting on select-ing his current college, he remarked:

> Well, what led me to go here was just, I'm really big on trusting god and believing god. At that moment in time I was just asking god where I was supposed to be because deep down I didn't really want to be here. It's not about my will but god and what he has planned on my life. So, I put my trust in god and he led me here and I've been here ever since.

Jordan, like many of his peers, was concerned about belonging in college and performing to a high level. They had witnessed other individu-als attend college and experience a disconnect in myriads ways. These experiences led Jordan to a critical self-awareness about his approach to college and how his faith played an important role in his understanding of his college choice and "place" on campus.

Bannon acknowledged that he had concerns about belonging on campus. In addition to the appeal of his college choice because of his football participation, he shared that he had a friend attending the school as well. Bannon expressed his concerns for college in the following ways:

> Basically with me being alone, would I be able to get things done. With it being a new experience, would I be able to take care of the things that I didn't have to in the past. Being around different ethnicities and seeing how I gelled; wondering how I would make my mark and leave a legacy at the college. And seeing how I would set up my life and things like that.

Similar to Bannon, Dwight also was concerned about being alone in college. He reported:

> Not being as close to family and definitely not growing on my own. Probably the fear of not being as social or separating myself from drama; trying to handle adversity on my own. In high school you had your parents and you could always go

and talk to them but just dealing with adversity was definitely a fear of mine.

Both Bannon and Dwight shared concerns about their social experiences on campus. Bannon was concerned about being alone on campus, which could manifest itself in a variety of ways. Dwight explained that his concerns revolved around being away from his family. Both of the students revealed how their respective family helped keep them grounded and deal with challenges and adversity. Additionally, their reflections also are important for helping to understand the critical role that cultural centers and student-centered organizations and programming play on college campuses.[30]

The student narratives about their anxieties and concerns help to nuance and complicate their in-college perceptions and experiences. Donald expressed a variety of concerns about going to college, which ranged from feeling that he would be alone to doubting that he would succeed. In expanding on his concern for being alone, he expressed:

> Well, I knew I was coming into college with some of my high school friends but I figured we'd all be too busy to hang out and do what we had to do. So, we'd end up going our separate ways. I didn't expect anybody to be friendly because I figured that they'd be busy pursuing the things that they wanted to do. I didn't think that people would have time to hang out and do different things.

Although he knew he would attend college with some of his high school friends, Donald thought that their friendship connection might be weakened by the academic demands and perceived social atmosphere of college. Embedded in this was his concern that he would struggle to make friends in college. And, additionally, his concerns about belonging in college led to doubts he held about his potential for success. Donald expounded on his reflection about not succeeding in college with the following:

> Because I simply couldn't see myself succeed. I couldn't envision a futuristic me doing anything meaningful or anything with purpose. That probably goes back to me being African

American and I've rarely seen African Americans in those fields. I don't have any incredible skills; I'm not a ball player, I'm not a rapper so I just didn't expect to excel at anything.

Donald's reflections provide critical insight on how students often internalize many of the impressions and messages that they receive or that are projected about their racialized and gendered identities. Additionally, his discernment reveals how many Black males might be praised and supported in athletic and entertainment endeavors but often lack support in academic and educational arenas. Thus, as various researchers have argued, many Black males are troubled in their educational pursuits precisely because they lack support, guidance, and access to capital that might enhance their academic efforts. Donald spoke specifically to his Blackmaleness and shared that he chose his current college primarily because of its convenient location. He added, "I didn't feel like I was prepared to go out of state—especially from cost and distance and things like that." As shared by Donald, and many of his peers, student concerns about belonging on campus were intricately linked to how they perceived their own ability to perform and, ultimately, persist and how Black male "success" is delimited in its projections to them.

Conclusion

Black males' college aspirations and college preparedness are a complex interplay of various factors that contribute to their sense of belonging in college. Examining students' precollege experiences is vital for shedding light on identifying areas of student needs and concerns. Additionally, this investigation reveals areas that can help bolster their future academic success. As we have seen, the men's aspirations and readiness were embedded across their family dynamics, family histories, secondary school experiences, and self-reflections.

As the students considered their college readiness, they learned to lean on a number of resources to help prepare them for college. Although they did not believe their secondary schools prepared them as well as they could have, the students identified parents and siblings, a teacher or class, community-based programs, sports, and their own motivation as key tools in their college preparation. For instance, they saw particular classes as beneficial to their future college efforts; they believed that the teachers taught the course like a college class, which helped them understand the types of teaching, the class pace, and the breadth of information that they would experience in college. Also, having cultural capital was important as well. Having parents or siblings who attended college was important because students could tap into this social and cultural wealth in order to help bridge gaps left by secondary schools. In these ways, some of the men learned to supplement their college readiness using alternative means to enhance their preparation. Still, in-school experiences are critical in preparing students for college. Researchers continue to note the importance of rigorous academic preparation during the secondary school years. All too often, too many Black males are excluded from rigorous classes, discouraged from opportunities to participate in advanced placement classes, and prevented from accessing educational opportunities that might otherwise support and encourage them. While the research focus here is on Black males in particular, these gaps remain true for all students and undoubtedly reveal areas of need in students' preparation for college and beyond.[31] To be sure, students' perceptions of their preparedness for college are correlated to their academic and social adjustment, their engagement on campus—especially early on—and their sense of belonging.

The men expressed a range of concerns as they thought about their matriculation to college. Students' perceptions and feelings about their preparedness for the academic and social demands of college are important not only during their precollege years, but in their college years as well. As students reflect on their academic and social skill sets, they also have opportunities to reflect on the capital and resources available to them along with their cognitive and noncognitive skills. Students expressed concerns across three main arenas: academics, finances, and belonging. These three domains are similar for many students in their preparations for college. Yet, for the Black men in this study, their expressions were critical for better understanding their transition, resilience, and persistence efforts. Given the ways that they felt underprepared because of their secondary school experiences, the men's academic concerns clearly were understandable. Academic concerns created anxieties for a number of students, some of which meant that students made a range of decisions regarding their collegiate efforts. For instance, a number of men shared that they attended community colleges because they did not foresee success at a four-year institution. These types of concerns continued to play out as the men matriculated to post-secondary institutions. Additionally, some of the men expressed financial concerns for college. They were unsure how they would pay for school, several imagined that athletics would provide them with scholarship money, and a number of other students did not want to burden their families with significant college costs or debt. Thus, in choosing colleges, the family was important for a significant number of the men. Finally, belonging in college was a concern for a large number of students. They expressed concerns about being alone, how they might be accepted on campus, being close to family, and persevering. This concern and desire for belonging in college left many of the men trying to find their place once they arrived on campus.

The findings in this chapter have important implications for students' in-college experiences. In particular, they call attention to the paths and pathways to college for Black male students. As articulated by the students, family was critical in developing their college aspirations and even played a role in their college preparedness and ultimate college choices. Indeed, the data suggest that families figure centrally in these Black male students' understandings, perceptions, aspirations, and cultural capital as they matriculated to college. Likewise, their levels of college readiness (and lack thereof) along with their concerns were critical connections that they took with them in transitioning to college.

CHAPTER 3

College as a Learning Experience
Transitioning to College and College Life

I failed my English class and that's where my poor writing came into play. That's when I realized this shit is *hard*; this shit is hard as fuck!

—Fred

My first year was like all Brothers & Scholars—for real. That was the only group that I was really involved in; that was the only group whose stuff I went to. I didn't really go to parties or anything. So, the only time I left my room was to go to class or a Brothers & Scholars activity. My first year was pretty point blank.

—Deondre

First year was probably my best year and it'll probably be my best year until I graduate. I met most of the people that I know now and we were in the same dorm. I was still trying to figure out the kinks and stuff and learn.

—Cameron

In this chapter, I focus on the students' early college experiences, paying particular attention to their first-year experience, how BMI helped them transition, and how they narrate their overall college experience. As discussed in the previous chapter, the students held a range of concerns prior to entering college. These concerns were academic, financial, social, and personal. Research has shown that many Black male students struggle in their first year of college.[1] For instance, Hausmann and colleagues (2007) identified sense of belonging as a predictor of intentions to persist for Black and White first-year college students. In particular, they found that those students with more peer-group interactions, interactions with faculty, peer support, and parental support maintained positive correlations with students' sense of belonging. Importantly, the researchers reported that, "how well a student adjusts to the academic environment of college is thus closely tied to their developing sense of belonging with college."[2] For Black male students, their adjustments to college and sense of belonging are impacted by their racialized and gendered identities. In an effort to investigate the men's experiences and transitions, these issues are explored in the current chapter.

As noted by the comments shared by Fred, Deondre, and Cameron, the students faced challenges, were focused, and had quality social experiences. The realization of the difficulties of college was impressed upon Fred during his English class in his first year. As he acknowledged, his poor writing skills undermined his success in the English class and ultimately resulted in a failing grade. Fred's experience is exactly the type of scenario that many of the men expressed apprehension about as they shared their precollege concerns. Deondre shared that his transition to college mainly centered on his academic work and his engagement in the Black Male Initiative program on his campus. He expected to face academic difficulties in college, especially given that he was self-admittedly "very unmotivated in high school." Thus, Deondre's personality, habits, and concerns converged into motivation and a fear of failure to perform well academically once in college. Thus focus—and fear—served him well in transitioning to college. Finally, Cameron noted that his social experiences helped him describe his first year as "probably my best year." In particular, although he was still learning to adjust, he cited opportunities to meet and engage with other Black males as the highlight of the year. Cameron's reflection helps highlight how Black men's social and emotional needs play a critical role in their peer associations, friendships, and engagement in college.

Investigating the transition experiences of Black male collegians helps us see the connections between their aspirations, preparation, and concerns with their actualized on-campus experiences. By paying attention to both, their academic and social experiences, we can craft a better understanding of their collegiate careers. Thus, what I discuss in this chapter helps reveal not only the students' meaning-making processes, but also their (continued) challenges, motivations, and successes in their early college experiences and adjustment to college life.

First-Year Experiences

As the men recounted their first-year experiences, they primarily focused on their academic adjustments and transitions to college. By centering their transitions within their academic experiences, the men reaffirmed the importance of college readiness for college success. In examining the transition from high school to college, researchers have argued that students' under-preparedness for postsecondary work was the result of differences between instruction, curriculum, expectations, and institutional structures.[3] The men in the current study had a range of experiences during their first year; some of them struggled in being away from home and transitioning to college, some identified the first year as a learning and developmental process, while others described their early years as a good experience. Along the way, and across experiences, the men shared that their early experiences helped them gain clarity regarding their purpose on campus, academic efforts, personal growth, and helped them obtain personal skills as well. Thus, even with their struggles, there was room for critical self-reflections and various learning opportunities.

First-Year Experience: "It Was Rough"

The interconnectedness between the students' preparation for college and transition to college was noted as a challenge to their academic success. Several of the students discussed how they struggled in their transition to college. Jordan's transition to college presented a challenge initially because the university where he was enrolled was not his desired college. As mentioned previously, he was not accepted to the college of his choice and he shared that many of his secondary school teachers thought he would not be accepted because of his grades and ACT scores. Once he entered college, he still was not keen on attending Lincoln State University. He explained:

> When I got here I was like, "Man! I can go home." It was hard because it was the first time I was away from home.

> Being away from home, that makes you independent and
> it makes you become a man. It makes you become a better
> person because you can't lean on your parents. Your parents
> are not always going to be there and throw you out that rope.

Jordan's reflection is revealing as it illuminates how he inscribes a gendered self-concept into his thoughts about college. Specifically, he asserted
that independence and self-improvement are masculine constructs, both
of which he inscribed into his own identity development during his transition to college. In his research on Black college men, Dancy (2010)
found that self-expectations (self-determination and answerability) and
relationships and responsibilities to family (positioning African-American
men as patriarchs, sons, and brothers) were two critically important manhood constructs that his participants engaged in.[4] Thus, for Jordan, being
on his own and trying to find his place on campus were two challenges
that he had to reconcile early in his college career, especially with regard
to how he constructed understandings of his Black masculine identity.
After self-reflection, and a variety of experiences on campus—including
participating in the Black Male Initiative program and pledging a fraternity on his campus—Jordan later acknowledged that, "I realize that I'm
here for a reason." Importantly, his engagement on campus provided him
with unique opportunities to continue developing and constructing his
manhood and masculinity. As he matured and gained more experiences,
he reframed his status on campus from one of limbo and discontent to one
more aligned with having a purposive presence. Here, in reflections such
as these, the developmental elements of the men's manhood are revealed.

Other students acknowledged that they also struggled in their
transition to college. Steven, a fourth-year sports administration major,
shared that his struggles were connected to his social and academic
experiences on campus. He reported:

> Oh, it was rough! [What made it rough was] being outside
> of the house and living on campus, meeting new people and
> having roommates and getting along with them. UPS kind
> of made it rough, working at night and not really sleeping
> and going to class in the morning.

According to Steven, he had difficulty in adjusting to campus life and
engaging in the social atmosphere as well. Academically, he was chal-

lenged primarily because of his work schedule. He attended classes during the day and worked at UPS during the second shift—from the late afternoon until about midnight. His work schedule and social experiences made his transition to college a challenge. Many of the men shared that a significant appeal of attending college was the opportunity to be on their own and establish a sense of independence. However, for students like Steven, settling into independence and adapting to college required them to be self-reliant and resilient. These demands also exhibit how the men (re)negotiate and (re)construct their masculine identities on campus. All too often, especially for Black men, the meaning of manhood has been treated as universal and one-dimensional, which reaffirms the need to examine the impact of students' social identities on their educational experiences.[5]

For Dwight, his transition to college was particularly tough because of early academic struggles that included dropping one class and earning a low grade in another class during his first year. He recalled:

> My first semester freshman year definitely was tough. I ended up dropping a class, ended up getting a D in another class. People say, "Oh you got a 2.0? You're oaky." But I'm like "No, that's not okay." Stressful, putting on weight and gaining a few pounds.

In specifically speaking about what made his first semester tough, he explained:

> Just me not applying myself and using the resources that were available to me: teachers, tutors, study tables, and stuff like that. I didn't take advantage of the resources and I didn't engage as much socially as I should have. I did do some modeling but I didn't apply myself like I needed to.

Dwight narrated self-expectations and responsibility in his manhood construct. He described himself as "partially prepared" for college primarily because he needed to be more responsible. In transitioning to college, he felt that he was ready for college life and ready to be on his own. Given his need to be more responsible and accountable for his own efforts and work, Dwight felt that he underachieved during his first college semester. He was not satisfied with a 2.0 grade point average that others considered a reasonable achievement. He believed that he could perform at a higher level and even experienced a great degree of stress during his first semester as he worked to reconcile his academic performances with his masculine constructs of self-pride and trying his best. These early experiences helped Dwight think more seriously about his academic future and the results he desired to achieve, which included applying himself more fervently in his academic efforts and accessing some of the resources available on campus. He further exclaimed:

> I feel like I fell . . . my freshman year I underachieved, my second semester I achieved and this semester I wanted to overachieve. I wanted to get a 3.5 but I've more like smoothed out—I'm at like a 3.0 to 2.8 range. I wanted to do better but when you start off slow it's hard to build up, so I still have my sights set on next semester.

Dwight remarked that he learned valuable lessons from his early college experiences, such as better time- and self-management and learning from his peers. He noted his in-class performances have improved and although he did not reach one of his academic goals (3.5 GPA) he maintains motivation to achieve at higher levels. In thinking about what helped him transition to college, he noted:

> Just seeing other people on campus having a good time; you see leaders on your campus and they're having a good time, they're getting good grades and then I'm trying to learn from them. Not that I'm trying to be like somebody else but learning from their experiences. Definitely can't procrastinate; if you want something then you have to go get it and want it. You have to apply yourself and you have to be open. I was afraid to open myself because I didn't want to get hurt. Learning how to create bonds with people too.

As they sought to adjust to campus life, a number of men engaged in behaviors intended to protect their masculine identities. Some of these protective measures, such as not opening up to others or only socializing with people with whom they had previous associations, reveals the delicate nature of their sense of self and highlights some vulnerable and fragile areas as well. Additionally, the men's experiences and concerns exhibit how engaging on campus in fraternity or ethnic organizations as well as institution-based Black male programs (or activities) could play a pivotal role in providing them space to further develop their manhood constructs. For instance, Dancy (2011a) found that mentoring helped his study participants better understand themselves as men and provided them spaces of vulnerability and coping. However, since some men's groups might endorse hegemonic masculinity, programs and activities intended to focus on Black men must incorporate opportunities and spaces for conceptualizing, exploring, developing, and reaffirming healthy masculine and manhood constructs.[6]

Finally, Black's reflections help further nuance the students' early college experiences. Specifically, he felt anxious about college, which led him to question his sense of belonging. In transitioning to college, Black noted that there are great opportunities for students to learn valuable lessons on being focused, learning the material independently, and expecting more from themselves. Another critical note is for students to stay focused on their academic success. After acknowledging that his first year was "very intimidating [laugh]," he expressed:

> It's like, it's a university; you have to be expected more of. I look at Monroe State as a prestigious university; this is like my Yale basically! You have to work your hardest to get the grade that you want. In high school I didn't have to work hard; here you have to work more because you don't get the same information everyday out of the week. You only get the information twice or maybe three times with classes in a week and you only get to see that information during a lecture. So you have to work hard.

In elaborating on what made his school intimidating, he reflected, "Maybe I just felt like I wasn't ready for it. Maybe I just thought that Monroe State wasn't right for me. Like I couldn't fit in here." Similar to a number of his peers, Black found adjusting and fitting in to college difficult. His concerns regarding the higher expectations reactivated his concerns about feeling underprepared for college. He attended a community college in his home community prior to transferring to Monroe State. In his eyes, Monroe State was the equivalent of an Ivy League venture for him. Prior to attending college, he did not envision himself as a college student—at least not one at a four-year institution. Thus, he felt that he needed a herculean effort in order for him to garner *any* level of success in college. Black has continued to internalize these conceptions. He described himself as an introvert and shared that he spends about 40 hours per week engaged in academic work outside of class. He quite frequently turned down opportunities to engage in social activities with many of his peers—such as social outings, gatherings, or events on campus—because he did not want to be distracted. He commented that he "could not afford" too much time spent in social activities, so he just focuses on his academic work.

A plethora of research, both historical and current, continues to reveal that Black students face a number of challenges while attending HWIs. The literature is replete with discussions about the educational experiences of Black males at HWIs, as structural racism, inequalities, and various forms of mistreatment and discrimination mire and constrain their efforts.[7] The majority of the men in this study narrated a range of challenging experiences that included microaggressions, campus climate, and separation and division on campus (these are discussed further in chapter 4). Some of the students' struggles also included their academic experiences—especially early in their college careers. Students explained that their lack of preparation played a role in how they performed academically. This manifested itself in their experiences of feeling overwhelmed, intimidated, and out of place. A number of students noted the need to improve their own efforts, as they transitioned to college with a similar mindset they had in secondary school regarding the effort needed to be successful. These students reported dropping a class (or two), not performing well academically, and feeling disconnected from the institution.

One of the key experiences in helping students transition during their first year was their involvement on campus. Research on Black students' Greek affiliation, for example, have shown the benefits of involvement that include being exposed to leadership roles, having opportunities for civic responsibility, and establishing a network of peers.[8] These opportunities for engagement often are even more critical for Black students at historically White institutions. Thus, investigating their transition experiences helps to identify Black male collegians' early college careers and how these matter in their belonging on campus.

As the students discussed their early collegiate experiences, a significant number of the men focused on their Blackmaleness and revealed how they constructed, and reconstructed, their masculine identities.

Some of the men constructed their manhood around self-expectations and responsibilities. Many narrated their early college years as a time when they were developing and renegotiating their masculine identities. For some of the men, this meant moving away from their parents' and guardians' homes so they could venture out to college alone. Here, being independent and self-reliant were critically important to the men as they started college.

Reflecting on the First Year: "It Was a Process"

Some of the students acknowledged that they tried to "do too much" during their first year on campus. This spanned the gamut of being heavily involved in campus life (such as registered student organizations and other campus activities), trying to balance the demands of collegiate athletics or work, and managing the range of classes they took. Yet, as a result of thinking through these experiences, many of the students acknowledged that their college careers had moved forward as a series of progressions. D'Angelo's and Marvin's experiences highlight the various processes that students experienced as they wove through their time on campus.

D'Angelo paid close attention to the college milieu and stayed mindful of his precollege preparation (or lack thereof). As a result, he remained focused on his academic performances and chose not to get involved in student organizations at the onset of his college career. He wanted time to get a feel of the college, and college life, and he wanted to be sure that he did not have any academic missteps. He expected college to be tough academically and imagined that he would spend the bulk of his time focused on academic endeavors; he expected "an 80-20 [split of time] with academics being 80 and activities being 20." Additionally, knowing that he was attending an historically White institution, he expected some racism and even acknowledged that his perception was based on his lack of familiarity with other racial groups. He described his first-year experiences in the following ways:

> Academically it was a struggle because my high school didn't really prepare me other than that one class. They didn't baby you so you have to stay on top of stuff. I can hold myself to accountability pretty well, so I kinda seen that and I tried to pick it up. I knew that I wanted to be involved but first

semester I didn't just to make sure that I adapted right. I met a few friends but I was worried about academics. I seen Greek life for the first time literally when I got here. I waited 'til second semester to be involved in ATP. I got involved in BSU.

Even with D'Angelo's determination to be focused on his academic performance, he earned a 1.9 grade point average during his freshman year of college. Thus, the struggle was real for D'Angelo as he tried to meet the academic demands of college and ease into campus involvement. He thought that his overall college experiences have been stressful; he explained:

> Stressful, still 'til this day! My main things academic wise I can be in there asking all the questions but when it comes to the test I just can't get it right. Even though I know I've tried hard, I know I haven't put forth the one hundred percent effort. I got a job, well my first stable job here. Involvement, I've been pretty involved throughout my first few years. Racism, I've experienced racism personally. It's the best of times and the worst of times.

The range of D'Angelo's experiences are plentiful, from personal relationships and a stable job to the stresses of academic life and dealing with racism. He asserted that his collegiate experiences have been "the best of times and the worst of times." Across this range, he still feels blessed for his opportunities on campus, which include pledging a fraternity and being elected president as well as serving on executive boards for a number of student organizations. Although he did not perform as well as he would have liked academically his first year, now, as a fifth-year senior, his grade point average is 2.7. He felt encouraged by his accomplishments in raising his grade point average and being sure to remain focused academically even though he participated in a number of organizations on campus. A number of the men credited their involvement in BMI with their satisfaction with and success in college. In particular, securing leadership roles provided them with greater responsibilities and increased their access to capital while developing relationships with other BMI members helped expand their social networks. These relationships offered the men critical support for their academic efforts and aspirations. Additionally, engaging in BMI also aided their personal growth and development as well.

Similar to D'Angelo, Marvin reflected on his academic efforts and saw room for improvement. He specifically identified that he needed to remain focused on his academic work and increase the effort he afforded to his academic performance. He looked forward to the social aspects of college but expected a lot of written assignments. Additionally, he figured that college would be a "new world; that whole concept of college in general where you have a lot of people from a lot of different backgrounds and a lot of new cultures." He visited the campus as a junior in high school and thought that the campus had a party atmosphere. In many ways, he was excited about his new experiences. However, he also acknowledged that he did not make the necessary transitions to college upon arrival; he reported:

> Found out that the work wasn't that hard or challenging. The quality of the work wasn't hard and second was that it was all on me. If I wanted to go to class then I would, if not then I wouldn't; nobody was on my back. I can say I blew them [classes] off a little bit trying to hold on to my high school tendencies. Trying to do just enough to get by.

Marvin described his first year as "Going with the flow. I really didn't stand out too much; I did just enough to get by. Just being average, being a statistic." In some ways, his attitude of "just being average" and behaviors of doing "just enough to get by" and "being a statistic" support conceptions of Black males' supposed opposition to school and their cool masculinity as well.[9] The students' experiences help to nuance notions of cool or oppositional behaviors and reveal how some African-American men have allowed oppressive ways of understanding who they are to cloud how they see themselves.[10] For many of the men, adjusting to and balancing their academic and social experiences in college was complicated by their identity development and negotiation. An important component of their identities was developing a sense of purpose about their time in college and their college efforts.

In doing just enough to get by, Marvin lacked a purposive effort and self-reported that he "skipped a lot of classes" and also "fit the profile of a typical freshman." Because he was more focused on his social experiences, Marvin's academic performances did not reflect his ability. Since his freshman year, he has been a lot more focused and much more aware of various opportunities on campus. He commented:

> I've been a lot more aware. Every semester I've tried to gain some skill or improve something that I've learned. I'm more aware of Lincoln State as a school. Freshman year and sophomore year I was just here, just going to class. Not really understanding what's going on. I saw there was Greek life and organizations, but I wasn't aware of the school; wasn't really aware of resources, tutoring, and things that could've helped me back then.

As he reflected on his academic experiences, and the lessons that he learned along the way, Marvin acknowledged a great deal of self-growth and self-awareness. His self-awareness has helped him increase his academic output and better conceptualize his place on campus. Additionally, he learned more about what campus had to offer and the various resources available to him. His heightened awareness was correlated with his self-growth; different opportunities and resources helped him expand his college experience beyond the often-held generic perspectives such as Greek life and parties.

What the students offered about their first year challenges helps to bring to the fore the importance of investigating factors that might help student success. For instance, in his study investigating the factors that contributed to Black males successfully completing a bachelor's degree, two key findings by Warde (2008) included (1) having an epiphany about the importance of higher education and (2) having access to the resources needed to attend and persist.[11] Some of the men's experiences echo Warde's findings given the revelations they experienced during their time in college (such as heightened awareness) and greater access to various campus resources. In addition, these experiences connect well with findings from other studies that student engagement in purposeful activities has positive correlations to academic outcomes.[12] Other students identified a number of stressors that impacted their college transitions. Similarly, in exploring persistence, researchers identified life-stressing events and environmental variables as key to persistence for Black males.[13]

First Year in Focus: "A Good Experience"

A moderate number of the students described their first year in college in positive ways. These students talked about their first year through descriptive terms such as a "good experience" and as "fun." In these ways, the students expressed that they had transitioned to campus smoothly and were able to enjoy a good mix between their academic and social activities and engagements. Most critically for those students who described their first year as "a good experience," was that they had performed well—or at least to their own self-expectations of their capabilities. Thus, their academic performances helped to alleviate many of their college concerns.

Myron described his first year as good and as a learning experience. He expected the transition to college to be a bit of a challenge academically—"I thought there would be a ton of homework"—but he believed that the college's proximity to his hometown might help him socially because he would know people and have some familiarity with the college community. In speaking about his first year, Myron described it in the following way:

> MYRON: It was, I'd say it was a good experience. It's the first time really, even though I'm not that far from home, but being away from home for an extended period of time. I learned a lot of stuff and I met a lot of people.
>
> DB: What kind of stuff did you learn?
>
> MYRON: I learned, well, you know, you learn uh book knowledge and stuff like that. But you also learn like personal skills. Like, I learned about professionalism and like how to get a job, how to present yourself; stuff like that, outside of education, per say [se] exactly.

For Myron, the quality of his first year in college was centered on meeting new people and his learning experiences. Although it was the first time he was away from home, he felt secure in knowing that the distance home was in close proximity so that he could maintain his connections with his family and could spend time with them frequently. Acquiring and enhancing their personal skills was important to a number of men in the study. Increasing their skills, such as professionalism and presentation of self, amplified the students' abilities to what they could deploy in college and in their lives.

Other students discussed their first year in similar ways. For instance, Arthur paid particular attention to finding a balance between being involved on campus and his academic work. He shared:

> My first year was, if I had to say, the prefect mix of being involved but also being aware of why you're here. It was my first year being involved, it wasn't a light commitment. I got involved [in Brothers & Scholars] and was on the e-board and got to make some connections. I was established in that first year . . . It was actually pretty easy, if I have to say so. The classes weren't too tough. The workload, in my opinion, wasn't too much. It was relaxing. I came from a high school where I kinda knew everybody and then coming here I had to meet new people. That was a good experience. Even though I had to meet new people, I bumped into people that I knew from elementary school, so I still kinda had some friends.

Arthur's thoughts about his academic experiences were important in creating balance for his first year. He noted that, other than holding the idea that it would be different than high school, he had no expectations about college. In expressing his trepidations regarding college, his two major concerns were succeeding in the classroom and thinking about (or knowing) what he would do after graduation. Given his academic concerns, it is clearer why he wanted to ensure that he was mindful about his purpose and responsibilities while in college. Maybe because of his hyper focus on academics, he found that his classes were manageable and he enjoyed meeting new people.

Similar to Arthur, Bruce desired to find a balance between his academic demands and social engagements. Bruce shared that he was involved in a number of activities during secondary school and this involvement helped provide meaning to his schooling experiences. Upon entering college, he knew that he wanted to be involved in campus life.

However, as he notes below, he tempered his social engagements so that he did not compromise his academic work. He explained:

> My first year, it was fun. I feel like most people come in and say, "Oh, I partied and I did this and all that" and their grades slip. I was a person more on the outside; I watched them do all the parties and watched their grades slip. I stayed focused on my grades. I was able to maintain my academic scholarship. I would say that at least fifty percent of people lost their scholarship or had to go back and reapply for it. So, I can say that I did stay focused and my grades reflected it. I did join three organizations during my first year and I'm still a member of those.

Bruce's experiences were similar to Arthur's in a number of ways, including balancing his social activities with staying grounded in pursuing his academic work. Both students displayed a level of maturity that allowed them to resist early temptations of focusing solely on their social lives. Both students joined a number of organizations during their first year and Arthur even participated at an executive board level of the Black Male Initiative program on his campus. Importantly for Bruce, and what helped make his first year experience positive, was that he stayed focused on his academic work. Arthur echoed this focus as well in his remark about "being aware of why you're here."

As noted in the previous chapter, many of the students entered college concerned about the academic workload, the college milieu, and belonging on campus. Thus, as they transitioned to college, students balanced these concerns with some of the "newness" of college life—such as attending parties, meeting new people, and participating in various organizations on campus. Based on the student narratives about their first year, taking into account their own self-described successes and failures, it was important for students to have balance. Some of the students were restrained in getting involved early on while some students shared that they tried to engage in too many activities—early in their college careers. Given these realities, trying to get adjusted to college weighed heavily on many of the students. They noted how being away from home, in a different environment, and on a college campus, provided them with unique opportunities to pursue interests, especially socially, that were meaningful to their college experience.

The Role of BMI in Transitioning to College

In talking with students about their BMI engagement, they shared a range of experiences that were critical to their college careers. Both Mighty Men and Brothers & Scholars were designed as social cohesion programs that included academic components as well. One of the major ways that the students discussed the impact of BMI was through what they experienced as a community. In speaking about the impact of BMI on their college experience, the men noted that the BMI community was important to their entry to the university because it helped relieve them of many anxieties of transitioning and provided them with a group of individuals with whom they could connect early in their college careers. Beyond the support group, students identified the impact of BMI on their college transition and their academic performance through social and cultural capital (sociocultural capital). Social capital refers to the ways that some individuals gain access to resources through networks while cultural capital is context-specific and refers to certain cultural signals or competencies (such as values, attitudes, and preferences).[14] Importantly, acquiring sociocultural capital increases one's competencies and resources than can be deployed in various settings to pursue different ends.

Arriving Early: "Becoming Very Familiar with the Campus"

Similar to Black Greek organizations, participating in Black Male Initiative programs can play a significant role in helping students transition to college, especially by exposing them to much-needed sociocultural capital.[15] For instance, the Brothers & Scholars program at Monroe State included an College Transition Program (CTP), which allowed students to move to college two days early, participate in bonding and social cohesion activities that helped them acclimate to college, and meet various staff, faculty, and administrators as well. Half of the students interviewed from Brothers & Scholars participated in the Early Arrival Program.

> CAMERON: That was the start of where I met the people that I hang out with today. It was a lot of exercises that we participated in that I really enjoyed. It started out good because we had assigned mentors but as the year went on the mentoring didn't turn out so well.

MYRON: Especially so early in the year, getting to know people and I already knew some people from high school, it was good. All of the speakers that they had and the activities that they had went in line with welcome week helped get our mind ready for school. And they hit on points that for African American males we'd need to focus on to be successful.

The CTP is a three-day program that included academic and social activities for first-year Black male and female students. While there are a number of activities that include both student populations (such as a college goal-setting session and a cook-out), six activities are designed to speak to Black males in particular. In addition to a program overview, other activities include sessions on relationship building and networking, Black male identity, and a mock classroom/student panel. The relationship building and identity sessions are geared toward social cohesion while the goal-setting and student panel are geared toward academic success. In addition, several BMI members volunteer as Ambassadors during the CTP. In this role, they greet and accompany students at various events and serve as tour guides to help students identify campus locations. During the panel discussion, student panelists respond to pre-identified questions about their college experiences (such as "What has your experience been like?" and "How did you decide on your major?") and field questions from new students. Cameron and Myron's reflections are representative of the group. Primarily, they appreciated opportunities to meet new people, learn about campus resources, and learn about college expectations from those who were familiar with the institution already. These activities aided students' transition to college as they "helped get our minds ready for school."

Further, several students shared that including sessions about identity and responsibility as part of the CTP program was valuable in helping them gain a sense of comfort on campus and introduced them to the bonding that was promoted within Brothers & Scholars. Renaldo shared:

As a student, I was at first a little bashful of the situation when I first got to campus being that I've never really been around a large group of Black students. I was slowly able to become more comfortable and know more people. It seemed that I was able to form a sense of brotherhood; I was able to gain more friendships and finding what I had in common.

As Renaldo reflected on what was memorable for him about his CTP experience, he added:

Becoming very familiar with the campus and having at least a small group of people that you knew on the first day. Whereas other people may only know who they came in with high school with—or their roommate or maybe somebody they met. But we had that and so much more . . . you're able to say "Hi" to almost 20 people; it makes you feel good.

In speaking about the impact of BMI on their college experience, the men noted that bonding with other Black males was important to their entry to the university because it helped relieve them of many social anxieties of transitioning and provided them with a group of individuals with whom they could connect early in their college careers. Connecting with other Black men not only provided the students with an early support group, but it increased their sense of belonging by making them feel welcomed and valued as well.

College Transition with BMI: "Gave Me Some Connections"

In discussing how BMI helped their transition to college, students discussed increased awareness and access to resources as key impacts. Of the students who said they gained access to resources, just over one-third reported that they learned about resources around campus and almost a quarter reported that they were connected to various people across campus—including faculty, staff, and peers. Students offered the following examples:

ELVAN: It's helped a lot. Especially with it being a support group, I've been getting a lot of advice about what classes to take, you meet people who are in your major, you find people who give you advice about when is the best time to take class. I have a couple of friends and if they have an assignment coming up we'll all get together, even if it's not that much, we'll get together and go to the library. We'll put the other plans on the backburner; like, it's not too much to put it off for a day and we'll focus on our studying.

KORY: At first when I wasn't social, I wasn't out there and didn't talk to that many people. I'm not going to say I didn't know what I was doing because I was going to class. But it helped me transition to college by getting to know all of the things about college. In high school they might prepare you for school or prepare you for a minimum wage job, but it doesn't prepare you for life lessons. And I feel like that's what Mighty Men has done; it's introduced me to networking, it's introduced me to different community service opportunities. It's helped me do more.

D'ANGELO: Mighty Men for me just helped me vent; it helped me be able to have people to talk to about whatever. Talk about how all the White boys say the "n-word" and thinking it's cool. Talking about how the teachers give us so many tests. It kinda made me feel more comfortable in knowing that I had a place that I could let it out. It helped me academically to stay on top and reminding us that midterms are coming up, career fair is coming up, so make sure you do this or do that.

Beyond the support group, students identified BMI's role in increasing their social capital. Elvan, a third-year accounting major noted that the program has been helpful in connecting him with people who can serve as academic resources regarding classes and class schedule, helping with assignments, and establishing a study group as well. Kory shared that BMI served as a resource socially and academically. He recalled learning about how to transition to college more effectively while also learning life lessons as well, such as networking and community service. Both Elvan and Kory affirm how BMI helped students access strategic resources on campus and increase their social capital. Researchers identify social capital as instrumental and productive relationships or networks. Additionally, social capital in college is often gained by student participation in out-of-class experiences such as clubs and organizations and may help students acquire the cultural capital that promotes success in college.[16] For D'Angelo, he specifically identified that his BMI program served as a counter-space, allowing him opportunities to counter much of the tension that he felt and experienced on campus. Thus, as a resource, BMI was critical to his college transition to better understand and articulate his experiences while also serving as a space that helped him academically and professionally as well.

Randy acknowledged BMI as a resource as he shared:

> It helped me meet African American males; gave me some connections, I got to meet some faculty and graduate students. They were able to tell me their experiences and I was able to learn from them and hear about the ins and outs of school. So having them as a mentor or somebody that you can talk to has definitely helped me.

Randy identified the social and cultural capital he was able to accumulate through his participation in BMI. This included opportunities to meet other Black males on campus along with establishing connections with graduate students and faculty as well. Randy believes these connections are key because graduate students and faculty were able to share their own experiences, and the knowledge they gained from matriculating through college has provided him with valuable insight on his own journey. Randy's experiences connect well with previous research that revealed that BMI programs play an important role not only in what students experience on campus but also how they experience campus. For instance, in a qualitative study of students engaged in a BMI program, researchers found that providing Black male collegians with opportunities to connect with others was a critical BMI experience as it had the potential to enhance their sociocultural capital.[17]

Bannon and Cameron shared this sense of connection. Cameron noted, "Just basically networking wise. I met a lot of faculty through BMI, which is helping me be successful in being here." Likewise, Bannon exclaimed:

> It got me connected with those that I would need to get connected with, people of my creed and people of my ethnicity, especially as an African American male because there's not that many on campus. Getting connected to people who cared and supported my efforts and then just being able to pursue my dreams and my goals.

Much like Randy, Bannon and Cameron also felt that engaging in BMI increased the capital at their disposal. First, Bannon acknowledged that BMI helped him connect with people in his racialized and gendered group on campus, which was important because of their low numbers on campus. Additionally, being connected to the group and the program helped Bannon enhance his sense of belonging on campus where he could pursue his dreams and goals without being deterred. This type of capital accumulation is significant given the myriad challenges and barriers that Black males face on campus. With increased capital, the men narrated ways that they were better able to be agentic, navigate the campus, tap into various resources, and persevere. According to Cameron, opportunities to meet faculty through BMI have helped him navigate campus more successfully. Darius also expressed this sense of comfort and connection as he shared, "Definitely made me more comfortable. Allowed me to see things in a different view in the Black community and even among myself." Thus, BMI operated in multiple facets on the students' transitions to college, which included increasing their capital and serving as a counter-space to the college milieu.

Academic Impact: "I Want to Be that Example"

Students also discussed the impact of BMI on their academic performances. They provided a variety of responses to their academic work and noted that they felt motivated by the positive and competitive atmosphere within BMI. Additionally, they talked about how BMI helped improve their academic performance as well. The following statements offered by students summarize this theme:

> TERRENCE: It has brought the competitor out of me. You know, if I hear a guy say they got a 3.3 or a 3.4 [GPA], it makes me want to do better. All my life I've gotten decent grades and I just didn't want to be that guy talking about a 2.2 when asked about it. It all goes back to credibility.

> MARVIN: It's made me hold an expectation within myself and as well as a bit of competitiveness with my fellow peers. I'm competitive so it feels good to be the best out of an elite group. The best of the best gets an award based on what you

did. It feels like a sense of accomplishment to me to say this is what you did. Like I said, I know I have to keep going to the tutoring, accessing the resources, [and] going to teacher's office hours.

The positive peer culture developed within these BMI programs creates an atmosphere that enhances Black males' academic performances. As expressed by the men here, they felt motivated to perform academically because of their participation in BMI. First, their peer group enriched this motivation where the academic focus helped bring out the competitor in some of the men. What is critical here is the point that many of these men welcomed the academic challenge to perform at a high level because they wanted to contribute to the positive achievements of the group. Second, the men saw themselves more broadly than individual agents but more so as members of the larger group. Whether it was the group setting a goal for a particular grade point average or because they knew that members of the group were mindful of their performance, some of the men felt motivated to achieve academically. Both of these findings support current research on the impact of peer support and relationships on Black male achievement.[18]

In addition to thinking about their peer group as friendly competition and feeling connected to the larger group, students adjusted their academic behaviors in an effort to meet the demands of college. Within the BMI community they were informed and reminded to access campus resources such as tutoring, the writing center, and faculty office hours. By engaging in behaviors such as these, students show how they worked to acquire dominant cultural capital as well as requisite knowledge to perform well (or better) academically. Students confirmed that these efforts helped them improve their grades, helped to display to professors the seriousness of their academic efforts, and showed how they invested both time and effort to the academic commands of college. In these ways, what the men offered also speaks to how BMI serves as a resource on campus. Finally, the men felt compelled to raise their expectations of their own performance because the supportive atmosphere of BMI helped the men re-conceptualize their academic performances. Reggie shared:

It's like competition, friendly competition amongst each other. It's not who sees your grades or anything, but we pushed for a group 3.0. So having somebody to compete with is good, because I'm a competitive person. So if we compete with each other and we're trying to push each other then we'll do better as a group. So it's like a driving for or a motivational force. I want to be that example for other males coming in to look up and see how we are and that way we can inspire them. And, then they see your grades, so they'll pull you to the side. So, knowing that they want you to succeed services as another tool. Knowing you have a support system pushes my drive and I'm sure it does other people too. So, it's like a support system.

Almost a quarter of the students (9 out of 40) declared that BMI either had a neutral impact or no impact at all on their academic performances. These students proclaimed an academic focus that did not rely on BMI; they expressed clarity about their academic goals and wanted to perform well regardless of what activities they engaged in. For the majority of the students, however, they made clear and explicit connections between their involvement in BMI and their academic work. A key point to maintain is the impact that the men saw in their own academic efforts. As Reggie attested, several of the students desired to perform well because of the influence this could have on the Black male collegians that would follow them. Thus, some of the men believed their academic efforts to be important for the group.

College Experiences Thus Far

Talking with students about their overall college experience is both necessary in getting to know them and their stories and quite informative. The students were eager to share the meanings they made from a full range of experiences and how those experiences mattered in their college careers. Importantly, the students' sharing also opens a door to better understand what they identified as significant moments and events throughout college, along with learning about their college journeys— even for those students who had only completed one year of college. As I discuss in the following sections, the student narratives reveal a complexity of reflections that highlight their social, academic, and personal lives in college. Additionally, some of the students still maintain concerns about their college success and their future endeavors.

College Life: "It's Been an Experience"

For most of the men who described their collegiate experiences in positive ways, their involvement on campus and social experiences were significant features of their narratives. Thus, confirming prior research, being actively involved and having high quality social experiences were important to the Black male students in this study.[19] Through these endeavors, they were able to meet new people, develop significant friendships and bonds, learn more about themselves, and acquire a range of skills along the way. D.J., a fourth-year student, shared that his college years have been a blast. He acknowledged that he was "just average" during his first year, mostly because he focused too heavily on the social aspects of campus life. He asserted that he was "trying to do too much and not balance it out," which ultimately resulted in him earning a 2.0 grade point average that year. In thinking about his overall experiences, he remarked:

> It's been a blast; I've met some lifelong friends. Like I said, I'm a very sociable guy. It's been an experience; I've had ups and I've had downs—man, college has been a blast so far. It's almost over now, but it's been dope. I've done a lot of networking too, so I think when I get out of here I'll have a lot of connections. So, I'll have some people that will be there.

Although he has had "ups and downs," D.J. still describes his college experience as "a blast" because he has been able to be active on campus, he has traveled throughout the state and region with a number of campus organizations, and he has made some significant friendships. He shared that his current roommates are two friends that he met during his first year on campus. D.J. placed a premium on his social experiences and the networking that he has been able to do.

As the students described their overall college experiences, they provided a view of their progression. Quite often, they discussed the friendships they have made along the way and the people that they met were significant and complimented their academic experiences. In the previous quote, D.J. specifically identified networking and human capital he has accrued while in college as important endeavors. The importance of the social experience was expressed by a number of students. Mark began his reflection about his overall college experience by framing it within his social experiences; he explained:

> It was great, starting back from freshman year just meeting new people from different backgrounds. Meeting guys from the inner city of [his home city] that was a different experience for me; growing up in the suburbs you just have a different experience. Just being able to adapt and trying to find out who I was. A lot of those guys didn't make it through whether they dropped out or transferred. Sophomore year was the year that I wanted to reach out and get involved. Freshman year I went to things like BSU but I wasn't heavily involved. My second semester I decided to join a fraternity and that really helped me find some social aspects of college because I wasn't really a social guy. I kinda just stuck to myself.

Mark described his college experience in positive ways. The social networks that he established and the diversity of people from different backgrounds that he met made a definitive imprint on his early experiences. He met people who grew up in different areas, which allowed him to learn about life experiences that were different than his own. This was crucial to his early experience as he explored self-discovery and heightened his self-awareness, as he noted he was "trying to find out who I was." In juxtaposing his experiences with those of others, he felt an accomplishment in still being able to persist as opposed to "those guys [who] didn't make it through." After his first year on campus, he increased his involvement, which ultimately allowed him to "find some social aspects of college" and expand his collegiate experiences. Additionally, he explained how his involvement shaped some of his experiences. He went on to share:

> When I joined a fraternity I saw the social side of it. Freshman and sophomore year were my best years academically and then after that I got into my major, which meant that academics got tougher. So, time management became harder especially since I became more involved. Once I got involved and trying to do something positive it was definitely difficult in trying to manage my time. Now, senior year, I've been able to get

> me a job and a pretty good position; I've been able to be a guy that other people can look up to. Now, I'm just trying to finish up. My senior year was a big year for me because this is the first time I had a job and I have different positions in my fraternity. So, overall I had a pretty good experience.

Although he had very positive experiences in his social engagements and involvement on campus, Mark found it increasingly difficult to balance time. Now, as a senior, it was important for him to stayed focused on engaging in positive activities and serving as a model (or mentor) to younger students on campus—especially in his fraternity and in the BMI program. In addition to his activities, he also garnered more responsibility because he secured a job and was thinking more about his future endeavors.

Several students reflected on their college careers in ways that included experiences well beyond their respective campus. Similar to D.J. and Mark, Jared, a third-year industrial engineering major, focused on his social experiences and also added off-campus connections he has made along the way that he identified as significant. He noted:

> Uh . . . gee, it's been a bunch of stuff. Gotten to travel a bunch, met all sorts of different people; I've met the mayor, I've met the athletic director at Ohio State. I don't know, I can't even think of everybody I've met a lot of different people. I met a lot of good friends; I've got to live with people from out of the country. I've gotten to live in the dorm and know what it's like to live away from your parents. And, I've pulled all-nighters. And, having a support system while I'm here. I don't know, my college experience has been pretty well.

As Jared recounted his college career, he made specific note of the opportunities afforded to him to travel, meet key people in the city and at other institutions, and establish important friendships as well. In addition to some of the traditional college experiences, such as living in a dorm, living away from home, and studying all night, Jared's sense of belonging on campus was connected to meaningful experiences, relationships, and having a support system. Given the interconnections across these three areas, he shared that he has had a positive college experience.

College as a Learning Process: "I'm in a Transition Period"

As the students shared their overall experiences in college, they also discussed college as a learning process that moved in a series of transitions. The first and most apparent transition was moving from secondary to postsecondary school. Within this realm, the students framed their reflections mostly through academic experiences. A second transition that was important to the students was moving into the independence they desired and reflected on their abilities to make their own decisions regarding how and where they spent time, the activities they engaged in, and being responsible for their actions. Third, the students also transitioned into a new, and very different, social environment where they met new people and had a variety of opportunities and challenges. Ultimately, across these transitions, the students learned a great deal about themselves—especially in terms of who they were and who they wanted to be.

Kory entered college primarily concerned about his academic performance; he desired to stay focused on performing well and remembering why he was in college. In thinking about his college expectations, he took heed to some of what he heard about college as that "real world" and his personal responsibilities. Kory moved to college during the summer and focused on his mental preparation; he wanted to be in the "right mindset" because he "didn't want to be that person who had to come home." In reflecting on his college experiences, he began by talking about his college transitions:

> It's funny because I feel like I'm in a transition period right now. Freshman and part of last year, I was real to myself. I don't think I'm anti-social but I'm not one of those people that are out there as much. I had a girlfriend at the time so it was go to class, maybe chill with her, and chill in my room. It was really structured in such a way that I wasn't doing anything other than academics.

Upon entering college, Kory mostly stayed to himself and did not engage in many social activities. He had a daily routine, which included spending a significant amount of time with his girlfriend, but mostly revolved around his academic life. He credits Mighty Men Mentoring for helping him create a transition in his college experience and expand it beyond academics. He continued and explained:

> Mighty Men was one of those things that got me out of my shell. Marshall got me going to the meetings and they said I should check it out. You get stuck in your ways and since you get used to doing things a certain way. They got me out to a meeting and had me go to the Summit; after that it grew on me. After going to Mighty Men and attending week after week, it motivated me to go into other things and speak up more. That's where I'm at now, doing the school and the social thing. I feel like that's what life is about; it's about the learning and you can't just focus on that because there's other things going on outside of that. My grades kinda slipped up last semester but I'm focused on bringing them up.

Participating in BMI for Kory, like many of his peers, was transformative. Most significant for Kory was that he felt motivated to get more involved in student activities on campus after regularly attending the BMI meetings. In addition to getting more engaged in campus activities, many students developed a greater sense of agency and self-awareness. Kory had transitioned from solely focusing on academics to now blending academic work with social experiences. Thus, he too saw college as this growing process where people learned how to get out of their shells and comfort areas and expand themselves. In the end, although his grades are not where he wanted them to be, he also credited Mighty Men with helping him see how he could learn and grow as a person, as he is focused on improving his academic performances.

As the students became more engaged on campus, their involvement helped provide new learning opportunities and opened up a variety of possibilities for them as well. Cameron shared that neither one of his parents attended college; thus, his college aspirations peaked as he would be the first college graduate in his family. He was motivated by internal and external factors that included his desire to succeed in life and better himself along with wanting to improve his community.[20] Keeping his aspirations in mind help to better appreciate his college experience, he explained:

So far, I'm really enjoying it. It's the best thing that could've happened to me in a while—a major chapter in my life. I feel like I've grown as a person; I met a lot of new people. I feel like it's like high school, not popularity wise, but a lot of people enjoy my presence. I'm stepping up and doing things, more involved than I thought I would be. . . . Sometimes I feel like I'm lost in a crowd in class. Profs say they have office hours and even if I go I still feel like I'm just a number because they won't know me personally. The other thing is job commitment with me working extra jobs and stuff, so just finding the time to balance everything out.

As can be gleaned from his reflection, Cameron believed that college has not only been a major chapter in his life, but it also is "the best thing that could've happened" to him and it helped him "grow as a person." A number of students, including both Kory and Cameron who are cited here, specifically referenced growing as people to be key processes and factors in their collegiate experiences. For Cameron, this growth was due to a number of factors, including a need to learn balance from working extra jobs, trying not to be (or feel) lost in a crowd in class, and getting his professors to know him personally. In these ways, Cameron's experiences help to reveal ways in which he sought mattering and belonging on campus. For instance, he clearly appreciated instances where people "enjoy my presence" and at the same he did not want to feel lost in a crowd in class. Additionally, he was involved on campus to an extent that surpassed his own previous conceptions of his involvement. Earlier, he shared that he expected college to be on his own in college and he saw college as a more individual experience. Thus, his involvement also can be read as his desire to be valued and seen as a positive contributor to the campus community.

College and Stress: "Hardship . . . and Complications"

A handful of students discussed the difficulties they faced in trying to transition to college, much of which was experienced during their first year on campus. Given the range of concerns that students held prior to college, and in part due to their lack of academic and social preparation, their struggles are not necessarily surprising. However, their struggles are important because they continue to highlight the intricate web of factors that contribute to student success, such as campus environment, preparation, academics, finances, and family to name a few. Below I focus on two student reflections as examples of this phenomenon. Raymond's trajectory to college was quite different from most of his peers in the current study. He initially desired to join the Marines. He enlisted voluntarily after completing high school and was not able to continue with basic training after a physical examination revealed that he was not "fit" to continue. Thus, he did not recall any expectations he had for college "except for extra work." He further added that he "expected students to be arrogant and conceited, I expected most of the teachers to be arrogant and conceited and I expected most of the work to be pointless." After what he described as an uneventful first semester of college, he faced a number of challenges his second semester—many of which continued (or contributed to others) through the remainder of his college career. He shared:

> First year was pretty basic, pretty much stayed to myself . . . Second semester is when everything started falling apart. I had to get another job to pay back my loans, my dad's house burned down and I had to pay for hotel rooms and had to feed people. So, I didn't get to focus on my schoolwork. And, I had to help my mama with some things too.

As his family faced difficulties, Raymond, a fourth-year exercise science major, played a prominent role in helping his family navigate difficult experiences. He shouldered financial responsibilities for the family and got "another job" to provide housing and food for family members in addition to paying some bills and helping family members try to find employment. At several points throughout his time in college, Raymond worked as many as three jobs at the same time to help provide for his family. His family connections and responsibilities competed with his available time to focus on his academic work. In speaking specifically about his first year, he added:

> Hardship, complicated; more so the personal life than college. It's not hard to keep up with college life it's just the personal life that makes it hard. I feel like if I could've just focused

on schoolwork I'd have a 3.0 or above but life didn't work out that way.

Raymond had no doubt that his academic performance easily would have been higher if his family life had not complicated his time in college. As he acknowledged, some of his personal life circumstances made focusing on college much more difficult. Raymond's experiences, and a host of aspirations from this student population, continue to identify the critical role that family plays in their aspirations, performances, and persistence. In her research on high-achieving Black males, education scholar Kimberly Griffin (2006) asserted that many Black students have to contend with family and friends in addition to balancing their college academic demands. In her study, she found that almost all of her participants identified their parents as a significant external source of motivation.

Another student, Terrence, a fourth-year Spanish major, initially decided to enroll at an HBCU (Historically Black Colleges University) because he wanted to attend school out of the state, he wanted to attend an HBCU, and he wanted to play football. After his partial athletic scholarship was not renewed for his second year, and given the lack of opportunities he was provided to contribute meaningfully to the football team, he decided to attend Monroe State University. He did not have a positive experience transitioning to Monroe State and described his early experiences in the following way:

> It was horrible. It was horrible because I already had the tensions coming in because [this] wasn't the city that I wanted to be in and I didn't want to be at a PWI [Predominately White Institution]. It took more energy to associate with White people. I felt lost. I knew just coming in that a lot of people from my high school weren't going to be here; it wasn't an HBCU. It was huge.

The most immediate factors that Terrence encountered was that Monroe State was not located where he wanted to be and he desired to attend a school where Black students made up the majority student population. Given these two reasons, he described his transition as "horrible." Even more importantly, Terrence did not have a sense of belonging on campus; he felt lost, believed that it took more energy to associate with the predominantly White student body, and felt disconnected from the school because of its size. In many ways, he felt alienated on campus and did not believe that he mattered within the college milieu.

As noted here, students maintained a number of experiences that fractured their sense of belonging on campus and, in some ways, jeopardized their academic performances as well. Family responsibilities, adding more work-related obligations, and college environment are all critical factors in student success.[21] Given the gravity of these external pulls, it is clear that students need a high level of support that incorporates a holistic view of themselves and is sensitive to the full gamut of their experiences.

Conclusion

In too many instances, what students experience in their first year of college is disconnected from their college aspirations and college preparedness. Often, students show up on college campuses with few ideas of what will be expected from them academically and socially. This is particularly true for the Black men in this study. Many experienced their concerns and ambivalences come to fruition during their first year while others tried to strategize around their concerns. Listening to and learning from the students' early college experiences helps to shed light on the strategies that the students adopted and deployed in their efforts to persevere to graduation.

What made the transition tough for many of the students was adjusting to the academic demands of college. Recall, one of the students' major concerns was their lack of academic preparation. We see these concerns realized across many of the student narratives regarding their transition to college. Both the academic workload and the pace of academic work were adjustments that students needed to make rather quickly. Additionally, their own personalities and personal characteristics were also factors, such as time management, responsibility, and academic performative aspirations. As they struggled to keep pace with the academic and social demands of college, attempted to balance their academic-social and work-school responsibilities, experienced being away from home, and tried to perform academically, their sense of mattering and belonging on campus wavered. Undoubtedly, as highlighted in this chapter, the men's identity negotiation and development influenced their early academic focus and performances as well as their social activities, peer relationships, and engagement on campus.

The students narrated a range of first-year experiences; each of their stories highlighted the nuanced ways that they attempted to adjust to campus life and how their institutions acted upon them—academically, socially, and personally. There is no homogenous story to the student narratives. As mentioned, some of the students struggled to adjust academically and found their transitions to college rather difficult. Some students narrated a more reflective stance and articulated their transition and early college experiences as a process. This "process" helped them grow, mature, and develop a range of skills—such as accountability and self-awareness. In addition, the process revealed to them how they could learn from their struggles and decisions (such as waiting to get involved in organizations and activities on campus) and see the results of putting their plan into action. For those students who underperformed to their own self-expectations, they specifically noted the need to apply themselves, better manage their time, access resources on campus, and garner social support as well.

In talking with students about their transition to college, they also noted how BMI played an important role as well. More specifically, participating in the Early Arrival Program played an important role in helping the men transition to college at Monroe State. In addition to gaining familiarity with the campus, many of the men's experiences helped them to develop and connect with a community as well. The community helped the men establish important connections, such as gaining a support group and developing their network, and enhanced their academic efforts as well. Thus, the CTP program helped introduce and enhance many of the students' navigational capital. Students reported that they learned about and how to access campus resources and they received insight about the college and critical advice about classes. Overall, students believed that they benefitted from the bonding experiences within BMI. Here, the students established a sense of connectedness as they were able to network with peers and other institutional agents and they developed relationships with other African-American males. These relationships were important because they highlight how many of the men sought to meet their emotional and social needs. For instance, students shared their experiences with others and developed cooperative coping strategies for some of the microaggressions and denigration they experienced. This cooperation also informed the men's masculine identity development. As opposed to working from an individualistic standpoint, cooperative masculinity is centered on working together to achieve shared goals and supporting each other for greater collective gain. Additionally, connecting with BMI helped the men establish a community for which they felt accountable to the group. This connection is important as we consider the men's identity development. Many of the men expressed that responsibility and self-expectations are critical to their early experiences and some even shared how they felt motivated to perform academically and how they envisioned themselves as examples for future Black male students.

Investigating the men's college experiences helps to reveal the interconnectedness of students' precollege efforts with their in-college careers. Many of the men described college as "a learning experience." They learned more about their strengths and weaknesses, adapted and adjusted some of their academic behaviors, and managed various stressors and challenges. Beyond academics, the social arena is an important location for men to make meaning from their experiences and continue to develop their social identities. Critical for a number of students was developing bonds and relationships across campus. Some men described meeting "lifelong friends" and asserted that they have had opportunities to meet people at other institutions. Thus, for some of the men, growing as a person was critical to their development. The men continued to search for ways to overcome their personal challenges; they saw their first few years of college as a "learning experience"—one that allowed them to grow as a person and move closer to becoming who they wanted to be. In the following chapter, I turn specifically to how the men experienced their racialized and gendered identities on campus.

CHAPTER 4

Being Black, Being Male on Campus

Experiencing the College Environment

> My first day on campus I was indoctrinated with confederate flags, confederate soldiers; this is before class had even started. Strange looks from others on campus; strange looks from people in general. And it was just very hard for me. At first I thought I was over-reacting . . . I realized that it was a whole different environment . . . It was very lonely. I remember eating by myself and studying by myself. Even in speaking to people, I just wouldn't get any responses.
>
> —Nathaniel

One of the main concerns with Black student success in college in general, and that of Black males in particular, is how they perceive and experience the campus environment. These perceptions and experiences have a profound impact on their collegiate career across their personal, social, and academic lives. How students feel about their campus, how they see themselves within the college milieu, and how the campus embraces their presence (or not) all matter. This is especially salient given the continuing significance of race within the United States and across colleges and universities as well. The reflection offered by Nathaniel, a third-year majoring in sociology, helps to discern how he was socialized to the campus environment and culture of his institution. He shares that he was taken aback by the combined impact of public displays of confederate memorabilia along with differential gazes from people on campus. For Nathaniel, these early collegiate experiences were hard and forced him to question his own perceptions and feelings. He felt lonely in the new environment where he often ate and studied by himself. And, he offers, even when he reached out to communicate to others he very often received no response. Nathaniel's experiences raise three fundamental questions that are at the heart of our colleges and universities. First, what does the campus environment convey to students about their place and how they might fit on campus? Second, how does the campus environment contribute to students' social experiences in communicating and interacting with others? And, finally, how do students make sense of the campus climate, especially within marginalized groups like Black males? These questions form the basis of this chapter.

How students experience college is complicated by the intersections of race and gender (along with other social identities) and, most significant to what is revealed here, their Blackmaleness has the potential to narrow their educational outcomes. To be sure, students' identities play a significant role in college, as is true for the men in this study. Many students narrated facing numerous challenges in navigating the college campus and persisting toward graduation. Most of the students clearly identified the continuing significance of race as a major component to their collegiate experiences. Yet, even more than this, it was also their Blackmaleness, the intersecting identities of being both Black and male, that foreshadowed how they experienced college. Past researchers have identified the importance of campus climate in the social adjustment and academic performance of Black male collegians.

Experiencing the College Campus

In discussing the general experiences of Black students on campus, about a third of the men offered some variation that their experiences were no different than those of any other student. In these remarks, Charles, a third-year majoring in political science, noted he is not part of campus life and therefore could not offer any insight, while Jared said he did not know but also offered, "I guess it's the same. At least for me it's the same. You go to class, do the work, take a test, and move on to the next semester. It's just an individual thing with college." For this student, he developed a strategy to focus on himself and do what he needed to do in order to persist toward graduation. In this realm, he perceived his experience to be the same as the majority population. In offering perceptions of Black students on campus, many of the men spoke from the "I" perspective and disaggregated their experiences from the larger group. As they discussed experiences on campus and their perceptions of the environment, the men's reflections focused on campus climate, communication, and racial intermingling on campus.

Campus Climate: "Comfortable and Uncomfortable"

In sharing their thoughts and perspectives about campus climate, the majority of the students described it in two primary ways. First, students identified and referenced the diversity on campus but noted the discomfort in many of the campus spaces that they navigated. Many of the students articulated this directly while others offered narrations that were related closely. Second, within the responses students also narrated a disparate environment that was filled with separation and division across racial and ethnic groups. In their descriptions, many of the students articulated that the campus was diverse. However, this was just part of their response. In their reflections students were clear that diversity did not automatically equate to harmony or inclusion. A good portion of the students associated campus climate as confining and even intolerable in some ways. Thus, the students experienced the college campus as a place where race and the realities of race were ever present. D'Angelo and Mark offered the following reflections about campus climate:

> D'ANGELO: Comfortable and uncomfortable. Comfortable being there's a lot of ethnicities from a lot of different areas so we're all just trying to go with the flow. In class, I know that I have different people in there that I can go to and ask questions about homework or anything. Uncomfortable because I'm walking on campus and we're about to cross paths and I've seen the double-take. I've seen the, "Why are you here?" look. I've seen the, "You're stupid" look and "Why are you talking?" look.

> MARK: From a racial standpoint, it's a kinda . . . it's a lot of . . . [long pause] . . . it's diverse but there's a lot of lack of knowledge of what the Black culture is about. So, some just looking out they just wouldn't understand it. They're kinda intimidated. Even when we're trying to do a fundraiser then participation from the masses is very difficult to maintain.

When you approach them on campus and ask for their support it's kinda like they didn't hear you or they're ignoring you. Even in Greek Court, there's not a lot of events together between PHC [Panhellenic Council] and NHPC [National Pan-Hellenic Council]—so it's a lot of division there. The racial aspect of it is really divided. Not saying that White students don't want to be involved with Black students they just prefer not to. It's not saying that we do something wrong but at the same time they have no interest in what the Black community is doing on campus.

Both D'Angelo and Mark noted the ways that campus diversity did not automatically translate into unity and cooperation on campus. For both students, this was exhibited in a lack of knowledge about Black culture, how Black students were ignored, and a disregard for the Black presence on campus. D'Angelo reflected that the campus was both comfortable and uncomfortable. He felt a sense of comfort in class as most students worked together and even provided support for classwork. However, this togetherness and sense of community was belied across the campus. Mark, a fourth-year business major, shared that he has experienced a White hegemonic gaze in racial interactions that question his presence as a Black male on campus. Historically White institutions have been identified as environments that are potentially threatening to the development of African-American students through the impact of social isolation and institutional and personal discrimination.[1] Mark's comments are similar to what D'Angelo offered; although there is diversity in the student population, he noted a chasm for Black students and Black culture on campus. In attempting to garner support on campus for various activities, Mark noted the tendency to be ignored, which contributed to the division on campus. Additionally, he identified a division even amongst student organizations on campus. He concluded his statement by highlighting the lack of interest expressed by White students in the activities sponsored by the campus's Black student community.

Mark continued his description of the campus climate; in the statement below he focused more on the relations on campus:

A lot of minorities get along pretty well; especially having the Minority Affairs as a resource group—Hispanics, African Americans, I'm not too sure about Asians. But as far as the masses it's not too much there. It's something that the school try to push out there and they try to advertise that diversity and say it's what they want but it's not something that the student body want. Basically because they're not willing to take the time to learn about what the different cultures are about.

A number of the men identified apathy towards Students of Color as a significant contributor and core feature of the campus climate. They also noted that the campus diversity was undermined by a lack of knowledge across racial lines. Importantly, various campus spaces, such as the Multicultural Student Affairs Office and Black Cultural Centers, help to facilitate strong, bonding relationships for Students of Color on campus.[2] Unfortunately, according to Mark, many White students on his campus did not use these types of spaces to connect with Students of Color. Although there was an institutional push for heightened social relations, this was not explicated or supported by student behaviors or desires. Mark asserted that White students generally refuse to invest in learning about other cultures. Maybe this was a result of intimidation, something that Mark offered earlier. Additionally, this could also be a function of Whiteness on his campus.

Marvin spoke directly to the unpleasant atmosphere as he shared the following reflection:

> At MU, it's. . . . it's distasteful. I would rather for a person to tell me straightforward why they have a problem with me as opposed to being around it and acting like their alright during the setting. I feel like the campus does little things to exploit so they can take away or make regulations for a certain group of people—minorities especially. Just seeing the pictures of the school, I saw a yearbook from the 1950s and there was a White fraternity that had nooses pictured. So, my perspective now is just like I'm here. There's only so much that you can do with regard to making change especially as one person. When it's disrespectful why should we have to hold our hands out and try to be friends.

In offering his perspective of the campus climate, Marvin exclaimed that it was "distasteful." First, he expressed concern over insincere and deceitful forms of communication. Second, he suggested a manipulative climate on campus that adversely affects Students of Color. Finally, he used the history of the university to help him make sense of the current climate. Environments such as these easily can create feelings of isolation and reveal the ways that Students of Color feel and experience being marginalized. Even when students desire to create change, their efforts could be undermined by incivility and disdain.

Several students spoke directly to racism and racialized experiences that were inherent to the campus climate. Nathaniel described his college campus in the following way:

> Confederate statues, confederate flags. Previous visitations from the Klan—that doesn't even sound right with me saying [it]. Racist legal situations with regards to young Black females defending themselves against drunk, angry White guys. Not many activities geared toward Black students with the exception of the Brothers & Scholars program. A very racially insensitive environment.

Similarly, in describing the college campus, Raymond offered:

> I've experienced some closet racism. Other than that, it don't really bother me—I don't react to that stuff because it's pretty laid back. I can't really think of anything else other than when they hung nooses from trees.

> DB: What was the noose incident like?

> RAYMOND: I think it was like one noose on a tree at Mendel Hall. I heard before that it used to be KKK members all the time coming [to campus]. I just ignored it; for me, a rope doesn't scare me. They did it at night and ran back to wherever they came from when the sun came out. They had some racist posters everywhere during sophomore or junior year; they were trying to get a White pride group started on campus. I have lot of Black pride so it don't bother me that they wanted to get White pride.

Both Nathaniel and Raymond identified racism and racially insensitive activities on their college campuses. Both of the students pinpointed the presence of Ku Klux Klan members on campus, which took Nathaniel aback. Nathaniel also cited confederate statues and flags on campus along with aggressive attacks on campus as elements that created "a very racially insensitive environment." Raymond identified a noose hanging on a tree incident, along with visits by KKK members, as contributing to a hostile campus climate. He noted that his high levels of racial identity and racial pride served as a buffer against these assaults. Examined collectively, as they share their perspectives and experiences on their campuses, the students clearly revealed the continuing significance of race, which made the climate both uncomfortable and oftentimes difficult to navigate.

Separate and Segregated Campus: "It's a Struggle"

In addition to describing the general campus climate, the men also shared their perspectives and experiences with interracial relationships and cross-cultural interactions. These narratives are important because they help reveal not only how these Black male students experience interactions and associations with other students but also how race and gender matter on campus. Cameron remarked on the issue of segregation and his observations are revealing as well; he shared:

> It's a PWI, so it's a lot of Caucasians. But I feel like it's really segregated. The Greek Row, we have a Greek Row for Caucasians but we don't have a Greek Row for Blacks. I feel like there's events for predominantly Whites and events for predominantly Blacks. Not saying that there are rules there but that's the way we see it. I feel like Blacks feel uncomfortable at an all-White event as opposed to Whites at an all-Black event.

Cameron also noted patterns of student groupings, which ultimately served to create divisions on campus. This is especially evident in the spaces that students occupy and at campus social events. Researchers have argued that focusing on Black student clustering often obfuscates the social dynamics of interracial spaces where Blacks face hostility and isolation.[3] An important element of the campus environment, which communicates to a full range of students how they belong and their place on campus, are the institutional spaces designated and assigned for various students and student groups. These spaces also inform where and how students might gather as well. According to Cameron, there were no overt "rules" informing students to differentiate; however, the result of institutional history, culture, and social practices created divisions between Black and White students. Additionally, because of negative feelings and possibly previous experiences, Black students seem to feel uncomfortable at events where White students are the majority. Highlighting Black student movement reinserts privilege to White students whose movements and homogenous clustering remain unquestioned.

The majority of students in this study insisted that Black students face various racial battles on campus. These struggles ranged from individual narratives, stereotypes, and misperceptions to a separated and segregated campus space. In discussing the campus climate and race relations, about a fifth of the students made reference to campus alerts—an electronic notice sent to the campus community via email and/or text intended as an "alert" of a recent crime on or near campus—that they believe typically described the offender as an African American. According to a majority of the students, the combined effect of low student population and campus struggles helped to create a separate community for Black students. Fred shared his reflections about the campus environment:

> It's kinda segregated for the most part. For events, it's segregated. Say like an organization is having a forum for marriage or something and only people of that ethnicity is going to be there. Or say there's a party, really only people of that ethnicity that's throwing the party will be there. But, socially, people get along. So, you can say the campus is diverse but as far as mingling, it's not.

Similarly, Charles saw segregation and division on campus and described it by noting that, "All the Black people know the majority of the Black people. And the White people know some of the Black people, but not most. It's divided." Both Fred and Charles suggested that their campuses were segregated. Fred referenced events on campus, student organizations, and social activities as ways that reiterated the separation on campus. Charles asserted that the campus was divided where many student associations were maintained in homogeneous racial groupings. With these differentiated experiences, meaningful cross-cultural and cross-racial relationships are difficult to develop and sustain.

Norman, a second-year pre-engineering major, explained:

> It's almost like a separate community almost because you know most of the Black people on campus. If you don't know their names, you know their faces. I went to [a Black Studies] class that my friend invited me to and I literally seen all the Black people that I knew on campus.

The low percentage of Black students on predominantly White campuses created opportunities for Black students to be somewhat familiar with each other—at least by face. This low percentage has the potential to create a context for establishing a microcommunity among this student population. In attending a Black Studies class, Norman felt connected to the community through his invitation and comfort among a large collection of Black students. This observation connects with findings by researchers who advocate for the need for institutional space for Black students. For instance, Adams (2005) found a statistically significant relationship between identity development and increased persistence for Black college students enrolled in Black Studies courses at a large, predominantly White university. For students in Adams's study and on Norman's campus, Black Studies classes offered a safe space for Black students.[4]

Outside of these types of cultural spaces, the men in this study identified a need for their campuses to improve their diversity and inclusion. Deondre noted, "I guess it's okay . . . I don't know what White students have, but Black students don't have much." The feeling of not having much suggests that Deondre and other students may find it hard to connect and engage with campus. Similarly, Monte discussed the separation on campus as well. He exclaimed:

> Everything is separate, that's just the best way to describe it. You have your people who hang with Black people and you have Black people who strictly hang with White people, you know how that goes. But it's just separate and I don't see it changing.

In observing how people navigate and cluster around campus, Monte believed that *everything* was separate. The separation impacts how students experience college and sends powerful messages about the climate. For Monte, he did not see any foreseeable change to the divisions on campus.

An observation by Randy helps to highlight the myriad ways that separation occurs on his campus:

> I think you see, the environment is very welcoming but if you sit and watch things you see the division among people. You'll see the cliques. You'll see Blacks in this area and you'll see Whites in this area. In the cafeteria you'll see the same thing. Everybody seems to get along but it's really like they just tolerate each other being here. But you definitely see a division among people.

Although he cited his campus as welcoming, Randy still noted division among the students. The welcoming atmosphere was belied by student practices on campus where students form cliques and hang out in their respective areas. For Randy, the appearance of harmony was actually a smokescreen for the divided reality. He finalized his comment with the following:

> I still feel as if people judge off stereotypes. You can see it in a lot of ways. You see people interact with White people as well. I still see a large amount of division and not a lot of interaction among races at all.

As many students have suggested, the separation on campus impacts students' social interactions and has implications for peer relationships as well. For a number of the men, they did not see or experience high levels of interaction across racial groups, which easily could lead to how students in different racial groups see each other. Low levels of interaction exacerbate the ways that people prejudge others and can create space for stereotypes to flourish. Although many students initially described their campuses as diverse, the majority of the men perceived a segregated campus that had gaps for this student population. Additionally, their campus environments are rife with areas that easily could cause unique challenges and struggles for Black students in general and Black males in particular.

Communication on Campus: "You Don't Know What to Expect"

In addition to describing their realities of the campus climate, which included racial hostility and dissonance, the participants also used communication to frame their racialized campus experiences. The men discussed the campus climate as separated with isolating social interactions where students are on high alert. In this way, social interactions and communication offered the students ways to construct meanings for themselves and other Black students. How they experienced the various forms of social interactions—both verbal and nonverbal—clearly communicated to students how they were to be placed within the campus milieu.

Sean, a second-year communications major, described the campus environment as diverse, but also spoke about experiencing a sense of dissonance on campus. He reflected:

> SEAN: It's like, it's diverse but you can tell people don't want you there. I have an elevator and I live on the 9th floor that's all the way on the top. We're on the elevator and say there's a group of White girls talking and they just get quiet. They stop talking [when we get on] and pull out their phones and act like they're messaging. It's like they're scared and they don't want to talk to you sometimes . . . and we're on a college campus.

> DB: How do you feel when they respond in these ways?

> SEAN: I just feel like, I just don't understand why they would do that. I don't have anything against any other races or anything like that. If you talk to me, I don't see any reason to get scared. I just think that's wrong of them; it's just reading a book by its cover. They may think I'm violent or hostile towards them; or, just hostile in general.

Sean's reflections are quite illuminating. On one hand, he noted that his campus was diverse but, at the same time, offered that he experienced some prejudice and stereotyping. In the quote cited above, he recalled being treated differentially on campus in what appears to be ongoing experiences. How students respond to Black males in common spaces, and public spaces, sends powerful messages to Black males about how their presence is unwanted and often unacknowledged. For instance, in speaking to these types of experiences, sociologist Robert Staples offered that there is "no solace against the kind of alienation that comes of being ever the suspect, against being set apart, a fearsome entity with whom pedestrians avoid making eye contact."[5] Sean felt wronged by these stereotypes, judgments, and slights and he was not able to fathom why other students might respond to his presence in these ways. Even without being prompted, the men often offered explanations and tried to unravel how their race and gender contributed to these types of experiences. Although he initially suggested that he did not understand why they might distract themselves, Sean later offered that the motivating factor may actually be fear. The sense of fear that Black males might be violent or hostile, even though the students refuse to talk with them or around them, connects well to the ways in which Black male bodies have been scripted historically. One popular inscription is that Black males are angry and volatile. The most insidious danger in these inscriptions is that personal prejudices have the potential to expand to institutional prejudices.[6]

Randy, whose observations about the cliques and superficial diversity were cited earlier, asserted that stereotypes and judgments often compromise communication on campus. Earlier he shared that stereotypes were prevalent across his campus and served as a basis for disunity. As a result, there are limited cross-racial interactions and dialogues. As he reflected on these challenges, he expounded:

> We're observing, some of the leaders in the Black community have noticed that. There are some White people who see that as well and they know that it's not right. You have some people who are against racism and I don't think that they're bringing it to the forefront and discussing it the way it needs to be. So I feel like if we interacted more then that will break down some of the stereotypes. So I see a lot of division. It's like every race just keeps to themselves pretty much.

Randy noted that the fissure on campus was not only noticed by Black students but by White students as well. The most significant challenge that Randy perceived was the ambivalence of White observers, and even those who oppose racism, to speak out about the challenges on campus. Although the division and self-segregation divides the campus, Randy believed that increased communication could help bring the students closer together.

Other students contemplated the difficult campus environment. Monte discussed how the separation on campus impacted communication as he offered:

> Um, separated. Separated amongst the Whites and Blacks. Everything, people talk about each other behind their backs. The Greek life in general will separate you from people that you didn't know. White people have their events and we come sometimes. We have our events and they don't come. But, everybody is on alert. And, that's one of the things that we have to work on, we can say all we want about the race problem, but if we don't work together then you can't say nothing.

Fred expressed a similar sentiment, he stated:

> It's like some White people they're nice—you can talk to them and have fun with them. And, others, they just don't want to be around you at all; they won't talk to you. It's really an on and off thing with many of the White students on campus and with others there's just no communication at all or anything.

As can be seen by what they shared here, students in the study clearly saw how race impacted interracial communication on campus. Moreover, the students interpreted the racial division as a significant area of growth for their college. Monte exclaimed that the division on campus dominates social spaces, especially with regard to meaningful and engaging communication. Monte's comment about divergent conversations connects well with work on the differing racial performances exhibited by Whites in public and private settings. Researchers have argued that White students' interactions were "two-faced," or markedly different, depending on if they were in a White-only social setting as opposed to being in the company with People of Color.[7] Similar to Mark's earlier comment, Monte also identified Greek life, where students have affiliations in fraternities and sororities, as a major instigator of campus division. Fred noted that some of the White students are nice, will engage Black students in conversations, and even have fun. Others, he offered, create an atmosphere of ambivalence. According to Frank, this wavering among White students made communication difficult across racial lines. Darius, a second-year majoring in sports management, echoed Frank's point as he described campus in this way, "I'm a Black man and I try to speak to everybody on campus. But some people don't even look your way. If you try to speak sometimes people just don't speak back; so judgmental." For Monte, Frank, and Darius, they experienced race through how some White students refused to look their way or ignored Black students on campus. As Monte noted, perceptions of race on campus and how they impact social interactions means that everybody is on high alert.

Jordan's experiences aptly summarize this theme:

I got a dirty look today from a White woman. I opened the door for her. I kinda just smiled and went on about my business. But, I thought about it later; was she intimidated because I opened the door or because she didn't know what to expect? This campus, from what I've seen, racially you don't know what to expect. Because I've met some good White people on this campus and they like Black people; but, I've also met many White people who just don't like Black people. I don't know why.

Jordan began his reflection by sharing how he was otherized by Black misandry earlier in the day that we conducted the interview. After initially shrugging off the incident, he later reflected on how his interaction was predicated on both racialized and gendered assumptions. According to Jordan, the White woman for whom he held the door, a gesture that is typically seen as courteous, elicited a negative gaze ("dirty look"). He surmised that she might have responded in this way simply because of his racialized and gendered identities. These types of experiences help reveal the Black misandric microaggressions and racial battles that Black male students experience during college. Importantly, Smith and colleagues (2011), and others, interpret these experiences as "excessive strains" that ultimately "require additional energy redirected from more positive life fulfilling desires for coping with and fighting against mundane racism."[8] Black misandric microaggressions are expressly aimed at and affect Black males, rely on pathological aversions enacted toward Black males, and are (re)created and reinforced within the fabric of societal, institutional, and individual ideologies, practices, and behaviors. Even further, Black misandry justifies and reproduces the subordination and oppression of Black males.[9]

Black Men on White Campuses

Most students expressed serious concerns for Black men at institutions that are predominantly White. The overwhelming majority of the men in this study provided examples of classroom environments, peer relations, interactions with faculty, and institutional culture that are challenges for Black men. These challenges made the men feel like outsiders on their own campus and, in many ways, created burdens for their collegiate experiences.

Black Males as Outsiders in the Classroom: "I Just Go to Class"

Across their narratives, students elaborated on the myriad ways that they felt like Black men are marginalized and otherized on their campus. Norman provided the following classroom experience as an example of challenges that he's faced, "In some classes I feel like if I answer a question wrong out loud I'd be kind of like that guy that represents all Black people. I don't know, that's just me." Chris also shared a racialized classroom experience:

> Sometimes . . . sometimes in my Anthro class my first year . . . one of our readings was about White privilege, it was the professor's fault, a lot people I guess didn't want to talk about race. I didn't want to say anything that would make people look at me funny; I didn't want to say anything that would make me look like an angry Black man in class.

For some of the students in this study, being a Black male on campus is mired in added stress and strain. Norman felt that his in-class participation was censored because his classmates might amplify his voice to be representative of "all Black people." Even as he offered this insight, he internalized the experiences and wondered if he was guilty of reading into the situation. Chris identified an experience where the professor allowed a classroom dynamic to develop that created isolation for him. In a class where the focus of the reading was about race specifically, students opted out of the discussion and reaffirmed how Whiteness was inherent within the space. This classroom atmosphere silenced Chris as an individual and served up an always convenient racialized frame of him as an "angry Black man" if he were to speak about White privilege. The professor and the students asserted Whiteness as the norm in the class. Thus, the privileges of Whiteness allowed White students to disengage from the conversation and put the onus of responsibility on Students of Color like Chris. The experiences of Norman and Chris reveal how Students of Color are burdened in classes and frequently are "objects of attention" when racial issues permeate the classroom.[10] Additionally, these experiences also amplify how Black males' presence is negotiated and, in some ways, controlled by others. For many of the men, being singled out for ridicule along with being positioned as the racialized spokesperson were commonplace on their respective historically White campus.

In addition to discussions, students shared classroom experiences where faculty denigrated their abilities and skills. Terrance expressed frustration in recounting his in-class experiences:

> I feel like the majority of the teachers outside of Black Studies class have been White. A lot of them I've been talked down on until I had to prove to them that I could do the work. I had a couple of teachers look down on me like I was a boy, but I'm a grown man. I haven't gotten any stare downs or anything like that, but if there's anything going on my focus and motivation just block those things out automatically.

Terrance and several other students spoke fondly of their experiences in Black Studies classes. There, they felt professors cared about them and created a welcoming atmosphere for all students. Outside of Black Studies, several students felt that they were belittled by many of their White professors. Terrance's mistreatment is much more than an individual matter and is not an isolated incident. Behaviors and actions such as these by professors, as well as the Black misandric ideologies that support them, are clearly an affront to Black males, their presence, and their sense of belonging on college campuses. Belittling Black men and the control mechanisms deployed against them reveal the links between racism as a system of social control and (the increased levels of) race-related stress experienced by Black men in higher education.

Deondre's reflection also highlights how professors play a critical role in students' collegiate experiences. He talked about the challenges he faced in the classroom as a Black male:

> I mean, it's just kinda it is what it is. I just go to class, I don't really talk to teachers after class that often and I don't think they want to talk to me after class. I'm a guy on campus . . . There have been some professors that I have been cool with. I had this one White professor and I told him that I was interested in astronomy and he told me that I wasn't smart enough for astronomy. He told me that I would have to take higher-level math and I'm pretty good at math. Instead of you telling me about the program you're telling me that I can't do the classes. It pissed me off a little. After that, I was just like, "It's whatever; I don't really care. I'll just do me."

Deondre's comments echoed the concerns and experiences of a number of students. The cultural dissonance that the students experienced revealed an environment with a litany of subtle and constant micro-aggressions and denigrations. As Black men, they recounted the ever-present racial battles that they faced—and even ones within the college milieu that posed constant threats. Ultimately, the racial battles, micro-aggressions, and Black misandry syphoned away some of their time, energies, and efforts from their academic pursuits and aspirations. These types of encounters, where their intellect and interests are disparaged, have compounding effects that create fatigue and stereotype threats. As noted by a number of men in this study, the compounding effects of these experiences create emotional, psychosocial, and even spiritual stressors during their college tenure.

Deondre recalled a particularly demeaning interaction with a professor who openly questioned his intellect. In questioning his abilities, the professor also denied him an opportunity to learn about career opportunities and expand his educational options. As a result, he asserted that he did not have much interaction with professors and felt that many of his professors did not want to engage him in serious conversations. Deondre had to manage the stereotype and denigration and, as it stands, he decided on a "just-do-me" coping strategy after being shunned by a White professor. According to researchers, "stereotype management" can be considered as a tactical response to myriad forms of racism and racialized experiences across school (and non-school) environments.[11] For a number of the men, interactions with peers and faculty were embroiled in microaggressive behaviors. These pressures, profilings, and insults all work to diminish the values that Black men bring to institutions and have the potential to create a hostile collegiate environment for Black male students. Scholars have defined microaggressions as subtle recurring acts (verbal, behavioral, and/or visual) directed toward People of Color intended to denigrate their racialized identities.[12] More specifically to Black male students, Smith and colleagues (2007) identified campus-academic, campus-social, and campus-public spaces as three racialized domains ripe for various forms of racial microaggressions that can threaten or impede the progress of Black male collegians.[13]

Black Males Targeted: "Same as It Is Just Being a Black Man"

In addition to classroom experiences, the students identified social interactions around campus that resonated with their feelings of being an outsider. Norman, quoted earlier about his in-class experience, also offered, "Sometimes when you're walking at night from the library or something you'll see people cross the street and I'm like, 'Dang, do I really look menacing?' [laugh]." Norman observed that Black males often are stereotyped as threats even while on campus. The idea of himself looking "menacing" elicited a laugh from Norman primarily because of his easily observable scrawny physique (I estimated that he might weigh 120 pounds). Students provided compelling observations of how Black male identity is contorted into negative images. Raymond asserted:

> I feel like, to be a Black male on campus, how should I put this? . . . I've been called a thug many times on campus, a gang member, and other stuff like that. I feel like Black students don't have a chance to show who they are because they're being judged by everybody else.

According to Raymond, his individual identity was rendered invisible because of the overly stereotyped perceptions of others. Being called "thug" and "gang member" is complicit with negative connotations that not only question Raymond's identity and character but they also problematized and "niggered" his presence on campus.[14] Raymond contended that these Black misandric microaggressive behaviors have happened on a number of occasions and thus are not a singular isolated incident. Additionally, profiling Black males as "thugs" and "gang members" pinpoints an already-made and convenient labeling of Black male identity that is replete with negative connotations. Labeling Black male collegians as "thug" suggests that this type of individual does not fit within the college environment, it taps into a highly contested notion of Black male as hyperaggressive (and prone to street-level physical violence), and also serves as a form of otherizing Black men to justify avoiding and scrutinizing their movements on campus.[15]

A significant number of students expressed awareness and concern regarding how Black men are perceived and the impact of those perceptions. As an example, Joseph spoke about how Black men are hypervisible on campus; he offered:

> You stand out [laugh]. Yeah, you stand out. I don't know, you gotta be strong. I guess when they see Black men, just from like looks from people's faces when I walk by and they've never heard me talk, they feel intimidated. I guess it's because of the dreads. But I guess it's from stereotypes . . . Because it's not a lot of us. You probably won't see a lot of us in one spot. If you're a regular student, not an athlete, you stand out. When I'm at my dorm it's like all eyes on you. It almost feel like they were looking for you to fail. Like, sometimes, I felt like people was looking down on me.

In expressing how Black men are targeted, Joseph's "laughter" was used to highlight his dismay at what he has experienced. He attributed the lack of representation on campus as the primary reason that Black men's presence on campus is scrutinized. Similar to Raymond, Joseph maintained that Black men stand out because of the stereotypes that others levy against them and he felt burdened by the "all eyes on you" inquiry. He expressed feeling denigrated and questioned about his status and belonging and he wondered what about his physical presence might trigger people's otherizing of him; he estimated it could be his physical stature or the cultural style that he wears his hair. As he considered each of these, he finally estimated that, "I guess it's from stereotypes." Finally, he asserted how the otherizing is complicit with negative views of him as he approximated that others were looking down on him and looking for him to fail.

Elvan equated experiences of being a Black man on campus to the everyday lived experiences of Black men throughout U.S. society. He reflected:

> Same as it is just being a Black man period. You know, you walk around, this is basically what I experience, you're walking on a sidewalk and you're walking by they just immediately get out the way . . . Especially like all of the police reports; every time it's a robbery the description is so general. It's usually a Black male between five-foot-six and six-feet tall, weighing between 150 and 200 pounds. That's just about every Black male on campus!

Elvan's observations connect well with the invisibilities that Black men face. Elvan's experiences also correlate with Anderson's (1990) "master status" concept. For Black males in public spaces, he argued the "master status" is a stigmatizing effect of "negative" status-determining characteristics that applies to them as a group. The trappings of master status and stereotyping render their individual identities and personas invisible. Elvan noted that the generic descriptors of police reports would render nearly all Black males on his campus as potential suspects. Thus, according to many of the students, a variety of campus spaces served to normalize how Black men are engaged in racial battles that often hinge upon their Black male identities.[16]

The experiences discussed by the men reflect the compounding effect of Black misandry as they routinely are stereotyped, profiled, and problematized. Raymond experienced name-calling and prejudgments, Joseph felt that others looked down on him in anticipation of failure, and Elvan saw no difference of how Black men are profiled throughout wider society and on college campuses. Black men face multiple stereotypes of being prone to criminality and aggressiveness and, as a result, are viewed as threatening and in need to be avoided.[17] Thus, Black males face a "paradox of invisibility" in that they are invisible and hyper-policed simultaneously and rendered to a "bipolar masculinity" as they are caught between vacillations of good/docile and bad Black male.[18] Theodore, a fourth-year psychology major, provided a lengthy statement about his college experiences that evince the systemic nature of confrontations that Black men face:

> My college experience is really what you go to college for; I learned about myself and I've grown. I've really opened my eyes to how the world actually is. And, just taking the classes that I've taken, I've realized what my color actually means. I remember my mother telling me, "Well, Theodore now, you're a Black man in America and now you're going to learn what that means." At first I didn't understand it and now I realize what she means. The fact is that I can walk somewhere on campus and the fact that I'm looked at as a Black male I'm automatically going to be blamed for something. For example, you get those emails and every time something happens it's a Black male. The craziest thing I've seen is there was this one announcement that it was a Black male between 5'7 and 6'2. That's a big ass range! I'm 5'7 and I know people who are 6'2, that doesn't look anything alike. Race just makes an impact on everything that I do. Basically just feel like a target. In class I feel like I have to act a certain way to go against a stereotype; I feel like I have to fight against a stereotype. I have to sit close to the front of the class just to send a message to the teacher. It's like I have to make an overt statement that other students don't. If I sit in the back [of the class] then the teacher is going to look at me in some particular ways and say it's normal. I've basically learned that people are not going to look at [me] as Theodore, they're going to look at [me] as a Black man. In one psychology class I read about the elevator effect; being a Black man means that you have no identity. I was looked at as the criminal, as the enemy; your Blackness is framed as a bad thing. Being a Black man in America means that you're going to have to work harder to not fit into a group. I mean at the same time I want to fight against the stereotypes to prove people wrong but it's also stressful because I shouldn't have to.

Theodore provided a number of insightful observations on the ways that his race and gender matter in his educational experience. He acknowledged his own individual growth and maturity while also becoming much more aware of the significance of his racialized and gendered identities. He insisted that one of the greatest lessons he has learned in college is that his individual identity does not matter; instead, Black male hypervisibility relegated him to a generic identity that made him susceptible to stereotypes in class and across campus. As a Black male, he felt targeted on his campus and expressed concern that he was engaged in a constant battle to belong and prove people wrong. Yet, even as he acknowledged his awareness of these challenges, Theodore also revealed that the burdens are stressful and cause him and many of his peers to be on a constant racial grind. This racial grind manifested itself in where he sat in class, how his teachers perceived him, his presence on the campus, and how his identity is criminalized on campus as "the enemy." He asserted that because these realities are pressed upon him, he has to "work harder" not to fit into the stereotypes; thus, in many ways, he felt confined by his Blackmaleness and engaged in an ongoing struggle against identity threat. At the end of his reflection, although he felt that he should not have to, he wanted to fight against the stereotypes so that he could be his own man.

As noted by the student narratives provided here, stereotypes, misperceptions, and mistreatment created challenges for Black males on historically White campuses that have implications for their academic performances, social and personal engagement, and mental and physical health as well. Nathaniel expressed his concern in being stereotyped and the weight this places on him:

> With the numerous emails saying 6'2 Black male robbed such and such it's very scary because at any time I can be arrested or hemmed up. It's very difficult because the statement that a 6'2 Black male or a 5'8 Black male did something, the statement is that you all look alike. So if I'm taken in for a lineup I have no chance because we all look alike. So, that's my future, that's my college education. So it's very scary. It's like being captured as a potential runaway slave.

Nathaniel and other students articulated that the narrative "Black male as criminal" is ubiquitous on college campuses and is steeped in a racialized imagining and construction of Blacks.[19] Nathaniel's criticism of the generic descriptor echoed Theodore's concern in that both men—and many of their Black male peers—could fit the description of the suggested offender quite easily. Thus, their presence on campus was available for scrutiny on an ongoing basis and, as expressed by Nathaniel, threatens their educational futures. Nathaniel's final statement is quite illuminating and sheds light on both the continuing significance of race and Black male criminality. He asserted that there is no safe space on campus and the criminalized threat is as widespread as nineteenth-century slave codes.[20] Nathaniel's connections are not far-fetched in a metaphorical sense, especially as racial profiling and policies such as "stop-and-frisk" have created what has been identified as the "new Jim Crow."[21] The result of the overly generic descriptors and bevy of stereotypes hurled at their racial and gender group means that Black males are targeted and profiled in public spaces, they are condemned in social settings, and they are constantly and concurrently visible and invisible.

Race Around Campus

The final theme narrated by the Black male students also offered an interior view of Black male identities from a broader perspective. Although students were asked about the school's campus climate and how they experienced race on campus, what they offered provided insight on the racial interactions from throughout the city as well. In doing so, students revealed Black misandry latent around the campus as they experienced racism and discrimination at local establishments and in interactions with community members. All of these experiences impacts how Black students are framed within and by the local community, which ultimately encroaches on their overall school experiences. D.J. reflected:

> I think it's diverse. It's a lot of White people but the Black people are really close knit. So, if you find one Black person then you can find a lot more. People talk about racism but that comes from the people that don't go to Lincoln, they're from Jefferson. I experienced this one incident where this White guy just called me the n-word. He said it 2 or 3 times.

D.J. began by noting the diversity and acknowledging the predominantly White presence on campus; he also suggested that there is a tight-knit

Black community on campus. He asserted that there are conversations about racism; however, while most believe it is on campus D.J. asserted that the racism was generated by Jefferson residents, the local city where his school is located. To make his point, he offered a personal experience in a local bar where a White male repeatedly called him a racial epithet.

Bannon also acknowledged Jefferson's environment. He shared:

> It's already known that the Jefferson area used to be real segregated and things like that. There's pictures in the history book with the ropes and things like that; so it's real racialized and segregated. Even when things go down with certain social events, you see on Facebook things like, "You need to get them monkeys out of here."

Bannon began his reflection by offering what he suggested is a widely known fact, that Jefferson has a history of racial strife. This history included a deep level of racial segregation in addition to a race riot and other racist acts.[22] Thus, the hidden injuries of race and racism still have the opportunity to manifest in the current time period. Bannon offered that the history of Jefferson was well-documented in local history books and social media was used to propagate racist attitudes and sentiments against Blacks. Marvin also used the Jefferson area to contextualize the campus climate. He reflected:

> We just a number; for minorities, we're just a number. Just to say we have a number. Like I mentioned about the nooses and the yearbook, last year there was an event at one of the local bars out here; they basically had a Lincoln State [Facebook] page and they had comments about Blacks . . . and they were saying Blacks need to go home. We had a town hall [meeting] but I feel like there was nothing about what was being done. I haven't seen a whole lot of changing on campus of the perception of us. Once a negative thing happen with anybody dealing with anybody of African de[s]cent it's just over the top.

Marvin initially asserted that while there are People of Color present on the campus and in the town, their presence seems not to be effectual because they are "just a number." Earlier in his interview, Marvin shared that he saw a 1950s university yearbook where members of a fraternity were pictured holding a noose and he also shared that there was another incident where a noose was found on a tree outside of a Black student's off-campus apartment. He contextualized a recent event at one of the local establishments within this history to suggest that racism and discrimination are inherent to the area. In the aftermath of the event at the local bar, where a fight occurred, people used social media to make denigrating comments about Black students and advocated for them to "go home." What Marvin offered connects with Bannon's contention that the local atmosphere was hostile to Blacks. Additionally, off-campus events have on-campus implications. Although a town hall meeting was hosted, no information was offered about what was being done about the local racial climate and there was no measurable change in how Blacks are perceived according to Marvin. Finally, Marvin revealed the racialized burdens of these types of incidents; he suggested that Blacks carry the brunt of the responsibility and any time Blacks are "involved" the response is usually "over the top."

Other students' reflections were similar about the local climate that surrounded their campus. Eric, a second year majoring in Black Studies, declared, "It's kind of racist. One time I was just walking down Devroe Street and some White dude in a car called me a 'n[igger]' for no reason; I don't know why." In contextualizing his school's climate to the local city, Sean remarked:

> Well, I'll say we're already being judged. A lot of community members are judging us . . . There's a lot of crimes going on and they'd be like, "A Black male, six-foot with a hoody on" and everybody was wearing hoodies. A lot of crime and they were blaming the Black people. I think they just blame Black people for a lot of things. We later found out that it wasn't even a Black person it was a White male in a Black hoody.

What many of the students recounted illuminates the powerful ways that Black male identities play out around his campus. The students continuously referenced how Black students in general, and Black males in particular, were being judged and how local community members contributed to the hostilities that they experienced. These prejudgments and misjudgments lend themselves to stereotypes where, according to the students, Black males usually are profiled as the offender. The generic

descriptor, "A Black male, six-foot with a hoody on," plays into historical framing of Black males as perpetual perpetrators and even into more
recent national events such as when Trayvon Martin, a young Black
male, was criminalized, attacked, and killed by a neighborhood watch
man in Sanford, Florida in 2012.[23] Martin's murder also served as a
powerful statement to Black males, and other men of color, that their
racialized and gendered bodies are still rendered as hyperaggressive and,
thus, in need of surveillance.[24] Yancy (2013) explained this phenomenon
as "walking while Black" where Black bodies are accosted by the White
gaze, continue to be reduced to their surfaces and to stereotypes, and are
racially policed. Sean's account echoes this rendering, and connects with
how many of the Black male students felt their racial and gender identities were confronted on campus, noting that Blacks are often blamed for
crimes in the local community. The rhetoric of Black male criminality
is powerful enough not to fathom its overuse and, in this case, misuse
since the actual perpetrator was a White male.

D'Angelo provided another example of racism around campus and
the emotional labor it engenders:

> Summer 2011 I stayed out here for the first time, I stayed for
> the summer and lived off-campus. Me and some other guys
> ended up having a routine of going out and playing basket-
> ball. We'll meet up around 8 or 8:30[pm], meet up outside
> of Thomas Hall and play on the outside courts. We invited
> people to play. There were a couple of nights in a row where
> a red pick up truck [drove by], there was a group of White
> guys [inside] yelling, "Go home niggers." It was all night long;
> they would yell, drive down the block and come back and
> yell it again. That was my first time experiencing anything
> like that and my initial reaction was just anger.

As noted by the student narratives offered here, the racial climate
around several campuses was both hostile and racist. Black male students
recalled multiple experiences where they were confronted by the continuing significance of race within the surrounding community and by
local residents. D'Angelo experienced racism during the summer while
playing basketball at an outdoor court. The repeated rhetoric of "go
home," which several students shared experiencing or hearing, is racially
charged given the racial dynamics of the interactions. In these instances,

local White residents continue to communicate to Blacks that their presence is unwanted both in the city and even as students at the university.

In speaking about his experiences in the local community, Theodore maintained that he has to manage his presentation of self on a constant basis. In the following quote, he reveals how he continuously self-polices his Blackmaleness by monitoring his volume, attire, and movement:

> Basically if I go out to certain parts of downtown and if I'm blasting my music then people look at me in a certain way. And it's like, "Why are you looking at me funny; I'm a college student trying to better myself." When I go to the mall if I'm not dressed a certain way then people may look at me funny or treat me differently or I might get followed around in the store.

Conclusion

This chapter focused on one of the most significant elements of students' college experiences—the campus environment. The voices of Black male students and their reflections about the environment are important precisely because they often are marginalized, overlooked, and rendered invisible on many college campuses by their Blackmaleness. As colleges and universities continue their efforts at diversifying the student population, how students experience campus has important implications for the college and students alike.

In sharing their experiences as Black men on campus, the majority of the students narrated a variety of racialized *and* gendered stressors that made transitioning to, navigating, and negotiating college and college life much more difficult. The men's narratives shed light on how projections about Black men—on and off campus—accost them in their educational endeavors. The gendered racism that the men experienced is testament to the ways in which they are confronted on both conscious and subconscious levels (such as gendered discrimination, implicit and explicit bias, and racialized stereotypes). These different experiences and the contexts in which they are engaged play a significant role in Black men's identity development during college. The men's masculine identities and manhood constructs are in constant negotiation and development. For instance, stereotypes of Black men as "thugs" and projections of Black men as unworthy denigrates their efforts, problematizes their presence, and troubles their identities, all of which impacts *how* they experience campus and campus life. Paying attention to Black men's gendered identity helps unravel how race *and* gender matter.

Campus-related pressures on Black men—in campus-academic spaces (i.e., classroom and library) and campus-social spaces (i.e., dormitories, recreation areas, and lounging areas)—and even in off-campus spaces (i.e., in nearby communities, downtown, shopping areas) all inform how the men feel like they fit and belong within the college community. The men are engaged in a delicate act of balancing the traditional schooling demands of college in addition to mental, emotional, spiritual, physical, identity-related, and psychosocial stressors.

Although the institution may be making efforts to improve diversity, members of the majority population may undermine race relations. These social practices on campus continue to create divisions between racial and ethnic groups, especially for Black and White students. More importantly, how White students act when they share campus spaces with Black students—and other Students of Color—belies inclusiveness. Campus climate is a critical component to harboring strong, positive experiences for students on campus. The majority of students identified a fissure between Black and White students, which was rooted in segregated campus spaces, negative experiences, denigrated perspectives of them as Black men, and perceptions of lacking campus resources. These concerns bring to the fore the need for campus climates that enhance the experiences of all students.

The great majority of the students insisted that as Black men on their respective campuses their struggle included apathetic classroom environments, strained peer and faculty relations, and a hostile institutional culture. In these experiences, Black male students continue to feel the brunt of racialized and gendered identities on predominantly White campuses. These challenges posit them and their Blackmaleness as "outsiders" on their campus where they experience variations of invisibilities and they are treated like *any* seemingly unworthy and unwelcome Black man in society in addition to being avoided, stereotyped, and profiled. Researchers contend that racial microaggressions exist in both academic and social spaces in the college environment and Black men often are viewed as threatening on predominantly White campuses.[25] Additionally, Anderson's (1990, 2011) concept of "master status" is helpful in revealing how many individual identities are rendered invisible as young Black males begin the great majority of their social interactions with non-Blacks from a deficit model. The compounding impact of racism, Black misandric microaggressions, and discriminatory treatment is that Black males feel devalued, suffer invisibilities, and may become less engaged on college campuses. This point further underscores the need for *holistic* approaches to enhancing the educational experiences of Black male students that include student-faculty outreach, mentoring, and student-centered programs and activities. Continuing to ignore the specific and particular challenges that Black men face on campus means that their low levels of recruitment, retention, and graduation will continue to plague our colleges and disharmoniously impact our communities.

In addition to the separation on campus that undermined diversity efforts, students also identified communication on campus as a significant contributor to social interactions. Much of the social interactions that the men recounted were mitigated through stereotypes that played on negative framing of their racialized and gendered identities. These permeating functions left some of the Black male collegians uncertain of what to expect on campus. Students felt accosted by the White gaze, which served to problematize the Black male presence on campus. Yancy (2013) identifies the White gaze as a racialized mechanism that brings Blacks into view while simultaneously distorting them at the same time. Thus, the men were stereotyped as violent and hostile, which translated into White fear. Some of the Black male students felt like "just a number" on campus, which denotes a clear lack of connection to the university. Even more than the stereotypes, the students cited Whites' unwillingness to confront and discuss racism on campus as another issue that created uneasiness on campus. This unwillingness to engage in critical conversations about race places burdens on Black students and other Students of Color for addressing and improving race relations and interracial collegiality on campus. Even further, not being attuned to the varied needs of diverse student populations threatens the progress and possibilities of many students, such as many of the Black men in this study. These dynamics all converged into the importance of increased dialogue the students suggested, not only as a way to break down stereotypes but also specifically to address race, racism, and Black misandry on campus.

Finally, interactions around campus had a significant impact on the men's experiences as well. The men specifically identified racism in the local community that included being called racial epithets and witnessing nooses placed outside of apartment buildings as examples of community-based animus. The use of nooses is a clear racist act intended to confront Black humanity. The noose has a long history connected to Black-White relations in the United States and is a racialized symbol of White terror in Black communities and on Black bodies. The dehumanizing experiences in the local community cannot be seen as individual acts or incidents, but rather should be seen as cumulative discrimination that potentially has a compounding effect on the men's collegiate experiences.[26] In one sense, racism experienced in the local community limits students' local options and forces them back to campus. Yet, Black men experience being avoided, shunned, and stereotyped on campus. Thus, the message is clear, even voiced by some local residents and used within social media outlets: these Black men should "go home." This message is amplified by social rejections on campus, strained social interactions, and racist episodes that confront Black men on an ongoing basis. The experiences that Black male collegians shared are powerful reminders of how race and race-based discrimination aimed at Black men are latent within institutional culture, permeate social interactions on campus, and are embedded within the local community as well. As Mutua (2006) argued, Black men as subordinated masculinities are subject to caricatures and are the target of efforts that seek to understand them not simply as Black but as the gendered multidimensional category Blackmen. For many of the Black men in this study, their very presence at the college and within the community was under constant attack. The men, however, were not passive in their experiences; the next chapter explores how Black men negotiated and managed the campus climate along with their racial and gender battles on campus.

CHAPTER 5

Black Men Emerging

Experiencing Self in College
and Engaging Resiliency

It's not the situation but it's the motivation that determines the person.

—Raymond

I don't believe my current GPA has anything to do with college not being for me, I just need to pick up where I lack at. Sometimes we allow our situations in life to detour us in the path that we're trying to go. Me, personally, I'm a strong believer in keep going and never give up.

—Jordan

The importance of campus climate on students' sense of belonging to the college community has been affirmed in a plethora of studies. A significant portion of these studies asserts that a positive racial climate contributes significantly to the social adjustment and academic performance of students in general and especially for Students of Color. The students in this study revealed in clear terms the types of institutional cultures they encounter, how these matter in their social relations, and how they impact their in-class and on-campus experiences. Yet, this is only part of the reality. Black male students are aware of their college settings and the various stereotypes levied against them as a group. In response, many of the men have learned to employ a wide range of resiliency strategies in order to persevere in spite of racial tension, racism, and discrimination. Researchers continue to note the need for more research that allows space to hear Black males narrate their collegiate experiences so that we can enhance their experiences. For instance, James Earl Davis maintained that, "Voices of African American males on college campuses echo their struggles . . . Out of these struggles, however, have emerged many Black men who are, although wounded, yet persistent in their reach for higher education."[1]

In this chapter, I focus on how Black males recount and make meaning from their experiences, assert their agency, and enact resilience on campus as they manage, negotiate, and navigate the campus environment. As the attestations noted by Raymond and Jordan at the beginning of this chapter reveal, they, along with many other Black male collegians, are not deterred by their encounters, but instead are determined to succeed. Raymond iterated the importance of motivation, a noncognitive variable, in helping people overcome obstacles they may face. Similarly, Jordan identified resilience as a key factor for his persistence efforts; as he noted, he focused on continuing to move forward despite the challenges he faced. I situate the men's experiences within resilience theory and identity to extrapolate how their race and gender impact the coping strategies they deploy. Black males, even on college campuses, are projected through pathological constructions that often diminish their identities, are always already under surveillance, and are marginalized in various ways.[2] However, by focusing solely on how Black males are problematized limits our scope and undervalues their persistence. Resilience, especially as expressed within these men's counterstories, offers a framework for understanding how Black male students go about negotiating the strategies they believe are required of them to successfully navigate college. Like other Students of Color, or those in marginalized groups, many college-aged Black males are engaged in racial and gender identity and other forms of self-development. On their campuses, the men construct and maintain identities that are racialized, gendered, and academic.

The men in this study give considerable attention to nurturing their identities and engaging strategies that allow for healthy self-conceptions and successful matriculation. On the one hand, academic coping strategies are necessary in the context of learning the college environment and meeting the academic expectations in place. On the other hand, they express concern over how they are viewed, stereotyped and profiled, and treated on campus. For these reasons, resilience strategies that incorporate racial and masculine identities emerge as central scripts among these students. In this chapter, I examine the resilience strategies that the men articulate and engage as counter-narratives to Black male mediocrity, disengagement, and deficiencies.[3] Importantly, as the men responded to the campus milieu, and bonded with other Black male students, they adopted a cooperative masculine construct that was used to leverage their bonding and collectivity to reach individual and group goals. The genesis of this masculine construct is the men's collective experiences and desires to achieve; additionally, this construct is dependent on the men's sense of cohesion and interconnectedness as well.

Engaging Resilience

The Black men in this study, as noted in the previous chapter, talked about feeling the gravity of outsider status and invisibility on their college campuses.[4] According to researchers, the "invisibility syndrome" takes the form of a struggle with inner feelings and beliefs that personal talents, abilities, and character are not acknowledged or valued by others, nor by the larger society, because of racial prejudice.[5] In discussing some of their collegiate experiences as an "outsider" or narrating feeling "invisible," the men used descriptive language to highlight microaggressions, racial battles, and the weight of these burdens. They maintained that the hostilities, microaggressions, and differential treatment made them reassess their place on campus and they began to focus on social and academic coping strategies in order to better manage their environment.[6]

Black Male Academic Coping Strategies: "Just Do Me"

Much of how the men made sense of their academic experiences was through assessing their interactions and relationships with classmates and faculty. In addition to managing academic expectations, they sought to find ways to negotiate academic environments and the social atmosphere that were healthy for their academic pursuits and individual personhood. Charles provided the following reflection:

> CHARLES: Your first year [on campus] it's odd. After that you don't care, you're like, "Man, I'm just up here to get my stuff and leave."

DB: What makes it odd?

CHARLES: You feel different. Me, personally, I feel different.

DB: What makes you feel different?

CHARLES: A lot of reasons . . . because most of these people ain't like me and they don't care about me. You look around and it's probably about two percent of us [Black males] on campus and that's low. When you somebody in that two percent people treat you like it. That's why I'm trying to hurry up and leave. I just want my stuff so I can leave.

Charles noted the oddities that Black males experience on campus confront their sense of belonging and creates triggers for them to leave. The challenges, as explored in the previous chapter, force students like Charles into an academic coping mode where he focuses on ways to just "get my stuff and leave." One of the main reasons that Charles was "trying to hurry up and leave" was because he felt that most of the people on campus didn't care about him. Earlier in the interview, Charles described his freshmen year as weak primarily because, "I didn't know anybody that went here but myself and I'm not really open to making new friends." Here, he acknowledged a challenge he faced during his first year, which could impact his integration to campus and because took a more private approach to social relations, Charles chose not to engage in many social activities on campus. Students' sense of mattering also is connected to their social practices and personality traits. A critical turning point for Charles was his engagement in the Black Male Initiative program on his campus. Although he expressed a desire to expedite his college career so he could leave, Charles acknowledged that he would not have made it to his third year at the university if he were not engaged in BMI.

The coping strategy used by Charles connected a number of the men's' narratives. For instance, as noted in the previous chapter, Deondre's desire to learn about the astronomy program was dismissed by a college professor. As a result of his denigration, he decided on a "just-do-me" approach as a means of negotiating his experiences on campus; Deondre shared:

Instead of you telling me about the program you're telling me that I can't do the classes. It pissed me off a little. After that, I was just like, "It's whatever; I don't really care. I'll just do me."

Researchers contend that many White faculty members view Black students in stereotypical group terms.[7] Additionally, it is critical to note that encountering even a single microaggression can set the tone for a student's experience of what to expect on campus—and this is particularly true for students across marginalized groups. Deondre simply asked a professor about an academic program and, instead of being engaged in a conversation about details or possibilities, he was belittled and denigrated. Thus, Deondre's "just do me" approach is a defiance strategy aimed at countering the hostility that he experienced from his professor and sustaining his sense of efficacy. Also, it could be easy to misread his "I don't really care" statement as disengagement; however, Deondre maintained a 3.4 grade point average during his first two years of college and was elected as president of the Black Student Union (BSU) at the end of his freshman year. During his second year, he pledged a fraternity, coordinated a major all-campus event for BSU, engaged in numerous hours of community service, and maintained active membership and participation in three other on-campus organizations. The notion of "I don't care" refers to his lack of desire to be insulted by Black misandry or to build relationships with faculty who clearly do not respect his intellectual ability or academic interests. Thus, "I don't care" and "just do me" can be read as ways to buffer the slights students experiences as well as masculine scripts employed by these men in response to attempts to marginalize them and diminish their sense of self.[8]

Researchers have theorized that Black men adopt and use "cool pose" as a way of surviving in a restrictive society. This expressive, cool masculinity entails behaviors, scripts, physical posturing, impression management, and carefully crafted performances to communicate pride, strength and control.[9] Several recent studies have focused specifically on Black masculinities and gender performance in higher education. For instance, Harris, Palmer, and Struve (2011) framed their study through "cool posing" to examine the masculinities and gender expressions among Black men at a private research institution. The authors found that the men in their study sought to express masculinities through leadership and

academic success while also maintaining ideas that resonate with hegemonic and culturally defined notions of what men are supposed to be.
Further, their participants engaged in behavioral strategies to maintain or
reclaim some dignity and respect as men. Much like their participants,
the men in the current study employed resilience strategies to keep their
humanity and manhood intact. Similarly, in examining how their gendered identity impacted their educational experiences, researchers found
institutional attention and avowal as key frames for influencing Black
males' college experiences and manhood.[10] The "just do me" and "get
my stuff and leave" narrations are employed *in response to* hostile campus
climates, racist stereotypes, and racial battle fatigue. Additionally, these
strategies connect to masculinity scripts that influence the behaviors
and responses of Black men in higher education.[11] One readily available
script is the "I don't care" mantra where Black men buffer their sense of
self from feeling isolated, rejected, or put down. Therefore, much more
work is needed at the institutional level to challenge the campus environment and support the men in their endeavors to pursue their higher
education goals. If only negative attention is given to a surface reading
of their responses, then the larger, structural impediments will continue
to exist and threaten the men's success on campus.

Two student experiences that were identified earlier are worthy
of reexamintion here. Raymond shared a particularly hostile event on
campus along with offering how he coped with the racial assault with
the following reflection:

> I think it was like one noose on a tree at Mendel Hall. I heard
> before that it used to be KKK members all the time coming.
> I just ignored it; for me, a rope doesn't scare me. They did
> it at night and ran back to wherever they came from when
> the sun came out. They had some racist posters everywhere
> during sophomore or junior year; they were trying to get a
> White pride group started on campus. I have lot of Black pride
> so it don't bother me that they wanted to get White pride.

Terrance expressed his coping strategy in recounting his in-class
experiences:

> I feel like the majority of the teachers outside of Black Studies
> class have been White. A lot of them I've been talked down

on until I had to prove to them that I could do the work. I had a couple of teachers look down on me like I was a boy, but I'm a grown man. I haven't gotten any stare downs or anything like that, but if there's anything going on my focus and motivation just block those things out automatically.

Raymond and Terrance identified personal characteristics that they incorporate into their collegiate experiences as measures to cope with their campus environments. As he narrated a potentially hostile event on his campus, Raymond offered that what mattered most to him was his own racial pride. This pride not only has helped him better understand the histories, traditions, and accomplishments of his own racialized group but it also buffered him from racial affronts. Raymond's assertions about self-pride is an important manhood construct and also connects with stage four, Internalization, of Cross's (1971) Nigrescence model. In stage four, Cross theorized that individuals accept their African heritage while also accepting the traditions, beliefs, and values of other cultures.[12] In examining racial identity development and psychological coping strategies of Black males, Bridges (2011) argued that they seek greater opportunities to express their emotions and feelings in productive ways.[13] Thus, racial identify development can serve as a protective factor in managing invisibility, microaggressions, and other forms of discrimination. In a similar vein, Terrance suggested that his focus and motivation do not allow attempts to denigrate his personhood from inhibiting his academic performance. By deploying these noncognitive traits—such as focus and motivation—Terrance was able to challenge and elude disparagement. Both of these men employed healthy identity and psychological coping strategies to help ensure a positive self-image and college experience.[14]

Black Males on Campus: "We Need More"

Researchers continue to note the impact of low enrollment of Students of Color at majority White institutions on race relations, diversity efforts, and student experiences. In Davis et al.'s (2004) study of Black undergraduate students at a large public university, "A fly in the buttermilk" was one way a participant described his perception of an experience that stood out for all participants: being alone in a class with many White students. All of the participants in their study reported how comforting it was to have other Black students in their classes and what a pleasure (albeit a rare one) it was to have a Black professor.[15] More than three decades ago, Fleming (1984) identified the crisis in social adjustment facing Black students in White colleges as one of three prominent issues in Black education. She maintained that low Black enrollment, social isolation, the small number of Black faculty and staff, and racial discrimination from faculty members and others served as major barriers of the Black experience.[16]

Saleem, a fourth-year biology major, needed a few moments to gather his composure as he began to describe the experiences of being Black and male on campus. He focused on the challenges that Black males face in transitioning from predominantly Black secondary school settings to historically White college campuses. In thinking about his experiences, Saleem recounted:

> SALEEM: [Deep breath . . . long pause] I mean . . . it's real hard. It's not that many Black males here. You just feel like a minority; even though you're a minority, you feel like you're really, really, really a minority.

> DB: What makes you feel like that?

> SALEEM: Compared to high school you see so many Black males there. And then you come here and you see less and less. You don't see so many faces no more and you want to see them here. We need more.

A number of men shared the stressors of low Black male enrollments on their campus, which easily lead to feelings of isolation and onlyness across both academic and nonacademic spaces. Saleem felt an enormity of weight in being one of very few Black males on his campus. During our interview, Saleem and I sat across from each other, within arm's length, at the corner of a table in a small conference room during our initial interview. After hearing the question, he took a deep breath in and stared at the ground for a long pause. His visceral response accompanied his revelation that "it's real hard" and created an indelible impression of the difficulties for Black male collegians on his campus—especially for those within the biological sciences. He clearly expressed racial battle fatigue and articulated the need for more Black males on his college campus. For Saleem, even *seeing* the faces of other Black male students on campus would have a significant positive impact on his collegiate experience. The low number of Black men on campuses is a reality that will continue to confront students at historically White institutions. In these types of scenarios, many Black students and other Students of Color have tried to carve out their own space on campus to serve as a buffer to an isolating campus climate through campus engagement in registered student organizations, fraternities and sororities, and gender-centered programming.[17]

Bannon illustrated the challenges of low Black male enrollment in the following reflection:

> [Long pause] It's interesting . . . [long pause] . . . I'm one of few. Sometimes I wonder how I want to react to a particular situation because I'm at a PWI. I feel like if I do respond to a particular incident then I'll be stereotyped as an "angry Black man."

Initially, Bannon needed to gather himself before responding to the question. After noting that being a Black male on campus was "interesting," he paused again to contemplate. For Bannon, the paltry number of Black males along with the campus climate demanded that he engage in a delicate balancing act as a means for managing his experiences. More importantly, he was aware fully of how his race and gender mattered on campus as he specifically identified how his social interactions and his identities are concomitantly intertwined within a narrowed view of Black males. His physical and verbal response to the interview question suggested that much of what he experienced was rendered invisible.[18] He seemed to carry a weight in suppressing ideas, thoughts, and reactions to what he saw and experienced. As researchers have noted, and as expressed by Bannon here, Black males' individual identities are rendered invisible on many college campuses. Instead of seeing Bannon's response to a particular situation as his own, manifest with multiple layers of his ideas and experiences, it could be interpreted by others as "anger." Patricia Hill Collins's work is instrumental in analyzing the ways that Blacks are confronted by "controlling images." These stereotypes allow for unequal power relations within social interactions such that the images deployed can control how marginalized groups are able to respond.[19] Oftentimes Black men face institutional norms that pressure them to appear friendly and cordial to undermine the controlling image of the "angry Black man."[20] Bannon's balancing act also highlights the emotional labor that Black males engage in during their college years. Additionally, researchers have argued that racial subordination not only creates difficult emotional expectations but may also create emotional dilemmas in which expected emotional displays undermine identity expectations.[21] By suppressing ideas, thoughts and reactions to various stimuli, this resilience strategy helps Black men stay focused on their goal of getting through college and, possibly, as a way to lessen the challenges of racial battles that they face on campus. Some Black men have learned to hold on to thoughts and reactions so that they can avoid being stereotyped as angry and so that they can manage social interactions on his own terms.

Earl's identity as a Black male also impacted his experiences on campus. This fourth-year psychology major discussed these challenges and provided some insight on how he attempts to respond. He shared:

> EARL: Actually, it's a struggle. When people look at you they treat you like you can't do nothing. I've actually experienced people say, "You can't do that because you're Black and you shouldn't try it because you're not good enough." I've tried to do things to show them different. I haven't been treated bad but I have experienced people looking down on me and having low expectations.

> DB: How does that make you feel?

> EARL: At times, I feel a little down about it. At times, I feel a little angry as well because I know they're treating me this way because I'm a Black male. I try my best at things that I might not be the best at just to show them that we're not all the same. If I can't get some stuff then I'll probably just learn on my own.

Many of the men's experiences continued to reveal a dire need for increasing the Black male population on campus, better appreciating Black male students, and a more robust understanding and imagining of Black men. Earl, like several other men, recalled being denigrated by lowered perspectives and expectations precisely because of his Black male identity. Although these experiences have been difficult for the men to handle at times, they remained resilient in his efforts to persevere. In response to explicit discouragement, Earl has still attempted to disprove the ways that people have tried to otherize him. Even in endeavors that may not be his forte, he defies expectations by asserting a desire to continue to pursue learning—even as an individual venture—and trying to help shatter the monolithic narrative and projections of Black men.

Black Males Focused and Determined: "Just Make It Through"

Several of the men offered that they felt like "walking stereotypes," they felt overly scrutinized, and acknowledged feeling that they had to prove their worth and belonging. These feelings and emotions emerge as a response to campus climates that they described earlier. In these instances, Black male collegians are forced to engage in a stressful range of emotional labor as they try to navigate racial realities on campus. As a targeted group within wider society, the men feel they often are treated like *any* unwanted and guilty-before-committing-a-crime Black man, as opposed to a male college student, and they feel they also are susceptible to being stereotyped on an on-going basis.[22] Thus, the strategies these Black male collegians employ are in direct response to how they make sense of their college campus and what they experience. These strategies clearly display how the men engage in identity work during their college years.

The men are not merely managing emotions, they are working to develop and project identities for how they wish to be seen as Black men. Monte reflected on the burdens of these experiences and shared:

> You're the target and you're aware of it. You know that you're the one that graduates the least. All that other stuff that happens outside of campus doesn't mean it doesn't affect us while we're on campus. It's just that we're the target group; we're the target group and we're aware of it . . . If I can just make it through this, then I'm good. I'll do a good job if I can just make it through. Just finish college. Doesn't matter what the GPA was, doesn't matter what I studied; just make it through.

Monte's reflection was both bleak and sobering. He felt that Black men on campus are targeted and he insisted that the weight that Black men carry as issues within wider society effect the Black male experience on campus. In the end, like many of his peers, his sole focus was to "make it through" college. For Monte, finishing college for Black males at a predominantly White campus is triumph enough and it supersedes a grade point average and one's choice of a major. In focusing his attention on making it through the college, Monte suggested a heightened awareness of the stressors and burdens that Black males endure in their college years. He identified that his way to manage these was to stay focused on graduating.

D'Angelo shared his insights on being a Black male on campus, which he identified as ranging between being the "best" and "worst" of times. He offered the following reflection:

> Campus life is crazy; like I said it's the best of times it's the worst of times. I've learned how to stay in my lane [and] not to step on any toes or overstay my welcome at someone's house. I've been invited to White parties before and those would be uncomfortable. The host would be comfortable but you see people drinking and looking at you funny. This college is honestly what you make it and depends on what type of person you are. I have a White boy or two that I can hit up and play Xbox with or play [basket]ball with. And you have the opposite as well. I still try to walk on campus with a smile, not to act like I don't know that things are going on but more so just keeping my calm.

D'Angelo began his reflection by acknowledging the chaotic nature of his college campus, which has provided him with both the best and worst of times. A significant lesson that he learned was to "stay in his lane." Here, D'Angelo offered that he treads his campus carefully in an effort not to overstep his boundaries or overstay his welcome. He noted how race plays a role in many of his social interactions. D'Angelo's coping strategy was to remain positive regardless of the situations that he faced. While walking around campus with a smile on his face may elicit scrutiny for being out of touch with reality, he asserted that this was his way to stay even-tempered. Thus, some of the men's emotional labor includes being aware of how Black men may be viewed as angry—or as threats. These types of experiences reveal how many Black men are embedded in pressures to negotiate self against being otherized. D'Angelo's welcoming smile easily confronts the stereotyped and overly projected image of the "menacing Black male." Similar to previous research, some of the men in this study used positive, restrained emotional displays as strategies to cope with the campus environment while some actively engaged in physical and behavioral acts to signify their racialized sense of masculinity.[23]

Student offerings on the ways that they cope and strategize to navigate the college campus, academically and socially, reveal the complexity of challenges that they face. In the previous chapter, the men described hostile environments where both students and professors were abrasive in their presence. In these ways, Black males described being in an ongoing racial grind in classroom settings, on and around campus, and in their social interactions as well. Yet, as articulated in the responses cited in this chapter, Black males display a keen social-emotional intelligence that helps them decipher the campus climate, discern impending and imposing threats to their personhood, and employ a range of strategies and scripts to cope with the environment. The scripts allow the men to diminish the blows of discrimination and hostility while also keeping their humanity and masculine identities intact. By employing these resiliency strategies, they are able to continue to persevere regardless of the obstacles they face, many relied on grit and others relied on various noncognitive skills (such as drive, determination, and focus). In speaking about how he has made it this far in his college career, Theodore shared:

> My determination. My determination to finish is what has drove me. I want to see the light at the end of the tunnel. I'm just focused on graduating. I have a goal and I know what it takes to get it; I have the determination to get what I want.

Similarly, Bruce reflected:

> I just believe that you have to stay focused, don't lose sight of your goal. My faith has really, really helped me out during this college thing. Some people come from such strict backgrounds that are just church, church, church and it's that way with me. I can't remember a single Sunday since I've been here [in college] that I didn't make it to church. Attaining my main goal, not forgetting where I come from, and leaning on my faith has helped me get to where I am today.

A number of men scripted resilience into their masculine identities and manhood constructs. Resilience was an important construct because it helped the men (re)center their focus while in college and helped them discern that many of the challenges they faced might be temporal. By contextualizing their experiences, and believing that they could perse-vere, the men activated resilience across a range of their experiences.

According to Theodore and Bruce, it is important for Black men to remain determined and focused. Theodore shared that his determination and focus motivated him and kept his goal of graduating within plain sight. Therefore, although he has experienced being racially stereotyped and profiled, none of the negative experiences trump Theodore's grit and goal of graduating. During our interview, Theodore and I sat directly across from each other in oversized chairs in a small room at the bot-tom of the library; there was a small table between us. As he began to answer the question and share his determination, Theodore sat up in his chair, clasped his hands so that his fingers touched lightly, and his eyes centered on mine. In that moment, I felt the intensity of Theodore's focus, which seemingly resulted from hours of hard work and study. He currently maintained a 2.9 grade point average and one of his goals was to graduate with at least a 3.0. Bruce expressed a similar approach as he used his faith to help him stay focused on his goals. During our initial interview, Bruce shared that during his two and a half years of college he had attended church every Sunday. Bruce's faith was instrumental to his personal grounding and his ability to persevere in college. He was raised in a churchgoing family in a small rural community about two hours away from campus. Still, his attendance at college did not supersede his continued engagement in religious activities. Specifically, he credited, "Attaining my main goal, not forgetting where I come from, and leaning on my faith" for getting him this far in his collegiate career.

Black Men Emerging

As Black male collegians continue to find their place on campus, through a variation of challenges and struggles along with progress and triumphs, many of the students described themselves as emerging victorious. The challenges that they faced both on- and off-campus are daunting; they have faced hurdles that other students may not experience. However, the men believe that the stereotypes levied against them, academic setbacks they have experienced, and even the personal trials that they faced all have strengthened their resolve to persist and strive for personal excellence. Their determination and perseverance are critical for their development, reaffirm their manhood constructs, and also clearly show the agency that they have embraced and engaged through their experiences. Their emergence and striving are highlighted below in ways that they sought to prove others wrong and how they felt empowered to defy stereotypes.

Responding to the Everydayness of Race: "Prove Them Wrong"

As has been discussed in this chapter, race and gender are salient, continuing, and chronic forces for Black males in higher education. Some of the men in this study discussed ways in which they were burdened by racialized and gendered stereotypes in their college careers in general and in their academic work in particular. Their narratives help reveal the barriers they face and the burdens they carry in dealing with these intersecting stereotypes. Even more importantly, their narratives reveal the everydayness of race, racialization, and Black misandry that are inherent in their college environments. One coping strategy that some of the men employed was motivated by desires to prove others wrong. These attempts are situated within an environment where Black male intellect and academic acumen are scrutinized. Researchers maintain that persistence plays a significant role in students' success in higher education.

The theoretical importance of persistence, especially within a racialized and hostile environment, reveals the need for Black males to become masters of their own fate. In their study that investigated the persistence of Black males in engineering programs, Moore, Madison-Colmore, and Smith (2003) found that students faced unique psychological and sociological challenges in engineering. The challenges they faced called for adaptive and nonadaptive coping mechanisms that promote academic persistence in unwelcoming and hostile engineering environments. They found that the students developed personality traits that embodied the prove-them-wrong syndrome whereby they became even more determined and committed to persevere when they perceived that their intellectual capability in engineering was doubted or slighted.[25] More recently, researchers have found that grit positively influenced grades in college for Black men at majority White institutions. Thus, researchers assert, persevering with passion is one strategy that Black males can employ to combat setbacks or, in the case of many students in this study, negative campus climates.[25] Focusing on the men's persistence also reveals their socio-emotional intelligence as well as highlighting how their voices matter in naming their own experiences.

Several of the men in the current study employed such adaptive and nonadaptive coping mechanisms and perseverance methods. Bannon shared the challenges he has faced in being a Black male on his college campus and he narrated applying a prove-them-wrong approach:

> BANNON: It's kinda hard because you have to deal with some of the things that goes along with being a Black male and the stereotypes that people don't know and they have stuff set about you. You already know what you're dealing with coming into college; your counterparts are perceived as more likely to going to college than you are. So you have to deal with the fact that you have to over excel in some areas knowing that.
>
> DB: How does it make you feel?
>
> BANNON: Like I said, I don't take it as an insult; I take it as an astonishing thing. People have these preconceived notions about people and they don't realize that they're doing it. Because of your background you already have these preconceived notions; it's crazy to look at some of these. I take it as a grain of salt and try to prove them wrong; I try to let them know that not all Black males are bad. Try to change as many minds as I can and then possibly start a chain reaction.

Several of the men asserted that being a Black male on their college campus was difficult primarily because of the general challenges that Black males face. They reaffirmed starting interactions from a deficit because of their identities and noted that many people they encounter already hold a particularly stereotypical view of Black men on college campuses. In a comparative sense, Black males are perceived through a deficit perspective, which for Bannon means that he has to "over excel" in some of his efforts. Additionally, in reflecting on his emotional labor, he was able to deflect a good deal of the scrutiny and preconceived notions because he anticipated these lowered views to be in place. Still, Bannon felt the need to "prove them wrong" in an effort to shatter their generalized conceptions about all Black males. In this way, he not only desired to carve out space for his own individual identity to reveal itself but he also wanted to help others see Black men through a refined lens. Additionally, his self-determination and resilience revealed how Black men construct manhood and masculinity within their collegiate experiences.[26]

Sean also offered that he wanted to prove others wrong; he shared his reflections about being a Black male on campus:

> SEAN: [long pause] . . . I just think it's like anywhere else really. Anywhere you go people are just going to look at you and judge you. It's like a different place and same attitudes. They're just going to look at you as "that" Black person. So, I just want to prove them wrong. Even though there may be people who act this way or that way, that doesn't mean it's me.
>
> DB: How do you try to prove them wrong?
>
> SEAN: Sitting in front of class, I know a lot of them say Black people sit in the back of the class. I get involved; people say that Black people don't get involved. I go to some of the meetings sometimes and I talk. I don't sag; some people might say Black people sag and they don't care how they dress. I try to make myself presentable and try to prove them wrong in anything that I do really.

First, Sean noted that being a Black man on campus was just like being any Black man in society. This means that although the college campus offers him an opportunity to improve his social capital and social mobility through involvement on campus and degree attainment, he is keenly aware of being prejudged for his racial and gender identities. Similar to Bannon, he engaged in a prove-them-wrong effort to help others expand their viewpoints of him individually and their perspectives of Black men collectively. The men's performative masculinity, in some ways, was in response to the culture and climate on campus and, in other ways, the larger societal pressures enacted upon Black men. These performances included navigating presentations of self, managing their presence and positions in the classroom and across campus, and negotiating social interactions as well. For many Black male students, these efforts mean that their racial and gender identity battles on campus are ongoing and they face them on an everyday basis. Given their experiences and involvement on campus, and their burgeoning identity development, many of the men refused to be labeled as just *any* Black man—who can be denigrated and dismissed—and intentionally engaged in actions that push back against the stereotypes and prejudgments. While there may be people who might fulfill stereotypes, these men desired to prove that they could not accurately apply them to all Black men.

Another student, Kory, acknowledged that being a Black man on campus is no different from being a Black man in any other segment of society. Thus, Black men constantly have to engage in identity work so that people can see them for who they are. He noted:

> Just like being a Black man anywhere else, like on the streets. You constantly have to prove yourself. If you don't show your worth then nobody will ever know. Just being about your business is one of the keys to being a [B]lack man on campus. If you not about your business if you not doing what you're supposed to be doing then it's going to be pushed down on you even more.

For Kory, two benefits of Black men proving themselves are noteworthy. First, in proving themselves Black men help to lift the veil on how they are perceived by others. As noted by Bannon and Sean, this has the potential of helping break the stereotypical mold of how many Black men are viewed. In articulating their identity work in these ways, the students invoke Du Bois's concept of the veil that grants Blacks a double consciousness. The students specifically speak to the ways that the veil serves as an intersectional lens through which Whites view them as Blackmen. In the experiences that the students share here, the veil of being Black and male casts them as different and thus in need of "proving their humanity" to others.[27] Second, "being about one's business," where students perform well academically and take care of their responsibilities on campus, combats attempts by others to diminish the worth and work of Black men. Although several of the men saw no difference in how Black men are treated in larger society and on their college campus, they were determined to shatter the negative and demeaning stereotypes of Black men. Thus, as these students adopted the prove-them-wrong resilience strategy in multiple facets of their everyday lives, they were engaging in identity work that potentially has broader connotations. For Black men in this study, proving others wrong is gendered work and a way of "doing gender" based on the routine and recurring practices that they engage in such as presentation of self, involvement, and other normative conceptions of respectability through a gendered lens.[28] Additionally, proving others wrong is identity work in that the men do not simply feel that they are trying to elevate just themselves but the much more broad spectrum of Black males at large.

Theodore expressed this sentiment of engaging in identity work and helping Black men emerge in the following way:

> In class I feel like I have to act a certain way to go against a stereotype; I feel like I have to fight against a stereotype. I have to sit close to the front of the class just to send a message to the teacher. It's like I have to make an overt statement that other students don't. If I sit in the back [of the class] then the teacher is going to look at me in some particular ways and say it's normal. I've basically learned that people are not going to look at [me] as Theodore, they're going to look at [me] as a Black man. In one psychology class I read about the elevator effect; being a Black man means that you have no identity. I was looked at as the criminal, as the enemy; your Blackness is framed as a bad thing. Being a Black man in America means that you're going to have to work harder to not fit into a group. I mean at the same time I want to fight against the stereotypes to prove people wrong but it's also stressful because I shouldn't have to.

Like many of his peers, Theodore attempted to find his place in college through perseverance and focus. He is acutely aware of the veil that permeates how Black men are viewed and projected on his campus; therefore, he engaged in resilience through specifically performing Black male identity against stereotypes. Theodore was mindful of where he sat in class as he revealed an understanding of where Black males position themselves in class can be interpreted to convey particularly negative messages about their seriousness as students. Thus, Theodore exhibited characteristics of a "Black male scholar identity" through his focus on future orientation, self-awareness, racial identity, and masculinity.[29] Additionally, he invoked an invisibility thesis in recognizing how

Black males are rendered invisible within larger society as having no individual identity.[30] Thus, in efforts to cope with the challenges that he faced, Theodore resisted by "fighting against stereotypes" to prove people wrong about himself and other Black men.

As noted by previous researchers, having to prove one's worthiness represents a potentially serious barrier to success for Black students attending an historically White institution. The students also were confronted by stereotype threat, the threat of being viewed through the lens of a negative stereotype, which has been found to impair academic performances of Black college students.[31] Both of these reaffirm the ways in which Black students, in general, and particularly the Black men in the current study were impacted by double consciousness. The students were engaged in an ongoing battle of perceptions and performances that connected how people viewed them as Black men and the ways that they thought about themselves and sought to persevere.

Self-Empowerment: "Be on Top of Your Game"

The final way that the men responded to the campus climate was through using problem-oriented coping strategies. Primarily, they focused on strategizing ways to excel and be at their best. Here, the men narrated ways that they were efficacious, maintained control over their actions, reactions and behaviors, and were self-aware. Cameron acknowledged the stereotypes that are levied against him and offered the following about being a Black male on campus:

> It's a walking stereotype. I feel like there are many stereotypes out here against me. And I just feel like I'm shattering them; I'm breaking the "Guiness Book of World Records": I haven't gotten anybody pregnant. I'm working at a fast food restaurant now but that's not my future, and I'm going to graduate. I don't sit in the back of the classroom. It's just defying all of them stereotypes and just shattering them, basically.

As mentioned by the men in various ways, being a Black man on campus is like being a walking stereotype. Many of the students perceived and experienced manifold stereotypes levied against Black men that constrict imaginings about them and often are used to create (and sustain) monolithic narratives about who they are. Cameron, along with several other students, felt empowered about overcoming the stereotypes because he was "shattering them." He specifically identified a range of behaviors such as teenage or youthful pregnancy that dominate many views of young Black men. Additionally, his current work at a fast food restaurant does not dictate his future and he was keenly aware of his presence in the classroom setting. Thus, through his own social, professional, and academic activities Cameron was motivated about his future possibilities and believed that he was shattering all of the negative stereotypes about Black men.

Similarly, Randy identified ways the he sought to overcome the stereotypes and lowered expectations that he has faced. He offered:

> I enjoy it. I feel like, I can't say I'm at an advantage, but I love being a Black male and do the things that I'm doing because a lot of people don't expect that. I enjoy it and I love when people see who's conducting this and they see it's an African American male and they're like, "Oh, wow! I wasn't expecting an African American male." But I feel like it's challenging in a good way. But sometimes it can be hard because you have to watch what you do because you are being watched. There are perceptions of African American males that are negative. So in that way you have to watch what you do and some are not allowed to be themselves.

What Randy shared in his reflection, both the triumphs and challenges, provides a key opportunity to see how the Black male collegians in this study made meanings from their racialized and gendered experiences and how they constantly worked to negotiate their place on campus. He noted that being a Black male on campus was hard sometimes because he felt that Black men were constantly under surveillance. The constant policing of Black men, even as "surveillance" on college campuses, is motivated by negative perceptions of them as a group, which ultimately results in some Black men not being able to be themselves or perform to their potential. What is evident across many of the men's narratives are the ways that their bodies, movements, and identities are policed constantly. The policing of Black males and Black male bodies adds another dimension of stress and stressors to their educational pursuits and, in some ways, is an ongoing threat to their sense of belonging and place on campus. Even with stereotyping and policing of the Black male presence as a backdrop, students like Randy identified perseverance and self-pride as important identity constructs that bolstered their persistence efforts. Randy asserted a self-love that was as reflective in the manner of how he said it as it was in what he said, "I love being a Black male and doing the things that I'm doing." He took joy in excelling against the odds and performing beyond others' expectations of him. Thus, both racial and gender identity served as key tools in Randy's ability to manage his experiences. In this regard, Randy highlighted self-determination in his ambitions to take the challenge and continue to rise above lowered projections or expectations. Randy's high academic and on-campus achievements included a 3.4 grade point average and participation in five different organizations including Student Government Association, the Black Student Union, and Pre-Law Society.

Fred asserted that being a Black man on campus is rife with challenges; some might be considered hard but he noted that college can present trials to all students. He acknowledged a coping strategy that relied on a positive reframing of the ways that Black men are confronted; in particular, he noted that the way to overcome much of the opposition that Black men face is to be focused. He explained:

> FRANK: I don't want to say it's hard because it's not necessarily hard because everybody's going through the same thing. But you kinda have that pressure on you that you're not supposed to be in the position that you're in and you're not supposed to be as successful as you are. Even though you don't represent all Black males you have to be on top of your game. So you kinda have that little chip on your shoulder that you have to keep going and you have to be on your stuff.

> DB: What do you mean when you say be on your stuff?

> FRANK: Like you just, even though people stereotype everybody, you can't just be no thug, you have to be intelligent and not just someone who hangs out all the time. You have to be on your work, talking to the professors and being on top of your work. So, like I said, you can't be a thug and somebody that's just smoke and drink all the time.

Although Fred believed that most college students were going through the same thing, he also asserted that Black men face additional and different pressure while being in college. Importantly, Fred's observations were problem-oriented as he identified the deficit rhetoric that is used against Black men as the main perpetrator. He noted that stereotypes of Black men as uninterested in college and as unsuccessful create pressures for him and other Black men because individual identities are compromised often by the group misperception and various controlling images. Thus, for Frank, Black men can reframe deficit thinking and use it as motivation to persevere in college and defy the racial denigrations held against them. He imagined and contended that Black men need to focus on their own intellectual abilities in addition to being responsible in managing their coursework and talking with professors as well. And, although individual Black men do not "represent all Black males," Fred invoked responsibility as a critical Black manhood construct in working to persevere in college and uplift Black men as a group.[32]

In discussing with Terrance his perspective of being a Black male on his college campus, he shared that he felt empowered and that he was leaving a legacy. He reflected:

> I feel empowered. I feel, I feel like a legend [smiles]. I feel like a legend because once I leave here there's going to be other guys who are going to have the same story and they'll feel motivated to continue on that path. I feel accomplished.

Terrance's smile after stating that he felt empowered and like a legend was both magnanimous and motivating. Upon graduating from high school, he shared that the only motivation he had to attend college was to play football. After attending an HBCU located in the South for one year, and not experiencing a great deal of participation in the football program, he decided to attend school closer to home. Initially, he had no desire to attend the local university and eagerly wanted to be away from home so that he could focus on his student-athlete schooling experience. In moving back, however, he was also closer to his toddler daughter and was currently seeking full custody. The semester following our interview, he was scheduled to study abroad in Spain—an experience he said he could not have imagined even just a year prior. During my observations and participation in BMI events, I witnessed his blossoming. He spent the majority of the year more reserved and he did not verbally share much during meetings. He showed his dedication to the program by attending every meeting and social outing and participating on the BMI's intramural football and basketball teams along with volunteering in the Black Male Connection program in which BMI partnered with two local high schools. On three separate occasions he brought his daughter with him to campus to attend and participate in a BMI activity because he was unable to secure a babysitter. Based on his character, desire to excel, and maturity, he was elected to a leadership position within BMI. In considering his journey, it is easy to see how and why Terrance might feel empowered and accomplished. Yet, a cursory glance at his racial and gender identity—through the White gaze or the stereotypical view that all Black males "seem" alike—means that the journey and accomplishments could be missed (or dismissed) quite easily. Still, Terrance has developed many characteristics of a "scholar identity" such as self-efficacy, willingness to make sacrifices, internal locus of control, and academic self-confidence.[33] In addition, establishing and leaving a legacy was an important manhood construct for a number of men as well as they wanted to use their successes to reframe the image and narrative about Black male collegians. Thus, in many ways, these students offer a different story about Black men that resist the pathologizing dominant tropes that often are held about them.

As we reached the end of the interview script, Monte sat shaking his head and smiling after I asked my last question of our initial interview. A former football player at both the high school and college levels, Monte's size easily belies his gentle spirit—Monte measures a solid six-foot-three-inches and I estimated he carried about 260 pounds. We conducted the interview in an on-campus office where we sat across from each other in chairs with just about a foot of space between us. We shared a four- or five-second moment of silence; I was still processing his last few comments and was in no rush for our conversation to end. I wanted to continue talking to Monte and learn more from his experiences. He maintained an energy that suggested he had more to share. His smile was infectious and I smiled in return—grateful for the opportunity to sit, talk, and share with him. After our silence, I asked if there was anything else he would like to share. He offered this reflection:

> I've had some experiences. I feel old; anything is possible. I feel like I'm strong enough to carry the world on my shoulders. As an African American male you have to have that. From the elementary school all the way up I feel like they trying to prepare us for prison; you just have to realize that you're better than that. Anything is possible. We have to stop as

a people blaming other people for what we're doing wrong. We didn't give teachers a chance to teach us. You want to complain to your parent, but we didn't give parents a chance to really parent us. We have to stop blaming other people. That's the one that I hate that I want to change and it starts with Black men. We have to start taking more responsibility.

Monte's reflection synthesizes a number of manhood constructs that were offered throughout the men's narratives. For instance, he conceptualized Black manhood as strength and responsibility; also, he asserted that he has to shoulder burdens and expectations as part of his masculine script. Thus, his college efforts are situated within his manhood and masculinity constructions. His conception of Black masculinity required him to conceive of his responsibilities in these ways. For Monte, being on top of his game meant that Black men take more responsibility for their actions in the home and in schools. Although they face grave challenges, such as feeling like they are being "prepared for prison," he advocated for a problem-oriented response where Black men acknowledge and accept their roles in understanding their current conditions and actively work to rectify their statuses. For instance, Monte asserted that Black men should focus on rising above any endeavor they encounter instead of blaming others. He encouraged a self-conceptualization of Black men that focused on self-esteem and self-awareness where they realize they are "better than" any lowered condition or projection because they are living embodiments of possibilities.[34]

BMI Supporting and Encouraging Resilience: "You Want to Achieve as Well"

In addition to examining how the men engaged in resilience through their individual efforts, some of the men also connected their efforts to their involvement with BMI. Primarily, the men credited BMI with providing a supportive atmosphere, a critical learning environment, motivation for Black male students, and a counter-space on campus. In this section, I focus the analysis on how the BMI program served as a counter-space for the men and helped support their efforts to responding to some of the hostilities they faced and the resilience strategies they employed.

Two students reflected on the benefits of participating in BMI that speak to how the program helps support the men's resilience strategies:

JORDAN: Reduced isolation, having a support system that's not prison, and being around people that look like you and are also motivated like you.

TERRANCE: If I wasn't engaged in Brothers & Scholars, I feel like I would be home more, I would be less motivated. I would be getting . . . just getting by. I feel like every African American brother is just getting by but that's not actually the case. There are people pushing for a 4.0. Staying at home will leave you in a one-track mind and that's not good.

For many of the men in this study, BMI's function as a counter-space helped to amplify their resilience and persistence efforts. The men identified that establishing connections with other Black males on campus helps the students overcome feelings of isolation and onlyness along with being motivated to achieve. The men acknowledged that BMI positively impacted their college experiences in not only what they experienced but also how they crafted (or re-crafted) their academic efforts. For instance, Jordan noted that BMI was important because it offered students agency in how they orchestrated their efforts ("support system that's not prison"). Thus, the collective nature of BMI helped the men feel more supported and helped them conceptualize how to respond to a variety of stressors and challenges and inspired them to achieve through cooperation with one another. These facets also inform how BMI contributed to the men's cooperative masculine identity development. Through their engagement, the men continued to develop a cooperative masculinity that was premised on a collective identity to support each other; in addition, the men worked together to achieve their goals—individually and collectively—and resist deficit framing.

Renaldo reflected on his BMI experiences and shared that the connections that Black men establish can help enhance their collegiate coping strategies and efforts. He shared:

You can get an idea of other people who are going through the same stuff that you are, familiar with other stuff . . . ability to be more open when you're really closed and not tell people much of anything. You feel more comfortable telling people those ideas. You feel challenged because other people are doing so well. It's not just because "Oh, you're Black!"

> Black people can do well . . . you're surrounded by successful
> people and you want to achieve as well. I know it helped me
> form one of my lifetime goals, which is to get a doctorate.

Important to the students' resilience narratives was engaging with the
Black Male Initiative program, which not only increased their sense
of belonging on campus but also bolstered many of the men's drive
and determination as well. A number of men highlighted how they felt
inspired and motivated, which was critical to their persistence. Students
felt connected with BMI and having cooperative support helped them
strategize their academic efforts on campus.

Several of the men asserted that one of their expectations of the
program was to have a brotherhood among the men who participate.
A comment by Justin, a fourth-year political science major, helps to
summarize how connecting with other men (as peers and other adults
as well) was critical to the success efforts for many of the Black male
collegians in this study:

> Bonding. Some people don't have fathers so just bonding
> with another male who's in the same position or circumstance
> as you, you need that. It has less to do with who I'm not
> and more to do with who I am; so I feel like the bonding
> you need that. You need to know how to bond with other
> males. That's how people remember you. You never know
> what the future holds and just building that bond may open
> up so many doors in life that you didn't know existed. And
> just holding each other accountable for whatever you need
> accountability for; if you need to be accountable for grades
> then there's somebody there for that . . . It's the bonding,
> that's what Mighty Men is providing.

Earlier in his interview, Justin expressed that he was invited to participate in Mighty Men by Vance, one of his fraternity members, who also
served as a Mighty Men staff member. Vance not only informed him
that he "should get involved" but, more importantly, that "we need
people like you to join it." This invitation appealed to Justin and he
held a positive initial impression of Mighty Men. Justin explicitly identified the opportunities for Black male bonding as the most important
aspect that Mighty Men offered Black male collegians. Even though he

was a member of a fraternity, he still maintained that Black men on college campuses "need to know how to bond with other males." For several of the students, BMI was different from and more attractive than fraternities, primarily because the program accepted *all* Black male students without regard to academic performance, college standing, or social clout and the men did not have to pay any monetary membership fees or dues. Thus, in some ways, several of the men experienced BMI connections as more organic. According to Justin, the brotherhood and bonding could deepen the men's connections—especially given some of the men's own personal backgrounds—and could help open future opportunities. Additionally, participating in BMI helped many of the men develop a cooperative masculine construct, which helped heighten and sustain their accountability for each other as well.

Conclusion

The Black male collegians in this study engage in a variety of efforts and strategies to be resilient and persist in college. In many instances, the stereotypes and discrimination that they endure have fortified their resilience and motivation and ignited a desire to excel against the odds. Importantly, their resilience and persistence was supported in and reaffirmed by their participation in BMI programs. Allowing space for Black males to articulate their college experiences opens a vast window of opportunity to learn how they see, understand, and make meaning of their own efforts.

The men's resilience strategies are deeply embedded within their academic goals, aspirations, and double-consciousness along with their masculine and scholarly constructs. Given the bevy of stereotypes and controlling images that the men face, a major factor in being resilient is having an awareness of how they are perceived on campus—and in wider society. Oftentimes, this knowledge informs the strategies that they employ.[35] Since academic coping strategies are critical to student success, the men attested to the need to reassess their place on campus and engage both cognitive and noncognitive skills in order to persist. More specifically, some men narrated how being focused and determined helped them stay on track toward graduation. In these instances, the men used active and positive reframing coping strategies that helped them deflect potentially frustrating experiences by being more focused on themselves and their efforts and goals. Additionally, the men engaged in emotional labor as well as they responded to negative and pathological framing of their raced and gendered identities (such as "angry Black male") by staying positive and focused.

Importantly, in investigating how they responded to being problematized on campus, the men also revealed how they imagined and performed their racial and gender identities. I identified three specific strategies that the men used to persist in college: just do me, I don't care, and prove them wrong. As previous researchers have noted, Black men do have a great deal of control over how they physically, behaviorally, and emotionally claim and reclaim their sense of self in public social spaces and within institutions. For many of the men in this study, they engaged in coping strategies that were in direct response to hostile campus climates and other microaggressive or discriminatory experiences. For instance, "just do me" and "prove them wrong" were connected to the men's self-pride, focus, and motivation. Each of these helped some of the men buffer their sense of self in interpersonal interactions, academic experiences, and events on campus. In thinking about and imagining their future selves, and constructing their individual efforts as part of a larger collective effort, the men also rejected one-dimensional projections of Black men. They scripted resilience into their Black male identities and tied their efforts to notions of responsibility, accountability, achieving against the odds, and trailblazer. As the men transitioned to college and responded to the campus milieu, they also developed a heightened sense of their social and emotional needs and identified intragroup peer relations as a key to buffering them against onlyness.

BMI provided the men with a different context to cope with their college experiences. Primarily, through BMI, the men's coping strategies focused on interconnectedness, where they relied on venting, emotional support, and institutional support to bolster their efforts. Thus, as established within this chapter, the BMI program also provided the men with a supportive atmosphere and served as a counter-space as well. The students were able to bond with other Black males, they shared and learned from and amongst their peers, and they felt accountable to the group. As a result, the students expressed feeling motivated and their sense of belonging increased as well. The BMI community also aided the men in their racial and gender identity development. In particular, the men revealed a new cooperative masculinity as important to their resiliency. Although some men initially responded to the campus milieu by turning inward ("just do me"), their connections to the group also allowed them to see and learn how cooperating with other Black male students could enhance sense of belonging and persistence.

The men's resilience strategies and identity work are not only embedded in their own individual efforts but also are connected to their involvement on campus. In the next chapter, I examine their experiences in a Black Male Initiative program, focusing specifically on the significance and meaning of their participation. Their meaningful engagement in the program enhanced their college experiences and strengthened their ability to persist.

CHAPTER 6

Brotherhood and Bonding

Shared Experiences in
Black Male Initiative Programs

In the beginning, I could kinda feel that it was the route that I was trying to take. I feel like it was to motivate us as African American males to graduate. I feel like even directly telling us that we needed to graduate wasn't enough because we knew we needed to graduate and anyone could tell us that. But they were giving us the big picture and pointing out the impact it could have on our communities and even the whole Black America.

—Donald

It's a great experience. Like, just like the brotherhood of the organization.

—Elvan

As the men in this study attempted to seek their place on campus, they engaged in a variety of on-campus activities that ranged from intramural sports and various clubs to registered student organizations, fraternities, and a Black Male Initiative program. The men's engagement in non-curricula activities is useful for better understanding how they connected and integrated with campus. More specifically, this chapter focuses on how the men engaged in a Black Male Initiative program at their respective universities and how they made meanings from those experiences. Previous research theorized that in order for growth to take place, students need to actively engage in their environment and the involvement must be both quantitative (amount of time devoted) and qualitative (the seriousness students approach a given activity).[1] The analysis that follows explores the quality of student experiences in BMI. Investigating the impact of BMI-type initiatives, from the perspectives of Black male students, can offer important insight into ways to increase engagement, persistence, and degree completion among Black males.[2] According to Donald, quoted above, he saw BMI as much larger than his own individual collegiate endeavors; he identified the work of BMI as one that has the potential to impact Black communities writ large.

Both of the BMI programs at Lincoln State University and Monroe State University are student-centered and give a high premium to building relationships. More importantly, the primary goal of both programs is to enhance the collegiate experiences of Black male students by focusing on strategies to retain them and help them graduate. Researchers have identified a range of factors that have been found to promote a climate of success for Black males; most germane to this research are three factors: peer group influence, identity development and self-perception, and institutional environment.[3] Similarly, Strayhorn (2008b) found that supportive on-campus relationships are positively associated with educational outcomes. He also advocated for a "multifaceted institutional response" where resources could be pooled from across the campus to enhance the plight of Black male collegians. Each of these measures, in addition to those identified by other scholars, is critical not only for enhancing the educational experiences of Black males but also in bolstering their retention and graduation rates. As the statement by Elvan notes, cited at the beginning of this chapter, BMI has been "great" precisely because of the brotherhood and bonding—the tight-knit relationships BMI members developed with one another—that the men experience through their engagement. Thus, in critical ways, BMI heightened and affirmed students' sense of belonging on campus.[4]

Experiencing Black Male Initiative Programs

In exploring how the men make meaning from their engagement in BMI programs, this chapter focuses on three broad domains that include BMI student experiences, BMI and collegiate experiences, and the significance that the men ascribed to BMI. Within each of these domains, students were asked questions that were designed to tease out their experiences.[5]

Getting Involved in BMI Programs: "It Might Be a Good Fit"

In an effort to understand the parameters of their entry points, students were asked how they got involved in the Black Male Initiative program on their campus. Student engagement happened in two primary ways: either through conversations and invitation from BMI staff/task force members or as a result of association with current BMI student members. Two students' lengthy responses to how they got involved in BMI reflect those of the group and are indicative of the qualities that many of the men say they experience through their participation.

> DONALD: My first year I attended just about all of the meetings and most of the events. And I became recommended for the E-Board, which is probably like the best way to get involved is to take a leadership role and take ownership of the organization itself.
>
> DB: What got you to go to that first meeting?
>
> DONALD: I felt comfortable around people like me and I knew that people like me were going to be at the meeting. Most of my friends were going to be there and all of the guys there were going to be African American males. I've had trouble with my own identity but when I'm there I feel comfortable. When we have conversations and talks, they've benefited you as an African American male and I felt like I needed to be there.

Donald asserted that gaining a sense of belonging motivated him to attend his first BMI meeting; his social identities as a Black male along with anticipated connections to friends and peer group all mattered to him.[6] Additionally, his participation provided him with a level of comfort and sense of security in how he might be received. Donald hoped to renegotiate and rectify his own Black male identity; and, as he sought to have a better sense of self, he valued many of the conversations and talks that occurred in and through Brothers & Scholars. Donald's sense of belonging was enhanced through his participation; one clear result was accepting a recommendation to be a member of the BMI Executive Board. In talking about what made him feel like being in Brothers & Scholars was necessary for him, Donald explained:

> Because I've always struggled with my identity and it's like I needed this because it was a way of helping me cope with that. I also wanted it to help me build my confidence and self-esteem, to give me a grounding of some sort that I could stand on so that I felt like I could become something more than just a Black kid. And I could begin to build an identity from that base and solid ground because I've never really had that. It kind of motivated me to try to change statistics and stereotypes that have been placed on my people. So, it gave me a purpose and a mission. And I needed that; I needed that as motivation to make it through college.

A critical self-assessment left Donald in search of enhancing his racialized and gendered identities as well as helping to ground his place in college. As students discussed why they felt like they needed to be engaged in BMI, many of the men centered their comments on their masculine identities and manhood constructs. Like many of his peers, Donald shared his belief that the organization could help heighten his confidence and self-esteem along with improving his self-identity. Importantly, helping to bolster student's self-esteem is linked to the concept of academic resilience.[7] Thus, many of the men envisioned and believed BMI as a space that would allow for their self-actualization: helping them to blossom into the individual that they hoped to become. Given this foundation, the men believed that their own lives could serve as testimony against the stereotypes that are levied against Black men and their success could help improve the educational and professional statistics of Black men as well. Additionally, as mentioned previously, BMI has been instrumental in motivating many of them to achieve and persevere in college by helping to sharpen their focus and work with greater intentionality ("it gave me a sense of purpose and a mission").

Similarly, Fred recounted his needs in initially attending BMI:

FRED: Well, I heard about it . . . I don't remember how I heard about it. I remember coming my freshman year and it was just like another meeting. I was meeting with Jason [a program coordinator] for TRiO and he asked, "Why don't I see you in Mighty Men?" And I just started coming and it's something that I feel good about.

DB: You said you remember Jason asking you to come initially, what made you go back?

FRED: It was really my mindset. Over the summer I was a little lost; I didn't know which direction I was going, I didn't know what I wanted to do. I had financial problems and I had girl problems. That's when I decided to change and I was like, "I'm about to get on my shit." And that's what Mighty Men is about; it's about Black males coming together and pursuing success and I knew that's where I needed to be. I looked at Mighty Men and said that's my beginning and I just have to set myself up right.

Similar to what Donald shared, Fred asserted that he knew Mighty Men was "where I needed to be." The major reason for "needing" to be there was because of Fred's own self-assessment that he needed to "get on my shit"—especially with the challenges he faced at the current time. Thus, Mighty Men appealed to many of the men precisely because they saw other Black men achieve and they identified the organization as one where Black men took care of business. Even though he had heard about the program during his freshman year, it was the invitation from one of the program coordinators that sparked his initial attendance. What Fred experienced at the first meeting, Black males coming together and pursuing success, was something that he felt good about and he also found that it was reaffirming to his own desires. He articulated his overall experience in the following way:

It's been pretty good, just to see older guys that have been here for a while that have done things and have gotten information and seen what they've been able to do. It's been a lot of learning and given me people to look up to. It's given me a way to keep me on top of my game. I don't compare myself to anybody, but it just helps me see what I need to be doing. I'm like, "He's doing this and I'm trying to do that, but let me see if that's something that I like; maybe I can try that too."

Many of the men's experiences in BMI have been critical to their development, connections with staff members, and access to resources. Fred shared that learning and self-development, both academic and personal, were critical outcomes from his engagement with BMI. He expressed being motivated to perform well and even wanted to try new ventures based on what his peers were doing. Many of the men shared that being in community with other Black men provided them with models of success that they could aspire to achieve. In this way, the BMI provided space for intragroup peer relations to directly and indirectly impact Black males within the program. Thus, for many of the men, the Black Male Initiative programs served much like "agents of socialization" that helped smooth the students' transition to college, provided them with connections to other Black men along with various staff and faculty, and served as a space for out-of-class learning as well.[8]

The men made definitive links between their peer interactions and academic success. Interaction with peers has the potential to contribute significantly to students' overall academic development, acquisition of knowledge, self-esteem, and self-efficacy. Additionally, peer-to-peer bonding can increase students' academic performances and persistence. These associations and relationships can improve persistence by providing access to academic and social resources and strategies. As the men indicated, a significant benefit of their BMI connections was the opportunity to access support, encouragement, and motivation. Thus, these BMI members provided each other with a significant source of social, cultural, and relational capital, which positively enhanced their college experiences.

BMI Experiences Thus Far: "Nothing but Positives"

As offered by the students in discussing how they got involved, what was critical to their ongoing participation was what they experienced through their involvement. Students were asked to share what their experiences were like in BMI thus far as a way to make sense of *how* the students experienced their participation. All of the students spoke about the positive qualities of their experiences in BMI. The quality of student experiences include students' thoughts and feelings about being a member of BMI, especially as it connected to their Black male identities and narratives of their experiences in the Black Male Initiative Program thus far.

IT'S BEEN GOOD

All of the students described the quality of their experience through positive adjectives such as good, outstanding, and great. Given the grand consistency of what they shared, a representative sample is identified here:

> DEVON: It's been good. It's cool. The talks we have, I wish we had more of them. It seems like there's a big time lag in between them—maybe [we could meet] every other week to keep everything fresh. Wish they lasted even longer but time flies when you're really engaged in talking. And then the outings after are just like icing on the cake; I'd be content with just the talks but I like the outings too.

> ARTHUR: I had a good experience in the Brothers & Scholars. The people that I met, you connect with the person outside of academics. It's a connection first off based on race but you develop the relationships outside of just race. You carry bonds and it's a very huge accountability piece that goes along with being in Brothers & Scholars.

> JARED: Nothing but positives. I got to travel with Brothers & Scholars; I got to have like a separate group of people that I can talk to and hang out with who are a lot different from the people that I'm with every day in the classroom. It's been a helpful experience as far as the transition from high school to college. It's given me the opportunity to share my experience with others to help their experiences. And I had a mentor as well, so that really helped.

For Devon, a fourth-year economics major, his experience in BMI has been positive. He specifically identified the monthly meetings as the key source to what he has enjoyed thus far. During these meetings, various faculty, staff, and administrators provided a targeted presentation to Black male collegians. For instance, at one meeting that I attended an education professor gave a presentation from national research that focused on the keys to Black male persistence in college. The 40-minute presentation was replete with data from current research, used voices from qualitative research studies, and concluded with specific action steps that Black male collegians could pursue in efforts to enhance their collegiate experiences—academically, personally, and socially. This meeting was held during the first month of the fall semester, which provided ample time for students to hear the presentation and implement some (or all) of the strategies. I sat next to three students who were taking notes during the presentation and, as I wrote my own notes, I observed that at least three quarters of the 41 students in attendance seemed to take notes in some form—most of the students had a writing utensil and paper, some borrowed paper from other students as the professor began his PowerPoint presentation, and others distributed paper (or note cards) after the presentation began. Four students who were seated near the door listening to the beginning of the presentation repositioned themselves in the room so that they could see the PowerPoint. According to Devon, the talks and discussions were of such quality that he wished the group could meet more often (maybe every other week as opposed to monthly) and the meetings could last longer. Arthur declared that he has had a good experience in BMI primarily through the people that he has met and the opportunities to connect with peers beyond the academic realm. Jared, in addition to traveling away from campus and having a mentor, also shared that relational capital, expressed by him as the opportunity to connect with others, has been paramount in his BMI program experience and his overall collegiate experience. For many of the Black male BMI participants, their relational resources and experiences in bonding with their peers and receiving support were critical to enhancing their collegiate experiences and success.

SUPPORTIVE ATMOSPHERE

In discussing the social dynamics that they experienced, several of the men focused on the supportive atmosphere of the BMI program and the people involved. The first two lengthy comments exemplify the breadth of these experiences; the third comment speaks specifically to the benefits of the supportive atmosphere.

MARK: My overall experience is speaking to other Black men on campus that I don't normally talk to. So, you're going to have different representation from various RSOs [Registered Student Organizations] and we're all just there and we kick it. We have freshmen there and they see something that's positive and they want to be a part of it. It's just being able to meet new guys and we're able to share conversations with these guys. When we meet, we discuss particular issues or things that are of an academic focus; we have mock interviews, [or] bring your resume in and get it checked out by the [coordinators], and things of that nature. It's been a great experience. It's not only good for me but even new guys that come in and don't even know how to start a resume. So, my overall experience with Mighty Men has been very good and it is a very positive group.

ELIJAH: So far it's been a good experience. I try to go every Thursday; like, that's one thing I look for during the week is to go to Mighty Men. [DB]: *What makes you look forward to Mighty Men?* Being around people that are trying to make it. It's like everybody is going through the same thing and we all come together to talk about what's going on. [DB]: *What's made your experience good?* Meeting new people. I've seen people around campus but I didn't get a chance to meet them like that. And knowing people that got my back and I got theirs if they need it.

SEAN: It's been good. I feel like I can talk to them about anything in there. If you have a question they don't sugarcoat it, they'll just tell you like it is. They're just there to help you and I think that's good to have on campus.

Mark acknowledged that BMI has fostered a supportive atmosphere among Black males on his campus. As a result, the atmosphere created within BMI has impacted Black male experiences across campus as well. Many of the men attested to garnering a range of capital through their BMI experiences, such as aspirational (feeling inspired and motivated), navigational (learning how to negotiate the campus), social (gaining access to various resources), and cultural (being in community with their racialized and gendered peers).[9] According to Mark, the supportive atmosphere has allowed students to tap into a vast number of people who can assist them with their academics and even in their professional preparations (such as developing their resumes and preparing for job interviews). He expressed positive experiences through his connections with the group. Elijah has made Mighty Men a priority and tries to attend each of the weekly meetings. The attraction for him to attend was the support group that is established through mutual and oftentimes interconnected experiences. An important element of his experience involves cooperative development and interconnected coping; that is, knowing he has a group of people that will support him and he is eager to reciprocate this to others as well. Similarly, Sean conveyed his BMI program experience was positive because he believed that the program and group of men involved were there to help him. They provided him and others with candid feedback on their collegiate performances and engagement.

LEARNING ENVIRONMENT

Similar to the supportive atmosphere, BMI members learned a good deal through their experiences. The following two comments by Kory and Joseph reflect these points. Kory offered:

> Mighty Men has honestly been, since joining Mighty Men there's been a period of enlightenment on my life. Mighty Men is probably one of the key factors in my growth; in sitting back looking at a lot of the guys who are in Mighty Men these are possibly guys, yeah they're my age, but as far as what they're doing it was like, "Wow!" They were doing things and people were like "Wow" and I was impressed. So that motivated me to contribute and get things going. You have presidents of other organizations like BSU, NAACP; you have all of these people who does [sic] so much for us at the end of the day. You have people you can look up to and you sit back and say, "All right, these guys are trying to do something." That's what drew me to Mighty Men—through consistently growing and seeing the growth not only in myself and in other people. I'm sure I wasn't the only person who sat back and didn't talk. You see guys who you see all the time doing all different kinds of stuff but seeing them in Mighty

Men was really like seeing them. You see guys with girls or tripping with his friends and you think, "Oh, he really ain't on nothing." But then you see them at Mighty Men and you're like, "Oh, wow!"

Kory identified his engagement in Mighty Men as transformative to his collegiate experience. He felt enlightened about his life through his participation and sees the program as a key factor in his growth and development. One of the ways in which he has learned about his own capabilities was through witnessing the efforts and accomplishments of his peer group. Thus, Kory was motivated to perform through his connections with other Black men on campus and learning about their collegiate endeavors. His connections to Black male campus leaders provided him with an opportunity to reflect on the organization and on himself as well. He expressed that he was drawn to Mighty Men precisely because of this legacy of leadership and positive productivity that many of the other members had achieved. Additionally, he was able to see growth in himself and his peers, which also compelled him and others to reassess early judgments and misperceptions of Black male collegians in different circumstances.

Joseph shared how he has learned through participating in the BMI program, he explained:

They exposed me to success and showed me the ropes. Had people come in and talked to us, they were rags to riches, on the road to glory. It was . . . if it wasn't for Brothers & Scholars, I don't know, I probably wouldn't come back this semester. Just sitting back and looking at the pictures we took in Ohio and, you know, I had a time I had to realize what I was really into. It was time to grow up, put all of that BS beside you; it was time to man up. You know, you're not granny's boy any more. It taught me a lot. And then, you know, it's survival of the fittest. Can you survive, are you going to give up? . . . Are you going to be a chump or are you going to be a winner? I figured that this semester I'm going to stay home and spend more time with my course work; getting away from my friends. Doing more of what's expected of me with my coursework and then going on with my day. I'm taking myself away from the crowd; stop following the crowd and

be on my own. I actually joined Brothers & Scholars just
because I wasn't involved in no other program. Like I said,
in high school I played football [and] they was on us about
getting our work done. So, coming here [in college] and I
wasn't into nothing and wasn't nobody on me. So, I guess
I need somebody on my back. I was doing stuff on my own
and doing it on my own wasn't working. So, I guess that's
why I joined Brothers & Scholars.

Joseph's BMI experience has been personally motivating. He notes
the quality of his experiences were so important that had he not been
engaged he might not have returned for the year. Reflecting on some
of the experiences that he has had helped Joseph put BMI in context.
Importantly, Joseph's manhood construct was centered on self-determination ("it was time to grow up") and revealed how he subscribed to
hegemonic masculine norms ("it was time to man up" and "it's survival
of the fittest"). Additionally, he identified self-independence as critical to his continuing masculine development ("you're not granny's boy
any more" and "be on my own"). Yet, as he continued to reflect on
his experiences, Joseph suggested that support was critical for changing
and enhancing the outcomes of his efforts ("doing it on my own wasn't
working"). His experiences and reflections reveal many of the men's
ongoing development and also shows how a cooperative masculinity was
appealing to their identity constructs and success efforts.

Many of the students suggested that being involved in college could
help them increase their sense of belonging on campus. For instance,
what Joseph learned about himself was that, similar to high school, he
needed to be involved in nonacademic activities while in school so
that he could be held accountable for his actions and behaviors. Thus,
participating in BMI provided Joseph with an internal familiarity. A
key component of what many of the Black male students experienced
through their participation in BMI programs was a heightened sense of
self and an increased self-awareness (discussed in further detail below).
Several researchers have noted the importance of critical pedagogy and
culturally relevant pedagogy for engaging Students of Color in general
and Black males in particular.[10] Here, I extend the context of these peda-
gogical approaches to nonacademic spaces including student-centered
programs and organizations such as the Black Male Initiative programs
that I observed and learned from through student engagement. Research-

ers contend that there is a critical need to engage students in ethnic identity discourse, even among elementary and young learners, which ultimately helps to affirm their ethnic identities.[11] Furthermore, as the narratives attest, students were engaged in a continuous process of developing their masculine identities and manhood constructs through their BMI experiences. Thus, identity discourse is even more important given the salience of racialized and gendered identities and how identities matter in students' schooling experiences. In addition to formulating and reinforcing a constructive image of self, support of this nature also may heighten students' self-efficacy and academic achievement.

Understanding BMI Through Experience: "Have Support that Motivates Them"

A key component of engaging in their BMI programs is for students to have an understanding about their respective program. Thus, students were asked to share their understanding of BMI based on their experiences. Student responses covered three main themes, which included academics, community, and responsibility. Each theme is discussed in greater detail below.

ACADEMICS

One of the main ways that students understood what BMI was about was expressed through an academic narrative. Seven students had comments that connected BMI to an academic focus. Several students offered the following:

> ASHTON: Making sure African American males have equal resources as everybody else. Not only having them but being able to use them, being notified about opportunities on campus, to help us . . . and keep up our grades.

> GEORGE: Challenging the disparity of Black male performance on the university campus.

> DEVON: Keeping   bringing together African Americans on campus and keeping them on campus. And try to figure out a way how if they're struggling then how do we help

them be successful. It's kind of an indirect way to keeping on track to graduate by keeping everybody accountable to some degree. Then you go to trips at the end to loosen the mood; some people would leave after the talks because they might get bored, so it helps to do activities afterward. And, you can build some camaraderie.

JARED: Brothers & Scholars is about making sure we graduate; African American males graduate. Helping the retention of African American males on campus and just making us better leaders overall.

According to Ashton, a second-year exercise science major, the purpose of BMI is to ensure equity for Black males on campus; this included access and usage of available resources and opportunities. George, a recent chemical engineering graduate, saw BMI as a program intended to improve the academic performance of Black males on campus. Devon provided a bit more lengthy response and offered that two of the key functions of BMI are to bring Black males together on campus and also to retain them. For those Black males who may struggle, Devon believed that BMI should be positioned to help support their efforts while also holding them accountable as well. Additionally, he asserted that coordinating social outings at the end of meetings was a good way to help people stay connected to the program. Jared's assessment echoes one of Devon's points, which is that the focus of BMI is to ensure that Black males graduate. Also like Devon, he believed that BMI is geared toward retaining Black males and improving their leadership skills. The statements offered by these students focus on the academic functions of BMI, which primarily included supporting their academic performances ("keep up our grades" and improving student retention) and working to help Black men graduate from college.

COMMUNITY

A second way that the students narrated BMI was expressed through the community that they experienced by participating in the program. Almost one-fourth of the students described and reported the importance of bringing Black males together and enriching their college community. Donald, Winston, and Elvan discussed the support system they experienced in BMI:

DONALD: I feel like Brothers & Scholars is about basically bringing African American males together and making them feel more comfortable on a predominantly White campus. Allow them to know each other and have a support system outside of their families. And have the support that motivates them to complete college.

WINSTON: Brothers & Scholars is about . . . I guess college community enrichment. I . . . after a while I realized that BMI is not just open to African American males, which I thought, I thought the case was different before then. I guess Brothers & Scholars is about African American male retention and it's about being a resource to a minority group on campus that . . . that otherwise would not have any more closer direction on the college campus. It's about leadership, diversity, it's about . . . uplifting, giving back.

ELVAN: Brothers & Scholars is about a brotherhood—us keeping each other in line to meet our main goal, which is to graduate from college. It's more of like a support group; whenever you're in trouble or something like that you have people there. If Keith [the program coordinator] can't help you then there are other people you can ask. Somebody will have an answer for you.

Donald, Winston, and Elvan each saw Brothers & Scholars as a support group. The great majority of students noted the importance of the community that is harbored by bringing Black males together on campus and the cultural wealth that is enriched and developed through the program. For Donald, he situated this collective effort as something needed to improve the sense of belonging of Black male collegians on a historically White campus. In building community on campus, by bringing Black males together for purposes of intentional interactions about their individual and collective experiences (i.e., campus climate, on campus experiences, and identity) and goals (i.e., academic success), their intragroup peer relations and associations can be made stronger as they have the opportunity to see themselves in each other. In many ways, the BMI program was built on the assumed cultural familiarity among this student population. Still, this community was a critical resource in helping the men persevere in college and many of the students expressed feeling motivated as well. Thus, similar to mentorships and Black student organizations, Black Male Initiative programs can serve as avenues of psychological and psychosocial support for Black male students.[12]

BUILDING RESPONSIBILITY

In addition to defining BMI through academic components and as a community, a number of students also discussed responsibility and accountability as key features of their understanding of BMI. The following statements by Raymond, Myron, and Monte are representative of this theme:

> *Raymond:* It's about holding Black people responsible for their own success, even though there's mentors and things like that we do hold everybody responsible for their own success. There's fun, bonding, mentoring, but we do make sure that everybody is about their success.

> Myron: It's about, really, getting African American males together, get them all on the same page, keeping them focused, make sure everything is going in order for them to graduate. I guess that's the end goal.

> Monte: Mighty Men is where Black men can come vent, what we can do better as people, what we can do better for our community and what you need to do to make it out of college. And it's like a stepping-stone to other things. Like most people who go to Mighty Men end up pledging to a fraternity, so Mighty Men is like a stepping-stone.

The students cited here saw and envisioned BMI as a space where Black men build and learn responsibility. Raymond stated this explicitly as he identified BMI's main purpose is to hold Black male collegians responsible for their own success. This is a critical insight and meshes well with the men's masculine identity development and manhood constructs. Thus, BMI served as an organization that helped to spawn the men's growth and self-awareness both individually and collectively. Myron and Monte echoed this sentiment, as they noted that BMI is not only about building a Black male community on campus but also making sure that they are staying focused and taking care of their responsibilities. Monte described some of these responsibilities as improving the plight of individuals and the community along with working toward graduation. By holding individual students accountable for their own success, BMI helps to engender agency among the students. Additionally, BMI helped these Black men see (and remember) their connections to the larger community. Importantly, as the men reflect on their learning and the values espoused within BMI, what they offer helps to nuance notions of success that are primarily articulated as college graduation. Instead, many of the men refocused and recentered responsibility as a critical manhood construct where they assert that success is encompassed by how their efforts connect to the community, which reveals another nuance of their cooperative masculinity. These messages and learning opportunities provide insight into how the men's gender identity and manhood constructs matter with regard to reaffirming (or heightening) their sense of and desire for responsibility. Additionally, as the men increase their abilities and display them in various ways, BMI helps springboard their activity into other student groups and campus organizations, such as fraternities, Black Student Union, and student government, which thereby impacts the larger university environment as well.

BMI Disconnects: "I Guess I'm Wanting a Little More"

As the men discussed their BMI experiences, they also noted that there can be disconnects between the program's stated goals (or goals articulated by program coordinators) and the men's experiences when it comes to cohesiveness. For instance, although both BMI programs are geared toward academic cohesion, almost a quarter of the students shared that BMI had little to no impact on their academic experiences. Thus, in addition to engaging students in conversations about how they benefitted from participating in BMI, we also discussed how BMI did not meet their expectations and what the programs could do better. Recall, many of the men credited BMI with making them feel important; one area of improvement was sustaining and deepening the connections of their intragroup peer relationships and associations. In speaking specifically about the brotherhood aspect, Renaldo exclaimed:

> The brotherhood aspect. I see groups of people that I've seen since day one, I see them all around campus and

everything . . . it kinda is insulting because here we were so close and now we're not. I've seen other groups of Brothers & Scholars guys hanging out . . . I kinda have to shrug it off because I can try to make other people fit in who are in that position—so the sense of brotherhood.

In relation to the brotherhood aspect, D.J. and D'Angelo's comments about students' retention in the program are noteworthy.

D.J.: Members, guys that come in. I don't see why, it's people that come in and they leave and it's like why? I just see the good that Mighty Men does so why wouldn't you want to be a part of this. But Greek life is so crazy; a lot of people get letters and they forget about Mighty Men. I'm one of those people that don't forget about where you came from. Kappa is an organization just like Mighty Men, so I'll be at Mighty Men. If I work 8 to 4, Mighty Men is at 5; I'm going to make that effort to get to Mighty Men.

D'Angelo: Retention. I used to say structure as far as having a president and VP and stuff like that but learned that we could still function without people having those official titles. Probably another is organization as far as what we're going to talk about when we say we're going to talk about certain subjects.

Given the positive attributes that students assigned to their BMI experiences, these discussion points about how some of the connections within the program did not translate to bonding across the campus are points that must be heard. Although many of the students attested that they did not have expectations about the program, the sense of bonding they developed in the program heightened their sense of what they wanted to continue experiencing and experience in the future. For D.J., Mighty Men was a foundational experience that he wanted to prioritize regardless of his engagement in other organizations. Additionally, D'Angelo's point about being more organized around topical issues in their "rap sessions" could relate to student retention as well. Assessments that focus on student experiences in BMI are a necessity as it relates to event and program planning and student experiences as well. These assessments could prove informative of how students experience the events, activities, and overall program and even how and why they choose to participate (or not).

As the men reflected on what they would suggest as changes to BMI, students reported greater student accountability as a critical area for improvement. The following student narratives accentuate how they see the importance of being accountable to the program:

> DEANDRE: I would have it so that, because I know they log who shows up to that, but I feel like there should be some award or something like that. I know some guys don't mind missing meetings because there's no penalty for it. There's no up or down to it. You might miss some stuff for yourself but there's no loss of benefits . . . Maybe like Brothers & Scholars Top 10; based on GPA, how many events you've attended, are you going out and being active in other parts of campus. The awards are real impersonal. Everybody wants an award and a lot of people get an award. Maybe get a custom shirt for people who are really doing their thing. Brothers & Scholars is all about inclusiveness not exclusiveness . . . I think people would want to get involved on their own if there was something that made you stand out.

> JOSEPH: Actually thought that the program was going to be a couple of times a week but it wasn't. Not just to say that that was one of my expectations but that's what I wanted. If I could have [the program coordinator] around and fellas and people with good grades that'll shape me up and keep me focused.

> WINSTON: I guess I'm wanting a little more oversight academically, maybe. Maybe I needed that mentor; maybe I needed that one guy who was an engineering student who could've helped me think positively.

> DENZEL: I feel that they could follow up with the students' grades more and help with advising as far as what classes to take. I feel like we don't get advised well [in the advising office]. On the advising part, they can totally screw up your

whole plan. I feel like they [the program coordinators] need
to step up and advise students even more—not six students
but everybody goes through the process.

What the students offer provides important feedback not only about
how they experience the program, but also the areas where they believe
Mighty Men and Brothers & Scholars can be even more effective. Listening to and using student voices in developing activities, events, and
outreach efforts can make BMI programming efforts more inclusive
and can help to ensure that the program remains student-centered. For
instance, in reflecting on what he would change about the program,
Winston stated, "It's not much, actually. I would like more academic
outreach because it's easy to get discouraged even if you got all your
eggs in a basket. I would just like more academic outreach."

Additionally, students also wanted administrators and faculty not
BMI related to be accountable for their success as well. Charles asserted, "Holding people of authority more accountability. Not Brothers &
Scholars staff, but teachers around the facility." Thus, as the students
have benefited from the program—academically and personally as well
as individually and collectively—their focus on improvement through
relational aspects cannot be understated. Clearly the efforts to impact
the college experiences of Black men collectively are critical, yet some
students still desire attention that focuses on their individual needs as
well. As has been expressed here, enhancing assessments of BMI programs is critical to speaking directly to the needs of Black male college students. Garnering feedback from students about their experiences
provides opportunities to learn more about the nuances of the program
and how to adapt to meeting the ongoing needs of students as they
matriculate through college.

Significance of BMI Experience

Many efforts have been made to enhance the collegiate experiences of
Black male students. As has been explored in this chapter, the BMI
provides a unique oportunity for students to be engaged in a student-
centered program that specifically sees their racial and gender identities
as strengths and from a postivist standpoint. As students discussed the
experiences that stood out to them during the interviews, they referred to

the benefit of having meetings that focused on their student population group—especially given the low number of Black males on both campuses. Additionally, they discussed opportunities to bond through social outings and participating in community service activities as important experiences as well. Thus, social integration is a key variable in what the students experienced through participation in BMI, which has been theorized and linked to student persistence.[13]

In an effort to engage students in a meaning-making reflection, they were asked a series of questions about the significance of the BMI program. These questions were spread across two broad themes: the importance of BMI to their college experience and their perceptions on the need of BMI at their university. In providing their responses to these inquiries, a third theme also emerged within student responses: BMI as a counter-space.

College Experience without BMI:
"It Would've Been More of a Struggle"

To explore the significance of BMI engagement on student experiences, students were asked how they thought their college experience would be different if they were not engaged in the program. This question provided a window to gauge how the men perceived and experienced BMI and how they made meaning from their experiences. Deondre and Kory offer lengthy statements that provide a broad canvass for understanding the context of what students offered collectively:

> DEONDRE: I don't think it would've been as good. Brothers & Scholars motivates me. I'm not saying I do good just to please Brothers & Scholars, but I don't want to let the guys down that believe in me. When you're around so many like-minded people it makes it easier for you to go out and do what you have to do to get success. My first year, I lived with a guy who was in Brothers & Scholars that did help me stay motivated and focused because I always saw him studying. It's important to have people around you that's about their business to help you know that you gotta get about yours . . . Especially like the Ohio State University [Retreat], that motivated me. I didn't go this year but I feel like that would've really helped me. It helps bring you back to the center. That program is

like a second wind to me. If I didn't have that stuff, I feel like I would fizzle out at the end of the year.

KORY: Ah man! I feel like if I hadn't continuously came to Mighty Men I wouldn't be talking to you right now. I'd probably still be in my room. I'd be wasting time. That's one thing that Mighty Men has taught me is to appreciate time; you can't get time back. Mighty Men has taught me that what you're doing, that's what molds the other stuff that's going on. I feel like if I hadn't come to Mighty Men I wouldn't be in the position that I'm in now like writing for the paper—and that's my major. They push us to make sure we have resumes and make sure we go to job fairs. That's not stuff that I'm thinking about, I know I should be but I wasn't. If Mighty Men wasn't there I wouldn't be 100 percent where I am now. I wouldn't be as on top of the things as I need to be on; they wouldn't even cross my mind. I feel like Mighty Men is a reminder that yeah you're in school right now but time is coming and you will need to know how to conduct yourself in a business-like manner. If it wasn't for Mighty Men I'd probably be in my room, chilling or playing games.

Although motivation was discussed earlier regarding the men's participation in BMI, Deondre's point about feeling motivated here is a bit different. He acknowledged that Brothers & Scholars has had a positive qualitative impact on his collegiate experience to the extent that he did not believe that his college experiences would have been as good. Even more than this, however, was the importance of Deondre's connections with other members of Brothers & Scholars, which fueled his motivation to perform well.[14] His early exposure to Brothers & Scholars was from a roommate his freshman year; his peer's studiousness and focus helped sharpen his own. Additionally, different programming efforts such as the retreat at Ohio State University kept him grounded and energized to finish the year with a strong effort. Similarly, Kory acknowledged the central role that Mighty Men has played in his collegiate career. The program has helped him think about his time very differently; in doing so, Mighty Men kept him centered on preparing for his future after college. Thus, instead of "wasting time" (being in his room, chilling or playing video games) Kory was working on a paper that was due later in the semester, he recently participated in a mock interview, and had plans to attend an upcoming job fair.[15] Although Kory was already enrolled in college, his engagement in BMI helped advance his realizations on timeliness and focus. For a number of the men, BMI served as a critical resource of not only keeping them on track but also helping advance their academic skills, such as learning how to plan and work ahead of schedule. As a result, BMI helped enhanced their academic agency, which they could employ at various junctures throughout their college careers.

In specifically reflecting on the impact of the BMI on the quality of their collegiate experience, a number of students offered much shorter statements that included:

> CHARLES: I probably wouldn't be here anymore. I probably would've been don' transferred out because I had no reason to stay.

> D.J.: It's hard to say because Mighty Men is such a vital role to me in college. I can't imagine my college experience without Mighty Men, I really can't.

> JOSEPH: I probably wouldn't have came back. Failure is not an option; I can get down on myself but I'm not going to give up. If I wasn't in Brothers & Scholars, I probably would've thrown that out the window.

> WINSTON: I think it would've been more of a struggle. I don't think I would've known where to go, I don't think I would've known about the resources. Without Brothers & Scholars, I would've been a lot lonelier when I needed assistance.

For the men cited here, BMI has been *foundational* in their persistence in college. Recall, in chapter 4 the focus was on the ways that students saw how their racialized and gendered identities matter on campus; thus, they cited racism, the continuing significance of race, and the impact of the campus climate on their experiences. In chapter 5 the men focused their attention on ways that they worked to persist and remain resilient regardless of the obstacles that they faced. In this chapter, we begin to see a more robust picture of how the students made sense of their college experiences and how they operationalized many of the lessons that they learned through their experiences. Consider, Charles and Joseph explicitly stated that they would no longer be enrolled at their current college if they were not participating in BMI programs. Another way to interpret their expressions is to consider how their personal and academic efforts might look different without their engagement in BMI and how they might have struggled (more) as well. That is, although they may have continued enrollment at their current institution, their academic engagement, motivation, and performance could be lowered without being connected to a community such as what they experienced in BMI. This critical participation, engagement, and benefit cannot be understated. As noted above, the ways that many of these college men experienced BMI was connected to the community cultural wealth of the program: it assisted their transition to college, helped them navigate the college campus by providing them with peer connections and a support group, provided access to resources and key university personnel, established a supportive atmosphere and space on campus, and helped them develop close-knit bonds with other Black male students as well.

For D.J., Mighty Men has been so vital that he could not imagine his college experience without being engaged while Winston noted that his college experience would have been more of a lonely struggle without Brothers & Scholars. Finally, D'Angelo articulated the significance of the BMI experience in ways that have helped him be more self-aware and find his place on campus. He shared:

> I'd say I'd have, not any built up aggression, but built up hostility. I feel like if I didn't have Mighty Men I wouldn't have met a few of my friends that I still have today. Mighty Men was the first group that I represented, so it kinda helped me start my progression in trying to be a leader as well as taking a role in being one of the main presenters—and being a leader. So, I wouldn't be as much of a leader as I am today. And the people that I met in the Minority Affairs Office like [two administrators], so it's helped to give me connections.

Being engaged in a BMI has been quite significant for D'Angelo as well as the overwhelming majority of the men in this study. BMI-type programs offer a unique opportunity for Black men to create community in college, which is critical in providing them with a support group, developing responses to microaggressions, and learning to cope with racial battles and the possible fatigue that results. D'Angelo's participation has helped him cope with the challenges he has faced on campus and diffused much of the hostility that could have built up. As students expressed the significance of BMI, their narratives help remind us of how the Black community has served as a buffer between Blacks and the dominant community in developing effective coping and success strategies.[16] D'Angelo's engagement in the BMI community has allowed him to navigate the campus climate and environment from a much less stressful mindset and he has applied a more focused mental and emotional approach. Additionally, the program has allowed him to connect with men with whom he still holds close relationships, along with administrators in the Minority Affairs Office. Finally, his participation also has allowed him opportunities to represent the program, provide presentations across campus and at a local conference, and develop as a leader on campus.

BMI as Counter-Space: "You Can Have an Outlet"

The notion and utility of *counter-spaces* within academic settings has been used to highlight one of the ways that Students of Color cope with hostile and unwelcoming environments. As an example, one study asserted that, "In learning spaces where Black students are the demographic minority, these spaces counter the hegemony of racist and other oppressive ideologies and practices of the institution and its members."[17] Given the various forms in which counter-spaces may be developed—formal or informal, academic or social—the meaning and utility of such spaces are critical for students to buffer hostile and negative campus climates and differential social atmospheres. For instance, in a study of a national organization for Black college men asserted the ways in which it functioned as a counter-space, as group members worked to build brotherhood to cope with the campus environment.[18] As has been noted throughout this study, BMI functioned as a counter-space for many of the Black male students precisely because it was an established space for the men to connect, thus bridging the gap of isolation and discrimination experienced on campus. The space allowed for cooperative learning opportunities, especially as it pertained to masculine identities and coping strategies. Students identified BMI as a space where they could be themselves, learn, grow, share, and connect with other Black men. BMI's function as a critical counter-space encouraged these men to share their experiences by bringing issues relevant to Black males to the forefront of discussions. The outcomes include learning from the experiences of others and also increasing their awareness of campus life, resources, and opportunities. As the men discussed the significance of BMI on their college experience, they specifically articulated how BMI operated as a counter-space for them.

Monte and D'Angelo responded to a question about the need for BMI on their campuses in the following way:

> MONTE: Hell yeah! You can put that as, "HELL YEAH!!" [smiling with a light chuckle] It is because if not you'd go crazy. Mighty Men is like a barbershop where you can come in, meet up, and talk about their problems.

> D'ANGELO: Yeah, there needs to be somewhere where you can have an outlet. It's not so structured that you have to stay on this subject because it's informal. I feel like it's needed. It gives you a way to talk about what you're dealing with and try to come up with resolutions no matter what you're dealing with.

Monte wanted to be clear about the absolute need for BMI at his campus. One of the main functions of his BMI experience was that it provided a space for Black men to maintain their sanity. Given the pressures of stereotyping, profiling, and racism that many of the men experienced personally and from the experiences of their peers (both on and off campus), a number of students believed that BMI also is needed so that Black men can discuss many of the challenges that they face. A significant part of these discussions was not only to release emotions but for the men to cooperate in working together to develop and learn ways to alleviate some of the challenges as well. D'Angelo echoed this as he cited the "need" for a space on campus that could serve as an outlet. Thus, he articulated how BMI served as a counter-space; he found the informal structure of conversations to be helpful in allowing ideas to flow and for "peer pedagogy" to develop.[19] Recall, at a different point in his interview (cited earlier in this chapter) D'Angelo offered:

> Mighty Men for me just helped me vent; it helped me be able to have people to talk to about whatever. Talk about how all

the White boys say the n-word and thinking it's cool. Talking about how the teachers give us so many tests. It kinda made me feel more comfortable in knowing that I had a place that I could let it out.

D'Angelo expressed how BMI offered a space for him to release and express emotions about his experiences as a Black man on campus—that is, how his race *and* gender matter. The key to D'Angelo's expressions was that he had a community of other men who supported his voice and, just as importantly, members also could affirm his experiences through the racial battles that they have faced.[20] He cites this opportunity as therapeutic and healing and he saw BMI as a conduit for Black men to express themselves.

Similar to Monte and D'Angelo, Bannon and Sean also conveyed the critical need of BMI and how it operated as a counter-space on campus. Bannon offered:

Of course! I feel like it's very important because it mentally prepares you for a lot of things that college is throwing at you. And they're your friend and everybody needs a friend. They might be going through different things back at home; when you're in Brothers & Scholars you get people who want to see you doing good, they want to see you succeed and they can help put you in that right mind set.

For Bannon, BMI was very necessary because it provided men with a counter-space to "mentally prepare" for experiencing the college and the campus. Just as important is that Bannon noted that BMI is a space that affirmed Black men through friendship and support. Whether students are dealing with issues from home or on campus, BMI can play a pivotal role in supporting and strengthening students' persistence efforts by increasing their mental resolve so that they can persevere on campus. Thus, BMI can play an important role in developing cooperative coping strategies for Black men and a cooperative masculine construct. Sean noted:

Yeah, I really do. Because there's no other place on campus where Black men can go and talk about what they're experiencing. We just need somewhere to talk and vent our problems or just help us with a situation that may be going on.

As has been substantiated by student narratives throughout this study, BMI functions as a counter-space for Black men as it is a space that is centered on Black male collegians, develops and implements programs with them as the targeted group, and allows space for healing. As Sean explained, BMI is a space like no other on campus and, as asserted by his peers, a space for Black men to talk about their experiences and receive help is much needed. Accordingly, as many of the students attested, BMI has the potential of cultivating resistance for Black male collegians (such as resisting being stereotyped and otherized on campus) as well helping them build a community of resistance (as they consider the impact of their collective efforts).

Conclusions

Exploring student experiences in Black Male Initiative programs is a fertile area of research, especially given the challenges this student population faces on historically White campuses and the critical need for Black male success in higher education. Both BMI programs established a Black male community on campus that revealed community cultural wealth, which allowed for relationships and bonding to develop, helped bridge the gap of loneliness and isolation, and fortified the men's persistence efforts (through increased awareness, mental preparation, support, and collective coping strategies). The community, relationships, and bonding matter significantly for the men in this study as they bolster the students in achieving their goals—both individually and collectively. Additionally, Critical Race Theory has proved quite useful in amplifying the voices of these Black male students in their experiences on campus in general and within the Black Male Initiative program in particular.

Throughout their experiences students narrated how BMI expanded the community cultural wealth at their disposal. Here, I use community capital (wealth) as the broad canvas to include academic capital and cultural capital as well. Academically, BMI members were connected to campus resources both individually and collectively; oftentimes this occurred via presentations where students learned (or were reminded) about available resources. Also, students' academic and social capital increased through the networks that were established through their BMI participation. Some students were introduced to and built relationships with staff and faculty across the university along with various adminis-

trators. Congruent with previous research, these connections are important to students' academic achievement and persistence as well their
academic and social integration on campus.[21] Given the difficulties that
Black students face in establishing relationships with many White faculty
members at historically White institutions, BMI's work is critical in supporting the men's efforts to overcome such challenges. They also were
introduced to various campus organizations through their participation
as well because many of the members maintained membership across
a number of organizations. These organizations spanned the gamut of
academic, social, and cultural groups. Students learned about organizations such as the National Society of Black Engineers, Collegiate 100,
and University Board to name a few. The men cited the importance of
learning about diverse campus resources and feeling connected to people
as key experiences for their college careers. The main tenets of their
increased community capital are that the men felt more connected to
the university, developed meaningful relationships across campus, and
strengthened their resolve to increase their academic performances. Each
of these was cited in how the students understood BMI through their
experiences and the significance they attached to their BMI experiences.
Still, as the students noted, there are opportunities and spaces that their
respective BMI program needs to improve, especially as it relates to
keeping Black men connected to the program, greater student accountability, and increased accountability for their success from administrators
and faculty.

In addition to increasing their community capital, BMI is a critical
counter-space on campus for these Black male collegians. I specifically
offer five ways that BMI functions as a counter-space. First, BMI created
a niche for Black males on campus to come together and connect. Given
the small number of Black males on both campuses this point cannot
be understated. Recall that in previous chapters the men pointed out
the loneliness and isolation they experienced in classrooms and across
the campus as one of few. Thus, BMI was pivotal in building relational
capital for students; BMI provided a space for them to meet, interact,
and connect with other Black males on campus. The formal gatherings
(at BMI meetings and events) also had informal implications as the men
developed friendships and bonded outside of the program—they played
pickup basketball together, attended parties at other institutions, and
engaged in various social activities. As a result, BMI helped to establish
a microcommunity for Black men where they felt included, connected,

and valued. The men articulate this mostly as a brotherhood, which denotes their shared collective identity. Second, BMI served as a healing space for many of its members. In chapter 4, the men described the challenges they faced on campus, which included a separate and segregated campus along with being racially profiled and stereotyped both on and off campus. BMI is a space that the men describe in ways that affirm their humanity, their racialized and gendered identities, and their manhood. The men cite the critical need for BMI on their campus so that they have space to talk, share and express emotions, and have an outlet. In addition, BMI helps them cognitively prepare for campus life, allows them to maintain their mental fortitude, and ultimately offers solutions—from peers, staff and faculty alike—for many of the academic and personal challenges they face. Thus, BMI is an emotional, social, and psychological counter-space.

Third, BMI provided the men with opportunities to enhance their agency. The men shared various stories of the meaningfulness in how they learned and enacted responsibility through their BMI experiences. These experiences help sharpen and deepen the men's sense of the qualities that they already possess as well as seeing their collective social identities. Fourth, BMI served as an important community for the men—both as a support group and a support space. Within this space, the students supported each other and also felt supported in their own efforts. This support was holistic, encompassing their academic strategies and efforts, social adjustments and coping, and personal lives and identities. As a result, the men believed that BMI supplied them with people who genuinely cared for them and wanted them to succeed. Finally, BMI functioned as a counter-space in the ways that it empowered Black men. This was most evident in how students' engagement in the program impacted the ways that they saw themselves and each other and how others perceived them on campus. In each of the ways specifying the functions as a counter-space, individually and collectively, BMI helped to foster and encourage the men's resilience and persistence in college and beyond.

The overwhelming majority of students found BMI to have a *significant, positive* impact on their college experience. Students stressed the importance of BMI in their academic performance, connectedness to other Black men, and personal growth and development. In particular, the connections, community, and counter-space helped the men develop a cooperative masculine construct where they envisioned their collective efforts could enhance their experiences. The significance of the men's experiences in BMI reaffirms the importance of student integration and engagement on campus in general, but more specifically for these men it revealed how this Black male-centered program connected to their belongingness, identities, and sense of self. Students felt invested in BMI through their individual and collective performances and many took on leadership roles as a form of further contributing to the program. Again, overwhelmingly, students believed that BMI is a necessity on their campus because of their acquired capital, the bonding opportunities, and in the ways that it served as a counter-space. The positive and supportive atmosphere of BMI along with the ways that the men were healed, enhanced, and motivated helped them identify spaces where they could find their place on campus and [continue to] aspire success.

CHAPTER 7

Black Men in College

(Re)Envisioning the Trajectory

Mighty Men is about, to me, it's about helping each other out—as African American men; holding each other accountable. Helping each other succeed in college and through college—and it's not just academic. Sometimes it's on a spiritual level, depending on the day. People where you can feel comfortable but where people are going to push you and want you to succeed in a lot of ways. So, it's a way of connecting you with people and your peers. And, also, changing the perception of how we are on campus of African American males and how to improve that.

—Reggie

With all of us coming from different backgrounds, you don't get a lot of people who've had a positive role model in their life. So for Black males to come in and see this it just gives them a boost. It gave the similar impact to me too; I see him doing it then I can do it. And, you get the real version of it, not just the . . . Just being able to have that camaraderie for Black males. It's not like a frat, you know "Oh nah, we don't want you." But Mighty Men is not like that, we accept everybody. We want people and it doesn't matter what your experiences were—good, bad or indifferent. So, Mighty Men offers that.

—D.J.

Being around people who truly care about your success as a student
but also care about you as a person.

—Arthur

The primary goal of this study was to explore the experiences of Black
male collegiate students with an eye toward rethinking the gaps between
retention (showing up to college) and graduation. In particular, I was
interested in investigating how this group of 40 Black men made sense
of their Blackmaleness in college, how being Black *and* male mattered
to their experiences, and the qualitative impact of their engagement
in an institutionalized Black male program. There is a great deal to
learn from Black men when their voices and experiences are received,
heard, and acknowledged. Importantly, this study offers an opportunity
to learn more about Black men personally along with their social and
academic experiences, identity development, and their efforts toward
success. The students entered college from a variety of standpoints. For
instance, some of the men's college aspirations were grounded in family
ties while others were concerned about their future selves. Throughout
the study, even before entering college, we learn of the men's concerns
for belonging in college; they expressed concern about being alone, how
they might be accepted on campus, and persevering. This concern and
desire for belonging in college left many of the men trying to find their
place upon their initial arrival on campus. Additionally, the men's masculine identities and manhood constructs were interwoven throughout
their narratives as well, which allowed a window to see how even some
of their aspirations and resilience efforts were gendered. If voices of
Black males on college campuses echo their struggles, then they also
echo their triumphs and successes as well. However, these efforts can
be appreciated only when we invite them in, willingly provide space to
hear their experiences and how they make sense of them, and talk *with*
them. As has been explored, in trying to find their place on campus,
the men have engaged and deployed a variety of strategies and efforts
throughout their college careers. Thus, one important facet revealed
was the self-reflexivity that the men offered in sharing their narratives.
In reflecting on their experiences and sharing their narratives, some of
the men expressed a deeper appreciation for their learning, bonding,
and persistence.

The most prominent findings in this study are that Black men *do* care about themselves, their education, and their futures. The men in this study wished to establish connections in college that would speak to their whole selves. As Reggie notes, sometimes the day or the events and experiences might determine what type of help Black men need to enter, succeed, and get through college. Key to the men's successes was the social and academic support they received. This support made them feel that they mattered and enhanced their persistence in navigating the academic demands and social milieu on campus. While there is no monolithic narrative offered from this study, as has been explored through the heterogeneity of the group, it is critical to understand that these men have multiple needs that extend from the time before they enter college through their graduation; and these needs incorporate personal, social and academic components. Importantly, as D.J. notes, many of the men believed in the camaraderie and connections that they established through BMI, even further, they could look to other Black men as models as well. These intragroup peer relations were motivating and uplifting, increased the men's self-efficacy, and helped sharpen their focus. Across the group, the men note the importance of feeling connected on campus. The BMI program was quite different from fraternities on campus as the men expressed their ability to be themselves and feel like they were welcome as they were. These connections allowed for deep and sincere bonds to develop, quite often articulated as a brotherhood, helped to motivate some of the men, and held them to be accountable as well. Primarily, the men expressed that the significance of the Black Male Initiative program on their campus was rooted in how it helped facilitate their connections, sharpened and informed their masculine and manhood constructs, and provided them with a sense of comfort as well. According to a number of students, they were highly aware of their Blackmaleness and, given how they often were framed in deficit perspectives, sought to contribute to a collective effort of improving the lot and perception of Black men on their campuses. Still, even the merits of their attempts to prove others wrong and improve the image of Black men are steeped in the men's Blackmaleness. That is, as many students attempt to resist being further marginalized on campus, their efforts to prove others wrong is layered with their desires to prove themselves and prove that they belong. Proving others wrong is not a neutral phenomenon; these students' efforts speak volumes about their place on campus and ongoing battles they face because of hostile climates and anti-Black sentiments. "Proving" means that these students must demonstrate to others their worth and value, which continues to position them as objects of subjective assessment and constitutes multiple sites of contention.

There are those who might argue that Black men are the primary agents and actors in their own underachievement and that the experiences of these 40 Black men do not warrant much traction. Yet, as documented in this study, a careful consideration of how they thought about themselves and their educational experiences reveal some of the complexities of Black men's race and gender on campus. Given some of the men's starting points and how they thought about college and their efforts, what should we make of their thoughts about being both Black and male in their college experiences? If they are in a constant search for belonging on campus, and some just want to "get my stuff and leave," then what can be learned from their insights and experiences? How do their experiences confront narratives about Black male mediocrity and other deficit-based narratives? And, finally, how much do higher education administrators, faculty, and staff, collectively, *really* care about Black males and their successes?

The simple response is that there is much to learn from Black men who continue to enroll in classes each semester, actively engage on campus, and matriculate toward graduation. Drawing attention to the men's personal histories, their academic and social experiences, and attempts for success has relevance for developing an agenda for the advancement of their efforts, and the efforts of other marginalized students. This research also has relevance for programing initiatives that are created specifically for minoritized students and their educational endeavors that rest specifically on their social identities. There is thus much to gain, both for practice and research, from these types of inquiries. In the remainder of this chapter, I turn to the ways this study can further these agendas.

Black Men's Race *and* Gender in College

As has been noted by a range of scholars, Black men's race *and* gender identities matter a great deal in how they experience college. In the current study, the men's race and gender identities were interwoven across their narratives. Studying Black men's constructions of masculinity and manhood and framing how they link these constructions to their college experiences, academic performances, resiliency, and engagement on campus are critical in unpacking their retention and persistence in college. The campus climate and college milieu are too crucial to leave Black men's voices silenced and reduced to national conversations about them, especially those conversations that do not include them. Assessing how they make meanings from their experiences reveals a great deal about how they navigate and negotiate their belongingness. Thus, by examining their Blackmaleness and engagement we have a unique opportunity to learn from the men's intersections. In particular, the men primarily centered their experiences across five identity scripts that were salient throughout their college tenure: (1) Independence and self-improvement, (2) Self-expectations and responsibility, (3) Self-disclosure and expressiveness, (4) Connectedness, and (5) Cooperative masculinity. These scripts, individually and collectively, provide further insight into how the men tried to find their place on campus.

Independence and Self-Improvement

As the men recounted how they thought about college and their early college years, they leaned on being independent and their self-improvement. A number of men asserted independence as a manhood construct. Additionally, being on their own and making their own decisions was consequential for how the men thought about themselves in the process of becoming men. Being men meant that students had to be self-reliant for looking out for themselves and their interests or, as one student asserted, "being away [from home] makes you a man." In many ways, this notion of independence was steeped in displaying physical and emotional strength, both of which are connected to heteronormative masculine constructs. Similarly, the men expressed a desire to improve their lives and become better people, which, for them, was contingent upon their independence because they could no longer "lean on their parents."

Self-Expectations and Responsibility

The men's constructions of their identities through self-expectations and responsibility played an important role in how they sought to reconcile their academic preparation and performances. Here, they expressed a self-pride in performing well regardless of their pre-college or early college experiences. The men discussed a sense of responsibility for their efforts to achieve. For instance, a number of men submitted that they were doing "just enough to get by" or, according to their own estimation of their abilities, had underperformed academically. Thus, they knew that they could perform better and felt responsible in taking or initiating actions to improve their efforts. Some of the men's self-expectations were heightened by campus climate and culture. Here they attempted to buffer their sense of self and feelings of isolation and, as a result, they responded by increasing their level of focus and sharpening their determination to succeed. Also, attending college was a way for them to continue or establish a new family legacy and, in some instances, position themselves as models for younger siblings.

Self-Disclosure and Expressiveness

As the men shared their experiences on campus, they expressed that some of the traditional norms of hegemonic masculinity clashed with their needs. For instance, some of the men discussed their initial fears of opening up to others while some of the men shared that they needed to learn how to create bonds with other men. The students' self-disclosure and expressiveness affirm the delicate nature of one's sense of self and how normative masculine constructs might limit one's development, social interactions, and engagement. Additionally, the men's narratives also provided insight into their interiorities and their social and emotional needs, especially as we consider their vulnerabilities and fragilities. Being able to "talk about" issues that affect Black men was vital to many of the participants; accordingly, some believed that being able to express themselves helped maintain their sanity and release some of the tensions they experienced given the college milieu.

Bonding and Connectedness

The men's engagement in the BMI program reveals essential insights about their masculine identities. For many of the men, engaging in BMI satisfied their desire for intragroup peer social relationships, which afforded them significant benefits. BMI helped increase the men's bonding opportunities and simultaneously revealed the importance of bonding for the men. For instance, a pivotal experience for the men through their BMI engagement was increasing their sociocultural capital. Being connected to others increased the capital and resources at their disposal and allowed them to access a supportive and nurturing counter-space. Additionally, BMI-type programs provide the men with an atmosphere of trust where they not only could take down their guard (and display their expressiveness) but they also could depend on others to help support their individual efforts. Also, through their engagement the men garnered leadership roles, which enhanced their responsibilities to the group and on campus. The men developed a tight-knit bond with one another, which most defined as a brotherhood, and connections with other Black men. This bonding expanded the men's social networks, provided support for their academic efforts and aspirations, and aided their personal growth and development.

Cooperative Masculinity

A final script that the men developed and subscribed to was one centered on collectivity and cooperation. The men's sense of, desire for, and commitment to cooperation are a clear deviation from an individualistic focus. Hegemonic masculinity is highly individual and often rewards individual success. The men's bonding experiences encouraged them to envision their linked fate on campus and helped them develop a collective conscious about their efforts. Critical to the men's ability to deal with the various stressors they faced was coping techniques that included social support and engagement on campus. For instance, the men's bonding helped to buffer them against isolation and affirm that they were not alone. The men's cooperative masculinity helped enhance their resilience and persistence efforts by allowing them opportunities to share academic and personal coping strategies with one another. Thus, in some ways, the men coached and guided each other in navigating and negotiating campus. As a result, the cooperation espoused and supported by the men mattered in three significant ways. First, it helped to increase the men's sense of belonging on campus. In particular, it helped (re)affirm and (re)center their sense of purpose on campus and made them feel valued. Second, the men's bonding increased their sense of accountability. As the men reflected on their own efforts, they also considered how their efforts might matter to the group as well. And, finally, the men's collective and cooperative efforts were envisioned as ways to reject one-dimensional images and projections of Black males.

Positioning Black Male Initiative Programs to Matter for Student Success

The increase in Black Male Initiative programs, along with mandates such as My Brother's Keeper Initiatives, signal some form of belief in these programs and what they might offer. These Initiatives and institutional-based programming must incorporate research in their design and implementation, be based on best practices, and use student experiences as driving forces. We need more research that either incorporates both quantitative and qualitative methods together in one assessment or design assessments whose methods can complement each other in providing a robust picture of Black male's experiences in higher education. Harper's (2014) recent charge is critical for researchers and education professionals as he called for and encouraged more attention on trying to understand which personal and institutional factors contribute to Black male persistence.[1]

Colleges and universities must continue to develop programs that engage students academically and socially, especially since both arenas are critical to student achievement and persistence. The impact of these programs on student experiences plays a critical role not only in what students experience but also how they experience campus. By focusing on the personal and institutional factors that contribute to Black male persistence, and the Black Male Initiative programs in particular, we have opportunities to learn about their motivation, resilience, and self-efficacy as well. This research advances the applicability of academic and social integration theories as well as identity and sense of belonging theories among Black male students.

Black Male Initiative programs are rife with opportunities that speak to how Black men can matter and be valued on campus. Based on findings from the current study, the following are offered as a list of possibilities for BMI programs.

Build Community

BMI programs can serve a critical role in supporting the retention and persistence of Black male students. The students in this study described BMI as nurturing, supportive, and encouraging, enabling them to enhance their sense of belonging and increase their engagement on campus. The BMI community can provide space to address and respond to the specific needs of Black males. These needs include access to capital, counter-spaces, and self-empowerment. Colleges and universities should encourage (or even require) administrators and other institutional personnel to support students' success actively and intentionally. These individuals can support, guide, encourage, mentor, and serve as models to students, thus, expanding the students' community network. Additionally, student affairs professionals can work to develop programs and work with students on an individual basis that encourage them to form supportive and nurturing relationships with their peers. The community might help students accrue a variety of capital, such as social capital (networks of people and community resources), navigational capital (skills to negotiate the institution), and resistant capital (knowledges and skills that challenge Blackmaleness). Gaining access to these critical resources can help build community on campus, which ultimately supports students' academic efforts, identity development, and can create (or reaffirm) a sense of purpose on campus. Additionally, these types of programs can help students feel included, valued, and like respected members of the community. Importantly, the community must establish an atmosphere where *all* Black male students feel welcome and valued.

Create Awareness of Campus Resources

Student adjustment to college life is impacted by their readiness (academic and personal), fit to the institution, support, and noncognitive factors (i.e., motivation and determination). A key for many minoritized students' adjustment and retention in college is helping raise their awareness of various campus resources. Building students' social capital via resources helps them transition to and learn how to navigate the institution. The transition experience is critical to students' early college academic performance and how they believe they matter on campus. In meeting the needs of students, and helping to bridge the gap in college readiness, it may be prudent for institutions to provide them with both academic and nonacademic resources and opportunities. Academic awareness events could serve a wide variety of purposes, such as: (a) orientating students to academic services (e.g., tutoring centers, mentoring programs) designed to enhance their success, (b) serving as a platform for students to inform campus personnel of their awareness, or lack thereof, of institutional services, and (c) introducing students to key campus personnel who could provide them with information needed to support their success. Consistent with research on college success, student experiences during the first year of college—both inside and outside the classroom—are crucial to their academic achievement, personal development, and retention.

Create Opportunities for Meaningful Interactions and Connections

Research continues to reveal that social networks can help students in their connections to college and various forms of human capital. Many students in the current study shared that they were informed and/or motivated by others to participate in BMI programs. Opportunities to interact and connect with other Black male students as well as university staff and faculty can be meaningful for Black male students. For instance, faculty should be included in student-centered activities, especially at research intensive institutions; there is a critical need for more collaboration between academic affairs and student affairs personnel. Too often, there is scant attention or appreciation for faculty service at these institutions, which can make working with students less appealing given the demands of research productivity. Still, at teaching institutions and community colleges there are great opportunities for faculty and staff to be engaged with student-centered programming efforts. These connections might inspire students to participate in other programs or activities (including internships and other organizations) and can enhance their linguistic capital and relational capital as well. Both of these forms of capital also speak to how students can be empowered. These interactions and connections help build their awareness about various opportunities and equip them with academic and social strategies that are critical to their successes. Additionally, students can make connections with individuals who later might serve in a supportive role, either informally or formally (e.g., as a mentor, role model, or recommender).

Empower Black Male Students (and Other Men of Color)

Learning about self is a significant finding regarding the benefits of education. Quite often, students who are empowered in their educational experiences develop the ability, confidence, and motivation to succeed academically—and personally. Providing opportunities for Black men to learn about who they are and who they want to be is powerful. One programming area that BMI programs might consider is Black men's own agency in their educational endeavors. Black men need to learn how to navigate and negotiate the campus across academic, social, and personal domains, which can enhance their self-efficacy and help equip them for success. BMI programs could develop activities that connect with students' academic focus and help bolster their noncognitive skills (e.g., drive and determination). In addition, programs and activities also can focus on areas for self-improvement, such as sociability, self-management, presentation of self, and professional skills as well (e.g., writing a resume or cover letter, interviewing skills, and organizing and facilitating events). Thus, BMI-type programs can offer unique opportunities for professional development, networking, and learning outside the classroom.

Create Space for a Holistic Focus on Black Male Identities

Black men are not just a raced group; their other social identities matter greatly to who they are and how they belong. For instance, their Black-maleness reveals how their race and gender matter to their academic pursuits, social experiences, and personal development. Thus, identifying the ways that they develop and subscribe to masculine and manhood constructs is critical. BMI programs can develop events and programming that focus on a full range of intersecting Black male identities that include space for the intricacies of class, religion, and sexuality. Additionally, Black male students can be empowered in better understanding their collective identities. Some of this work includes shattering negative stereotypes, especially through the experiences of Men of Color who have achieved on campus, the lives of men who have achieved in a variety of fields, and healthy conceptions of their self-identities. Thus, BMIs can provide alternatives to the images of Black men and what Black men can be that are prevalent across U.S. society. This focus can help Black men define and redefine their self-concepts and bolster their identity constructs, which has cognitive and noncognitive benefits.

Improve Campus Climate and Culture

The need to improve campus culture and climate continues to plague many historically White institutions. Clearly, diversifying the student population is important, but what is even more critical is *how* these students matter on campus, the resources and opportunities available to them, and how inclusion is incorporated in the institution's strategic plan (including in hiring faculty, staff, and administrators and in programming efforts as well). Although there are a variety of benefits that BMI programs might offer, the shortcoming is that there is still much more progress to be made at colleges and universities, especially historically White institutions. A clear goal for colleges and universities is for its students to persist and graduate. However, how students are valued as members of the institution and the holistic support they receive varies greatly across different student populations. Beyond BMI spaces, institutions need to create and maintain an inclusive environment that is beneficial to students' academic and social success and their personal development and well-being, especially those from marginalized groups.

BMI programs cannot be relegated as a "one stop shop," either intentionally or unintentionally, for all of these students' needs. Instead, they must be woven into the fabric of the institution so that students can reap the full benefits of their engagement and the institutional commitment to their success. Intentional efforts must be made for holistic institutional support across the students' whole selves and critical funding and human resources need to be committed and part of the institution's strategic plan. Establishing a BMI-type program is not the end of the work that institutions need to do; in fact, it must be a point within the larger structure (and plan) that supports student success. Additionally, Black Male Initiatives must be backed by strategic resources that help counter some of the institutional culture that students encounter and enhance student opportunities for success. The BMI programs at Lincoln State and Monroe State exist in the midst of oppressive and hostile institutional climates that denigrate Black male students. Even though these programs provided key resources and a safe space for students, the men still had to navigate and negotiate apathy, indifference, profiling, stereotyping, and hostility on campus, in classroom spaces, and in interactions with faculty and staff.

To be sure, a legion of Black male college students have persisted and graduated from historically White institutions—and all other types of institutions—well before BMI programs were established. Given the hostile environments that they have experienced since they began enrollment at HWIs, one can posit that Black men often demonstrate resilience and competence and many of them succeed *in spite of* the campus culture, not because of it. The need to improve these climates and environments cannot be overstated, and lead to a range of questions: Where and how is BMI aligned with the institution's short-term and long-term goals regarding inclusion? In what ways is BMI supported by the institution's administration beyond the program's existence? And, finally, how can future research and practice capture and assess experiences from student-centered programs that further inform efforts to enhance students' success? Black males, and other marginalized students, need to be nurtured throughout their developmental process, which includes various campus spaces. Ventures such as Black Male Initiative programs can play a unique role in increasing the sense of belonging for Black male college students and establishing activities and events that speak to their racialized and gendered identities.

Finding One's Place and Succeeding on Campus

For the men in this study, finding one's place on campus occurs across four broad domains. First, it can be argued that finding one's place begins with college aspirations and pre-college experiences. Research continues to document the significance of academic preparation and exposure to college during the secondary school years. Importantly, these experiences provide students with opportunities to explore both academic and intellectual interests that have the potential to stimulate interests in a range of fields. Thus, academic, social, and cognitive preparation is important individually and collectively. These preparations and the experiences that students have within each realm converge to inform students' perspectives about their future prospects. In addition, they also inform and cultivate students' self-efficacy about their abilities to garner success in college. As the men shared their college aspirations they also shared their concerns, which primarily centered on believing that they could persist in college and believing that they would belong. Again, both of these concerns were birthed out of their pre-college experiences, which were connected to experiences in school and family dynamics.

In addition, many students harbor concerns about belonging on campus and fitting in with the college culture *prior* to attending. Many of these concerns center on their academic skills (feeling underprepared for college), being away from family and friends, their ability to complete college successfully, and their fit on campus. The students' expressed concerns reaffirm the need for belonging. Even further, having a sense of belonging to one's institution connects to one's sense of self. In their various experiences and engagements on campus, the men also helped reveal how their sense of belonging was heightened in different contexts—such as transitioning to a new environment and their experiences around campus—and was salient precisely because of their Blackmaleness—such as being one of few (on campus or in a class) or being stereotyped and profiled.

Second, in addition to pre-college experiences, students' adjustment and transition to college is critical to their sense of belonging as well. As students transition to college, they must balance their preparation and concerns with their academic and social adjustments on campus. Similar to the benefits of exploring their precollege experiences, investigating their early college experiences can reveal the delicate balancing act that students engage in. For instance, some of the men struggled academically during their first year of college, some men enjoyed the opportunity to be more responsible about how they spent their time and used the new college context to explore a range of social and personal interests, and some of the men expressed their concerns with over-involvement and how it might create academic challenges. Throughout these experiences, some with better outcomes than others, the men continuously negotiated their place on campus and sought to affirm their belongingness. Additionally, these experiences provided them with experiential knowledge about who they wanted to be, how they believed they could perform, and how they desired to belong. These critical self-reflections revealed to the students some of their strengths and weaknesses, informed them of continued adjustments they needed to make, and helped them learn more about themselves and the college environment. With each new experience, and many of the new contexts that they engaged, the men made meanings from how they mattered and how they were valued on campus.

Third, how students develop coping and resilience strategies is situated within their identities; for many of the Black male students in this study, there strategies are situated within their Blackmaleness. In many ways, their resilience and persistence can be seen as resistance. Their determination to just make it through, focus on their own efforts (i.e., "just do me"), and remain positive and optimistic all reveal how they imagined and conjured resilience as an important aspect of their collegiate experience. Additionally, these efforts also center on how the men attempted to find their place on campus. Given the challenges they faced—academically, socially, and personally—and the college milieu, the men's resilience and persistence incorporated psychological, social, emotional, and mental efforts. And, finally, students are engaged in an ongoing process of finding their place on campus. Efforts to engage these students and support their success must take into account how the institution acts upon them, their experiences, and their social identities. Researchers, practitioners, and stakeholders must examine the diversity of Black male experiences and be mindful of the various factors that impact their experiences as well. In these ways, others will be positioned to narrate new stories about Black men and be better able to confront and understand their collegiate experiences.

Conclusion

> In those sombre forests of his striving his own soul rose before him, and he saw himself,—darkly as through a veil; and yet he saw in himself some faint revelation of his power, of his mission. He began to have a dim feeling that, to attain his place in the world, he must be himself, and not another. (Du Bois, 1995, p. 3)

Exploring the nexus between Blackmaleness, engagement, and sense of belonging for Black males' educational experiences at HWIs advances discourse regarding student achievement in higher education. Many of the men in this study drew on the collective and cooperative support from the Black Male Initiative programs to affirm their racial and gender identities and masculine constructs, engage in acts of resistance, and hone skills needed to persist in college. Nurturing Black males' belongingness, and paying attention to how their identities matter on campus, can enhance their academic and social outcomes and have a profound impact on how they pursue success.

Appendix

I collected the bulk of the data for this study between November 2012 and December 2014. A phenomenological approach was used to explore how students' race and gender identities mattered in college and how they made meaning from engaging in a BMI program at two historically White institutions. The benefit of a phenomenology approach is that researchers seek to understand and describe the lived experiences of research participations (Denzin & Lincoln, 2005). In particular, phenomenology is used to capture what participants have experienced, how they experienced it, and the meanings they make of their experiences. In my conversations with the men, many offered that beyond BMI staff members or a student affairs professional they had not spoken at length with anyone about their collegiate experiences. The interviews ranged in length from 75 minutes to three hours and I transcribed each of the interviews.

Before beginning data collection, I identified six colleges/universities with Black Male Initiative programs. These programs were selected primarily by accessibility, as each was within a five-hour driving distance from where I was located. I reached out to the program coordinator at each institution via email to inform him or her about the study and followed up with a phone call as well. I was able to connect with four coordinators and inquired about their interest in partnering in the study. After several conversations, during which I discussed the purposes of the study and my interest in the program, I secured agreement from three coordinators and later set up a date and time for me to attend a meeting in person to inform students about the study. My initial goal was to interview 15 to 20 students at each institution. As I tracked my progress during the first nine months of data collection, I only was able to secure five interviews at one location. I added two interviews shortly after but determined that I would center research for this book project on two of the original locations so that I had a balanced representation of students. As a result, the findings that I present here focus solely on students from Monroe State University and Lincoln State University.

As mentioned previously (chapter 1), the institutions used in this study varied in geographic location (one urban, one rural), size (medium-sized and large), and Carnegie Designation (Master's granting and Research I). Monroe State is a large, public university located in an urban city in a Southern state. The university enrolls just over 15,000 undergraduate students and Black students account for about 11 percent of the population. The Brothers & Scholars program was developed with a specific aim to improve the retention and graduation of Black male students. During the time of data collection, Keith, a middle-aged Black male, served as the program's coordinator and was the sole staff member responsible for all outreach, programming, and assessment efforts. The Brothers & Scholars program incorporates monthly meetings where students gather for lectures and presentations (from a faculty member, administrator, or community member) and afterward participate in social outings that occur both on and off campus. Often, students meet one-on-one with the program coordinator, coordinate academic study tables, participate in community service activities, and engage in various other activities as well.

Lincoln State is a medium-sized, public university located in a rural city in a Midwestern state. There are about 10,000 undergraduate students and Black students account for 16 percent of the population. The Mighty Men Mentoring program was established to increase support for retaining and graduating Black male students on campus. Jason and Andre, two Black male staff members, served as the primary cocoordinators for the program and William, a third staff member who also holds a position on campus, assists them; they oversee all facets of the program including programming and activities. Mighty Men meets every week and they conduct a small number of university-wide events each year.

The 40 Black men interviewed for this project represent a diverse collection of students at each classification level; the participants included 4 first-year students, 8 second-year students, 15 third-years, 9 fourth-years, 2 fifth-years, and 2 recent graduates. Student engagement in BMI programs ranged between one semester and three years of participation—one student participated for four years, as he was a member of the design team who developed the program on his campus. The students also represented a variety of majors; the most common student majors were social sciences (8) (i.e., sociology, Africana Studies, communications), engineering (8), and political science (6). The overwhelming majority of the students (36 of the 40) were from urban cities and all of the students were aged between 19 and 26 at the time of the interview. As a measure to protect the students' identity and provide confidentiality, I asked the students to choose a pseudonym at the beginning of each interview. In a small number of instances, the men asked me to choose a name as they did not have one that they could think of in the moment.

The students were recruited using a purposive and convenience sampling approach (Weiss, 1994). In this approach, I worked with the BMI program coordinators at each institution to identify students to participate in the study. In addition, I personally invited students to participate in the study while attending a BMI meeting at each institution. For this invitation, I verbally provided students with my personal background (e.g., currently serving as a faculty member and teaching and research areas) and a background of the study and identified the purpose and goals of the study as well—which were to learn about the college experiences of Black males and their experiences in BMI programs. Both of these efforts, working with BMI program coordinators and inviting students at a BMI meeting, were used to help facilitate recruiting students for the interviews. The outlined parameters for participating in the study were race, gender, current college enrollment, and participation in the BMI program. A total of 50 students were individually invited to participate in the study; I was able to secure one-on-one interviews with 40 students. The great majority of the interviews took place in a small office on campus. I worked with the program coordinators to secure a space that would be convenient for privacy. Several of the interviews were conducted off campus at a local café.

In addition to conducting interviews, I engaged in ethnographic fieldwork—primarily at Monroe State. I attended activities that included on-campus events where BMI members would be in attendance, BMI meetings, events, and social outings. As I built relationships with the men individually, some of the students invited me out to other activities, such as fraternity events. Additionally, they invited me to participate (and attend) events that they sponsored on campus as well such as Black History Month events. Through my attendance and participation, I was able to observe the men during their engagement on campus, which helped me to better understand and appreciate what they offered during interviews. I also observed some of the men in leadership roles. My observations, along with reading and rereading the interview transcripts, helped inform my follow-up interviews.

Given my range of professional and academic experiences, students engaged me in conversations about their lives and trajectories as well. For instance, we discussed navigating college, they had inquiries about graduate school (including identifying and applying to graduate programs) and my own professional path, and we talked about some of the current and ongoing challenges facing Black communities. I have remained in communication with a significant number of men and, as a result, we update each other on current work, our well-being and, for the men, their school status. Based on my last communication, 24 of the men had graduated from college (including the two men who graduated recently during the data collection). Thus, as a group, 60 percent of the students had graduated college within six years of enrollment (21 of the 24 had graduated in 4 or 5 years) and seven more were on track to graduate during the 2016–2017 school year. Several of the students formally invited me to their graduation and/or their graduation celebration and several others have engaged me in conversations about graduate school.

As I talked with the men during the interviews and engaged them in conversations at events or activities, I often thought about my own college experiences. In particular, I often reflected on being both Black *and* male in college and how my own identities mattered in some of the choices I made. Although we shared racial and gender identities and had many similar personal interests, I did not assume that I knew these men. On a number of instances during our interviews, a few of the men framed a comment, response, or question through a shared knowledge about being Black men. Statements like "I know you know what it's like" to signal an expected familiarity from me. These statements helped me be more mindful of some of the men's pauses and visceral responses. One of the elements from the interviews that stands out most for me is our discussion about the campus environment. In developing the questions, I estimated that some might require more recall than others, but that the flow of questions would aid the men in reflecting on their experiences. I was blown away completely by how the men received the question, "What is it like to be a Black man on campus?" I was shaken further by their nonverbal responses that communicated or hinted at the burdens that they shouldered. Some of the men disengaged from eye contact with me, some hung their head, and some shook their head side to side while focusing intently at me. Some of the men shifted their body position and some of the men took more than five seconds to utter any initial verbal response. These nonverbal responses, in addition to the stories and experiences that men shared, reaffirmed to me that their race *and* gender, their Blackmaleness, were at the core of what they experienced in college. In addition, I thought about the ways that some had defied the odds in getting to college or continued to pursue college degrees even though they experienced a variety of hardships and challenges.

For some of these men, I imagine that our discussions helped them gain greater clarity on where they were and what they had experienced. The conversations might have helped them think about the remainder of their time in college or their post-college plans as well. I think both of these contributed to their willingness to share. Another reason, as many of them shared after the formal interview ended, was that they did not think anyone (beyond a small circle of people such as an advisor or BMI staff member) would be interested in their experiences and what they thought. Their responses, and some of their queries, continued to remind me of the correlation between listening and understanding. At the heart of inviting me into their world and allowing me to gain a perspective of their interiorities, the men desired that I understand who they are and who they can be. Studying the experiences of Black male collegians offers a wealth of opportunities to investigate areas of interests and, in many ways, can allow us a chance to confront some of the rhetoric about them as well.

Notes

Chapter 1

1. The names used throughout this book are pseudonyms to protect the confidentiality of research partners and institutions.

2. Throughout this book, I primarily use the term "Black" to denote the racial identity of the men. In large part this is to connect with the nomenclature used by scholars who seek to nuance identities of U.S.-born Black Americans from those born in and throughout the wider African Diaspora. In their self-descriptions, the men were split pretty evenly about their racial identity; about half identified as African American and about half identified as Black. I use the men's own nomenclature and terminology in each instance where their voices appear throughout the book in an effort to respect their words and what they shared. Additionally, as is consistent with critical race scholars, I capitalize Black/s, Students of Color, People of Color, and Faculty of Color to reposition individuals and groups who are often minoritized within dominant culture. Being Black, or members of other Communities of Color, should not be reduced to a hierarchal relation to the assumed White majority. Importantly, Critical Race Theory, the central framework used for this book, challenges dominant ideology within the United States. Therefore, capitalizing these terms continues to interrogate institutional practices that minimize the significance of race, problematize Communities of Color, or replicate how they are marginalized.

3. Much of the research attention on Black males' educational experiences has focused on providing summative details about their status and performance during the time of review. For example, Michael J. Cuyjet's *African American Males in College* published in 2006 is an edited volume that focuses on improving the general condition for African-American males in higher education. This attention extends from the status of Black males (Garibaldi, 2007) to (re)setting the agenda for Black men in college (Harper, 2014) and surveys of Black males in higher education (Wood & Palmer, 2015). Most of this work is aimed at detailing, subscribing, and ensuring success for Black male students. The major questions under investigation are (a) what is the sustainability of

increased attention on Black males, and (b) how will this attention impact the condition for Black males in the United States?

4. In examining the "trouble with Black boys," Noguera reveals the implicit and explicit ways that schools and other institutions (such as the criminal justice system) trouble Black boys. He pays particular attention to environmental and cultural factors on the academic performance of Black males. He also examines the ways in which environmental and cultural forces shape the relationship between identity, particularly related to race and gender, and school performance. See *The Trouble with Black Boys: . . . And Other Reflections on Race, Equity, and the Future of Public Education* (San Francisco, CA: Jossey-Bass, 2008).

5. In her study on Black boys' educational experiences in a public school, Ann Arnett Ferguson argued that the school incorporated a hidden curriculum that had differentiated rules and processes for White male students as opposed to Black male students. She found that an important component of the school's "hidden curriculum" was through the labeling practices and the exercise of rules that marginalized and isolated Black male youth in disciplinary spaces and, quite often, they were labeled as bad boys. The interpretation of "bad boys" was intended to project these youth as criminally inclined. See *Bad Boys: Public Schools in the Making of Black Masculinity* (Ann Arbor, MI: University of Michigan, 2000).

6. Harper and Harris (2012) outline an agenda across institutions and states focused on improving college completion and increasing postsecondary degree attainment rates among Black male students. They identify many of the programs listed here along with others as well. Similarly, as mentioned, Cuyjet's (2006) edited volume profiles programs targeted for Black male success. Some of these programs mentioned here are included in the volume, such as African American Men of Arizona State University, Black Men's Collective (Rutgers University), 100 Black Men of America, and Student African American Brotherhood. Additionally, the White House's "My Brother's Keeper" is aligned with these efforts as well (White House, 2014).

7. Similar to other researchers, I use historically White institutions (HWIs) instead of predominantly White institutions to identify the historical and contemporary possessive investment in Whiteness. The use of HWIs helps to reveal the racialized infrastructure that is in place, the current racial campus culture and ecology, and how these modern-day institutions still benefit Whites at the expense of Blacks and other Students of Color.

8. In conceptualizing intersectionality, Crenshaw (1991) writes about the unique compoundedness of Black women's intersectional experiences and the centrality of their experiences to the larger classes of women and Blacks. She contends that Black liberation from racial subordination necessitates theories and strategies that include an analysis of sexism and patriarchy. Additionally,

research has shown continuously that Black students face a number of barriers at HWIs (a few earlier studies include Allen, 1992; Epps, 1972; Feagin, 1992; Fisher & Hartmann, 1995; Fleming, 1984; Sedlacek, 1999). With regard to campus climates, researchers have identified racial microaggressions as a cause of stress for its victims. Scholars have defined microaggressions as subtle recurring acts (verbal, behavioral, and/or visual) directed toward People of Color intended to denigrate their racialized identities (Harper, 2009; Pierce et al. 1978; Solórzano et al., 2000; Sue et al. 2007). Racial microaggressions are prevalent across various social institutions, such as in the workplace and at schools or across campus environments. In addition to microaggressions, Smith's (2004, 2010) work on "racial battle fatigue" is critical to better understand experiences of People of Color in historically White environments, and more specific to the current project, the experiences of Black males at historically White institutions. Smith et al. (2007) defined racial battle fatigue as "the result of constant physiological, psychological, cultural, and emotional coping with racial microaggressions in less-than-ideal and racially hostile or unsupportive environments (campus or otherwise)" (p. 555). Researchers assert that the most damaging aspect of experiences within these racially toxic environments is that the collective memories often become part of a person's life history and, therefore, they seldom fade. The racialized experiences one encounters ranges from racial slights and discriminatory or unfair treatment to indignities and personal threats (see Smith 2004; Smith et al., 2007; Smith, Hung, & Franklin, 2011; Smith, Yosso, & Solórzano 2006).

9. Lorde argues that self-definition is a critical establishment of self and one's relation to others. Additionally, defining self in a collective sense also helps to broaden the perspective and allows for multiple truths and stories to be heard. See *Sister Outsider: Essays and Speeches* (Berkeley, CA: Crossing Press, 2007).

10. In their discussion of "new possibilities" for engaging Black male youth, findings from Baldridge, Hill, and Davis (2011) assert the need to create new and relevant educational models that address the unique and complex circumstances of young Black men. These challenges, such as social hardships and structural constraints, reveal the need for alternative sites of education and youth development).

11. Bell argued fervently about the permanence of race throughout his scholarship. In *Faces at the Bottom of the Well*, as in many of his other works, he argued that race was neither a passing phase nor could it be swept away with some of the short-lived judicial and legislative victories. Instead, race is a permanent feature of American life that compromises relations, growth, and opportunities. See *Faces at the Bottom of the Well: The Permanence of Racism* (New York, NY: Basic Books, 1992, p. ix).

12. For a concise history of Critical Race Theory, from its early origins to its connections to other social movements to its major tenets, see *Critical Race*

Theory: The Cutting Edge (Philadelphia, PA: Temple University Press, 1995). Additionally, other scholars have argued for the permanence of race and examined how race acts as a major organizing principle in U.S. society (e.g., Alexander, 2010; Bonilla-Silva, 2010; Feagin, 2014; Muhammad, 2011; West, 1993).

13. The major tenets of CRT have been identified by a range of researchers (for example, see Delgado, 1995; Solórzano, 1997; Solórzano et al., 2000).

14. Yosso, Smith, Ceja, and Solórzano (2009) use CRT to expose some of the ways racism on college and university campus has morphed into more subtle forms that still have pernicious results (p. 663). For instance, their respondents identified interpersonal racial microaggressions, racial jokes as microaggressions, and institutional microaggressions as key barriers in their collegiate experiences. Importantly, the effects of racial microaggressions can lead to rejection, race-related stress, and stereotyped threat.

15. Although Collins focused on the experiences of Black women, her insights and analysis on the interconnectedness of race, class, and gender are important to the current project. Primarily, the point here turns attention to experiential knowledge (p. 222).

16. James and Lewis (2014) began their inquiry into Blackmaleness by examining the connections and contradictions of W. E. B. Du Bois's (1903/2005, p. 2) quip, "How does it feel to be a problem?" and Carter G. Woodson's (1933/2011, p. 5) critique of the educational process that "depresses and crushes . . . the spark and genius in the Negro by making him feel that his race does not amount to much and will never measure up to the standards of other peoples." The authors asserted that the insights accrued by examining the cultural, social and emotional needs of Black male learners can help "redress hegemonic educational philosophies, practices and pedagogies that counter or ignore all together the unique development trajectories of Black males" (p. 105).

17. Dancy (2014) asserted that separating masculinity and manhood is important so that we can see how they are connected but are different concepts. By examining these independently, we can better appreciate the expressions/behaviors and the "constructed meanings that inform, undergird, or are potentially concealed by these behaviors" (p. 150).

18. Dancy (2012) also used Du Bois' double-consciousness to frame his study on Black men's masculine identities and manhood constructs. See *The Brother Code: Manhood and Masculinity among African American males in college* (Charlotte, NC: Information Age Publishing, 2012).

19. Anderson introduces his concept of Black men's "master status" in his early work and continues to develop this thread throughout a number of subsequent manuscripts. See *Streetwise: Race, class, and change in an urban community* (Chicago, IL: University of Chicago Press, 1990, p. 163).

20. These authors examine invisibility syndrome in counseling and psychotherapy of Black males (see 2000, p. 33).

21. Here, I borrow the analysis provided by Mark Anthony Neal in his investigation of Black male expressive culture. In examining a variety of Black masculine identities, Neal analyzes the nuanced ways that these identities are queered simultaneously as legible and illegible (p. 8). He asserts that Black male bodies, identities, and masculinities often are always already under surveillance. See *Looking for Leroy: Illegible Black Masculinities* (New York, NY: New York University Press, 2013).

22. See Strayhorn (2014) pp. 212–213.

Chapter 2

1. For instance, Freeman (2005) explored the disparity between the number of Black high school students who aspire toward higher education and the number who actually attend. She explores specific factors that contribute to attitudes and disposition toward college, including gender, finances, and high school curriculum (see also Jackson & Moore, 2006; Howard, 2003; Toldson, 2008; Toldson, Braithwaite, & Rentie, 2009).

2. See Campbell (1983).

3. Researchers have found that three particular stages connect Black students and their families with regard to their college success: precollege events and experiences, early college influences, and late college influences. Across these stages, students are working to negotiate family expectations, college environments, and their perceptions of their status on campus (i.e., as a minority at an historically White institution), developing community and fictive friendships on campus, and garnering spiritual support (see Harris, 2006; Herndon & Hirt, 2004; Ladner, 1998). In her classic study of Black families, Carol Stack focused on the extensive kin networks that helped Black families develop adaptive, resourceful, and resilience strategies to survive desolate poverty. She asserted that the extensive kin networks were functional and stable, which refuted much prior research on Black families. She identified cooperation and mutual aid as two critical survival strategies. See *All Our Kin: Strategies for Survival in a Black Community* (New York, NY: Harper & Row, 1974).

4. Jawanza Kunjufu (1995) noted that Black boys' educational inclinations and efforts halted around the end of their elementary school years. He contended that teachers halt their efforts to nurture and promote achievement among Black males as early as fourth grade, thus inciting apathy and disengagement among those students. As a result, and given the easily accessible negative projections of Black males in the wider public, one might assert that Black males do care about their education—especially as they transition to secondary school. However, a plethora of studies have revealed Black males' care and concern for their educational status, experiences, and accomplishments. For instance,

Akom (2003) framed his study in "organizational habitus" to problematize the oppositional culture thesis and to illustrate the ways in which a group of low-income Black students subscribed to and endorsed academic achievement (also see Carter, 2003; Harris, 2011).

5. For example, Zaback, Carlson and Crellin (2012) analyzed U.S. Census data to demonstrate the value of a college education and found correlates between earning a formal education and self-efficacy and improved life chances. They contended that people who earn a bachelor's degree have a median income of $50,360 compared to a median of $38,607 for individuals with an associate's degree and $29,423 for people with only a high school diploma. Additionally, individuals with a graduate degree have a median income of $68,064—35.2 percent more than those with bachelor's degrees (also see Howard, 2013; Ng, Wolf-Wendel, & Lombardi, 2014).

6. In his study of Black students' academic identities and college aspirations, Howard (2003) argued that it is imperative to understand how they maintain their academic integrity in pursuit of their educational goals especially as they continue to be marginalized academically and socially in schools. Given the challenges that they faced, students felt that they were in a tug-of-war for their minds. Howard found three contributing factors that influenced their academic identities: the role of parents, the perceptions of teachers and counselors, and the role of college. Thus, students' early schooling experiences (Allen, 2015; Brooms, 2014ab; Davis, 2003; Howard, 2013) and how they balance both internal and external factors in developing and maintaining their academic identities (Brooms, 2013; Howard, 2003; McGee & Martin, 2011; Polite & Davis, 1999) are critical in their aspirations and orientations to college.

7. Yosso (2005) identified familial capital as those cultural knowledges nurtured among families, that carry a sense of history and memory and it helps to forge a heightened sense of consciousness. Familial capital is connected to kin, denoting both a close family knit and including a broader network of community, and thus is nurtured by extended family as well.

8. Herndon and Hirt (2004) maintained that the family is a conduit for educational attainment because they are primary sources of academic potential, they set the parameters of community standards within the home environment, and they serve as the primary socializing agent for establishing meaning in life and the world and creating a social environment that influences how students view education.

9. A score of researchers have provided thorough analyses of the challenges that Black students face in traditional school settings and how after-school and community-based education spaces [can] play a pivotal role in reaffirming students' identities, providing them with socioemotional learning opportunities, and supporting their whole selves (Baldridge, 2014; Baldridge et al., 2011; Fashola, 2003; Woodland et al., 2009).

10. In examining the current landscape of educational reform, Baldridge (2014) argued that many discussions about Black youth were framed in a deficit model. Funders, board members, and even CEOs of various organizations often framed their work in "saving" Youth of Color and, thus, neglected the strengths and assets that they brought with them into educational settings. Thus, Baldridge argued for relocating the deficit away from youth and instead placing it in the structures and systems that continue to marginalize these youth (p. 463).

11. See Baldridge et al., (2011) p. 133.

12. See case studies by Fashola (2003) and Woodland (2008) for insight on engaging youth during after-school hours.

13. In examining the factors that promote pathways to academic success for Black male students, Toldson's (2008) findings reinforced the need for stronger academic preparation and college access programs that emphasized college preparation.

14. Noguera (2003) asserted that schools that serve Black males often fail to nurture, support, and protect them. As a result, they are more likely to be excluded from rigorous classes and prevented from accessing educational opportunities that potentially could support and encourage them. Additionally, researchers have identified a variety of characteristics of effective schools; most germane to the current discussion is: (a) a rigorous curriculum; (b) high expectations; and (c) a commitment to educate all students. A lack of appropriate preparation could threaten to impede the progress of success of Black male students (Noguera, 2003; Palmer et al., 2009).

15. In assessing students' college readiness, ACT (2006) reported that nearly one-third of students entering some type of postsecondary education need to take remedial courses in one or more subjects because they lack the skills to take standard credit-bearing courses (p. 1). This lack of preparation is exacerbated for marginalized students, especially those attending high-need schools (Ladson-Billings, 2006)

16. In a recent study by Lewis-McCoy (2014), he found inequality among suburban schools, which often have the presumed reputation of better access to resources. More specifically, he identified "opportunity hoarding" as a key strategy of White middle-class parents to secure resources for their children. In effect, structural factors, social and class positions, and past experiences limited access to resources for many racial and economic minority families.

17. Diamond and Lewis (2015) and Lewis-McCoy (2014) detail how White parents in suburban schools hoard resources, which contradict and undermine equitable educational opportunities. In addition, Diamond and Lewis found that teachers engaged in active policing of Students of Color and the incongruity between the school's stated policies and how they were practiced helped create an atmosphere for racial differences in academic outcomes. They found disconcerting differences in grade point averages, graduation rates, test score performances,

and placement in gifted, honors, and AP educational tracks between Black and White students. See *Despite the Best Intentions: How Racial Inequality Thrives in Good Schools* (Cambridge, MA: Oxford University Press, 2015).

18. Tyrone Howard argued that sports have played a damaging role on Black male development. He coined "athletic seasoning complex" to describe how Black males are encouraged to develop their athletic identities and engage in an intense pursuit of superior ability in playing basketball, football, or baseball at the expense of their academic development. He contended that the athletic seasoning complex is built on four key components: (1) early and persistent exposure to sports, (2) inordinate time commitment to developing high-level competency in sports, (3) the holdback phenomenon, and (4) the save-the-family syndrome. See *Black Male(d): Peril and Promise in the Education of African American males* (New York, NY: Teachers College Press, 2013).

19. Various researchers have acknowledged the importance of investigating the motivations and self-determination of Black students. Specifically, research by Griffin (2006), Brooms (2013), and Allen (2015) is informative. Griffin (2006) found that Black high-achievers reported being motivated by both internal and external factors. The student participants connected their motivation to internal drive and desire to be successful in addition to achieving highly valued goals (such as career), making their families proud, and being a positive representative of the Black community. Additionally, in exploring the educational experiences of fifteen Black males, Brooms (2013) found both internal and external factors as important supports for their achievement. Students reported drive and determination as critical internal factors while peers, teachers, and mentors were important external factors. Similarly, Allen (2015) found students enacted agency in their own academic pursuits and drew on parent and teacher systems of support to experience academic success.

20. Researchers note that by taking into account various forms of capital, such as dominant and nondominant cultural capital or sociocultural capital, we might develop a more complete and nuanced understanding of how it affects students' academic orientations, performances, schooling experiences, and outcomes (Carter, 2007; Harper, 2008, 2012; Hotchkins, 2014; Lareau & Horvat, 1999; Stanton-Salazar & Dornbusch, 1995; Yosso, 2005).

21. Stanton-Salazaar (2011), p. 1074.

22. ACT (2006) p. 3.

23. The ACT Report included five key action steps that included: create a common focus, establish high expectations, require a rigorous curriculum, provide student guidance, and measure and evaluate progress.

24. Fergus and Noguera (2010) used data on the academic performance of Black and Latino males in New York City to analyze a host of challenges that might impede their achievement and graduation rates and negatively contribute to their dropout rates. In particular, they examined the distribution of

quality school contexts and examined the academic pathways and trajectories of a graduating cohort of Black and Latino students. They found that across K–12 schools, there was a disproportionate distribution of quality schools represented in schools rated C or lower, which ultimately serves to reduce the students' opportunities for college readiness. Additionally, they found that the pathways for those who later developed into regents earners developed quite different paths during elementary school.

25. See the following for varied perspectives on the matter: Allen, 1985; Fleming, 1984; Fries-Britt, 2002.

26. Jonathan Kozol (2012) argued that many poor families are cheated out of opportunities for higher education, social mobility, and future possibilities because of the gross inequalities in funding and resources in many inner-city and less affluent suburban schools. Given the cultural framing often used to discuss achievement and academic performance, all too often students are positioned as the unit of analysis while the structures that allow for inequality receive less attention. See *Savage Inequalities: Children in America's Schools* (New York, NY: Broadway Books, 2012).

27. Several researchers provide critical analyses of Black males' athletic experiences and its impact on their academic efforts (see Beamon, 2009; Harris, 2014; Howard, 2013).

28. See Harper's (2012) research on Black male students' success efforts in higher education.

29. Strayhorn (2012), p. 3.

30. Patton (2006) found that Black Cultural Centers (BCC) represent safe and welcoming spaces for Black students at historically White institutions. In making meaning of their interactions within the BCC environment on campus, the students found BCCs provided them a sense of historical and personal identity and they perceived the BCC as "home" (also see Bowman, Park, & Denson, 2015; Guiffrida, 2003; Strayhorn & DeVita, 2010).

31. Palmer and colleagues (2010) exclaimed that all racial and ethnic groups in the United States must be included in high educational preparation in order to "enhance and sustain its global competitiveness in the knowledge-based, global economy" (p. 112).

Chapter 3

1. Black males' struggles during their first year are similar to other students in their adjustments to college (Astin, 2003) and at the same time are differentiated by their race and gender identities, their family backgrounds, and previous schooling experiences (Allen, 1992; Douglas, 1998; Harper, 2012; Hausmann, Schofield, & Woods, 2007; Palmer & Young, 2008).

2. Hausmann and colleagues (2007), p. 829.

3. Venezia and Jaeger (2013) argued that there are many reasons that students are unprepared for college-level coursework, such as the dissimilarities between what is taught in high schools and what colleges expect as well as the disparities in instruction based on students' socioeconomic status—that is, high schools with high concentrations of students in poverty are disparately different than those with more financially advantaged students. Additionally, the authors also asserted the importance of nonacademic variables, such as peer influences, parental expectations, and support.

4. In addition to self-expectations and relationships and responsibilities to family, Dancy identified two additional constructs: worldviews and life philosophies (beliefs about others) and double-consciousness (attempts to think and act according to others' expectations).

5. Hunter and Davis (1994) argued that this unidimensional focus (i.e., men as economic providers for their family) limited our knowledge about how Black men made meaning of their masculinity and manhood. In seeking to unravel the "hidden voices of Black men," the authors provided a conceptual map of Black men's meaning-making. A central challenge to manhood that the men in their study identified was what they expected from themselves. Additionally, Davis (1999) asserted the need for research that focused on how gender informs the experiences of Black males on campus. Recent research has provider a more robust perspective of Black men's masculine identities and manhood constructs that has informed our understanding of how Black men see themselves and the ways that they are projected and represented as well (see Cooper, 2006; Dancy, 2011b, 2012; Hammond & Mattis, 2005; Harper, 2004; hooks, 2004; Mutua, 2006; Neal, 2013).

6. Ford (2006) and McClure (2006) both provide critical insight on Black men's interiorities regarding their gendered identity constructs. Ford explored how Black masculinity is physically, behaviorally, and materially constructed from idealized images resulting in a contextually adaptive sense of self among Black males at a large research university. McClure's study explored the meaning and function of fraternity membership in the lives of Black men on a predominantly White campus. She found that the men subscribed to hegemonic and Afrocentric masculine constructs, thus revealing the complexity of Black male identity. McClure concluded that the men used their fraternity membership "in ways to reflect the Afrocentric model of cooperation and connectedness to the Black community and more specifically to other males" (p. 68).

7. The findings from this research are important in (a) documenting Black student experiences and (b) revealing some of the cultural and institutional barriers to their success efforts (Allen, 1992; Chavous et al., 2004; Davis, 1998; Feagin, 1992; Feagin, Vera, & Imani, 1996; Fleming, 1984; Jackson & Moore, 2006; Jenkins, 2006; Sedlacek, 1999; Smith et al., 2007; Solórzano, Ceja, & Yosso, 2000).

8. Black male experiences in fraternal organizations have been documented in the literature on how this engagement contributes to their collegiate experiences (Harper & Harris, 2006; Patton & Bonner, 2011) and how it impacts their sense of self (Harper, 2008; McClure, 2006).

9. The oppositional culture theory was popularized by Fordham and Ogbu (1986) in an attempt to explain the gaps in achievement between Blacks and Whites. The theory posits that students underperform in school primarily because of a group culture that devalues learning and sees academic success as "acting White." Although it lacked sufficient evidence and ignored external factors, it continued to grow in popularity and put the onus of responsibility on students for their academic performances. A range of researchers have criticized this approach for its limitations and for how it marginalized Black students. Ainsworth-Darnell and Downey (1998) provide a powerful counter-narrative while other scholars continue to show that Black students in general, and Black males in particular, do care about education. For instance, Harris (2011) tested the empirical implications of oppositional culture theory through quantitative analysis and found several shortcomings, such as Black students value schooling more than their White counterparts and their skills are inhibited by socioeconomic and health factors in addition to lowered teacher expectations.

Majors and Bilson (1992) suggest that "cool pose" is a distinctive coping mechanism that Black males use partly to counter the dangers they face on a daily basis. They further explain that "cool pose" is a multidimensional survival skill and a coping strategy. Cool pose encompasses a set of language, mannerisms, gestures and movements that "exaggerate or ritualize masculinity" and although it might allow young Black males to deflect some of the negative confrontations they face, it might also be dysfunctional in some ways. For instance, adopting a cool-pose stand could limit one's ability for emotional developments and connections, might be interpreted as irresponsible and unconcerned by those outside of the group, and might unintentionally welcome physical confrontations (i.e., feeling compelled to respond physically to an affront or slight).

10. In exploring the cultural constructions of manhood as defined by Black men, Hunter and Davis (1992) found that the Black men in their study conceptualized a multidimensional construction of manhood. In part, this was due to the ways in which they subscribed to the ideals of hegemonic manhood (such as being a provider) and felt restricted by some of the social and economic ills that they faced (such as racism).

11. Warde's study of 11 African-American male graduate students identified a total of four factors as being significant contributors to their successful bachelor's completion. In addition to an epiphany and access to resources, he also found having a mentor and being resilient are key factors.

12. Kuh et al. (2008) measured "academic outcomes" as (1) first-year student grades and (2) by persistence between the first and second year of college.

13. Although Wood and Williams's (2013) research focused on persistence factors among Black males in public two-year colleges, their findings are still salient for the current study. They asserted that social involvement, by itself, did not facilitate persistence for Black male collegians. These efforts must be joined by academic involvement in order to increase persistence; these include faculty-student interactions and study habits.

14. Bourdieu (1986) identified social capital as an aggregate of the actual or potential resources that one might accrue and asserted that it was highly dependent on the size of the network of connections at one's disposal. Coleman (1988) contended that social capital is productive in that it makes achieving certain ends attainable that otherwise might not exist. Similarly, Portes (1998) acknowledged that one of the most critical functions attributed to social capital is as a source of "network-mediated benefits" beyond one's family connections. Cultural capital can enable or limit an individual's ability to negotiate social groups, organizations, or institutions. Young (1999) used cultural capital to refer to the "adoption of social practices as well as the acquisition of understandings that help one to navigate social life in ways that lead to increased personal efficacy" (p. 204).

15. In their study of a Black Male Initiative program, Brooms, Goodman, and Clark (2015) found that meaningful interactions and connections along with opportunities for personal and professional development were critical for the Black male students that they interviewed. Importantly, students interpreted these experiences as opportunities to expand their social and cultural capital, which they believed would help them in better navigating the college milieu.

16. Over the past 30 years, the formal use of the term "social capital" has increased in popularity among academic researchers, policymakers and educators alike (Portes, 2000). Bourdieu (1986) framed the concept as "the aggregate of the actual or potential resources which are linked to possession of a durable network of more or less institutionalized relationships of mutual acquaintance or recognition" (p. 248). Additionally, its meaning has been associated with influencing human potential on an individual and collective scale in the arenas of education, economics, employment, politics, and health, as well as access to advantageous quality of life resources (Coleman, 1988; Portes, 1998). The progressive benefits of social capital are transmitted to recipients through formal and informal networks across multiple sectors of life (Portes, 2000). Social capital has been deployed in a number of education studies. For instance, Strayhorn (2010) found that African-American male college students achieve more favorable academic outcomes through social capital benefits derived from activities such as student organization involvement and volunteerism and exposure to interactive settings which are valued in educational contexts.

17. The majority of participants in Brooms et al.'s (2015) study cited that they were motivated to participate in the Black Male Achieve program

because of the potential for meaningful interactions and connections with other Black men. The students asserted that these interactions and connections helped build their awareness about various opportunities and equip them with strategies (academic, social, and financial) that were critical to their successes on campus.

18. This finding connects well with research by Harper (2006) and Strayhorn. Much like the men offer in the current study, Strayhorn found that supportive relationships are positively associated with educational outcomes for Black men.

19. Using a representative sample from national data of nearly 8,000 Black students, Flowers (2004a) found that in-class and out-of-class experiences positively impacted students' development and outcomes. Additionally, as noted by previous scholars, involvement has been identified as a key variable to student persistence (Pascarella & Terenzini, 2005; Tinto, 1993).

20. Motivation has been identified as an essential component of the academic experience because it can play a significant role in students' thoughts, beliefs, and behaviors. The intrinsic and extrinsic factors that motivate students is related to their academic self-concept, orientation toward their future selves, influence of family and friends, and educational environment (Brooms, 2016a; Cokley, 2000, 2003; Garibaldi, 1992; Griffin, 2006).

21. Kuh and Huh (2001) proposed that a variety of factors—such as socioeconomic background, financial aid status, and family background—can influence student achievement. Similarly, Braxton, Millen, and Sullivan (2000) identified family problems and financial aid assistance as two key factors that impact why students leave college.

Chapter 4

1. For instance, Chavous and colleagues (2004) examined how African-American students experienced racial stereotypes and gender across both predominantly Black and predominantly White colleges. They found a range of stereotype expectations, which included students' perceptions of biased treatment and evaluation within their major classroom settings. The authors assert that a critical area for further inquiry is "men and women at PWIs may experience different types of racial discrimination or race-related treatment on campus" (p. 12). Importantly, their findings support the research efforts of the current study as they noted a need to "examine both individual perceptions of institutions as well as institutional structures, instructional practices, policies, and other sources that may convey messages about belonging and fit to African American students" (p. 14).

2. Patton (2006) argued that Black Culture Centers (BCCs) represent safe and welcoming spaces for Black students at Predominantly White

Institutions (PWIs). Amidst a climate of covert racism, separatism, and apathy, a number of Black students in her studied asserted that need for the BCC on campus. Additionally, she found that students perceived the BCC provided a sense of historical and personal identity and a "home" for Black students at these institutions.

3. Researchers continue to identify hostile campus environments as one of the major challenges that many Black students encounter at HWIs. Due to their minoritized status on campus and their underrepresentation, their efforts and presence on campus are scrutinized and even policed. As a result, a plethora of studies discuss their cultural alienation and isolation (Feagin et al., 1996; Fleming, 1984; Nagasawa & Wong, 1999) as well as gendered racism, blocked opportunities, and environmental stress (Fitzgerald, 2014; McCabe, 2009; Smith et al., 2011). Smith and Moore (2000) argue that Black students often are lumped into a singular frame based on assumptions that they represent social, cultural, and economic homogeneity. These assumptions mask the context of student experiences based these differences and how students develop closeness or not at historically white institutions.

4. Adams (2005) examined the experiences of Black students at a large, predominantly White university. She conducted an analysis of student responses on "The Black Ideology Scale" and conducted six focus group interviews as well. In the first phase of the study, she found those students who enrolled in Black studies courses felt less pressure to focus on extraneous issues. Students reported feeling engaged in a significant learning experience (i.e., gaining more insight into their ancestry and culture because of the focus of classes), they had opportunities of having Black faculty members as well as being in a class whose "content directly related to issues that impacted them" (p. 291). Importantly, Adams found that these courses "created a space in which students could discuss issues of race, develop pride in Black culture and find a 'voice' with which to express their identities and social concerns" (p. 292).

5. In sharing his own experiences, Staples (1986) asserted that Black men in public spaces often are viewed as threats and menaces. He shared that young Black males are overrepresented as perpetuators of violence and this creates fear in public spaces. Although he often sees people who fear the worst of him—and other young Black males—these truths still do not mitigate being otherized and problematized simply because of group membership (p. 196; see also Staples, 1982).

6. In his study of Black masculine identity and discourse, Jackson (2006) traces the origins of Black body politics and its contemporary manifestations in televisual and cinematic images. He argues that the vast majority of social interpretations of race "are predicated on difference and devaluation, and the body is often conceived as a mere physical vessel that links human beings and their differences to the social world" (p. 5). In scripting Black masculine bod-

ies, Jackson asserts that stereotypical portrayals of Black males as angry, violent, and criminal are heavily prevalent and readily available for public consumption. The implication in these projections and inscriptions is the idea that "the Black masculine body is viewed as a threat" and has "deleterious effects" on one's growth and development (pp. 99–100).

7. Picca and Feagin's (2007) study is important here as they investigated the front-stage and back-stage racial performances of Whites in public (multiracial) and private (all-White) discourse. They exclaimed that, "Much of the overt expressions of blatantly racist thought, emotions, interpretations, and inclinations have gone backstage—that is, into private settings where Whites find themselves among other Whites, especially friends and relatives" (p. x).

8. Smith, Hung, and Franklin (2011) argued that for far too many Black men, HWIs represent racial climates that are replete with gendered racism, blocked opportunities, and mundane, extreme, environmental stress. They examined the experiences of 661 Black men and found that both racial microaggressions and societal problems in predominantly White environments contributed significantly to increased contexts and instances of racial battle fatigue among Black men (see pp. 66–67).

9. A host of researchers have investigated how racial microaggressions impact Black men. Smith and colleagues' (2007) study examined the psychosocial experiences and racial battle fatigue among Black male college students at HWIs. Their participants' experienced racial microaggressions in three domains: (a) campus-academic, (b) campus-social, and (c) campus-public spaces. Black males reported being stereotyped and placed under increased surveillance by community and local policing tactics on and off campus and were defined as being "out of place" and "fitting the description" of illegitimate nonmembers of the campus community. The authors concluded that the culmination of the students' experiences "reflects the racial microaggressions they encounter as they negotiate their identity in a world that marginalizes their existence and transforms them from a Black male to an object, from a student-scholar to a racial target, and from a potential protector to a potential predator" (p. 573). Other researchers also find that many Students of Color at HWIs report campus environments to be unsupportive and racially hostile and thus ripe grounds for gendered racism, stereotypes, racial microaggressions, and racial battle fatigue (see Robertson, Bravo, & Chaney, 2014; Smith 2010; Smith et al., 2006; Steele, 1997).

10. Feagin, Vera, and Imani (1996) reveal how different forms of racialized space, time, and recognition shape the everyday life experiences of Black students. In their study, half of their respondents noted that at least once or twice they were mistreated by White professors on campus. Students experienced racialized stereotypes, insensitivity to Black culture, and isolation. In particular, students felt that they were objects of attention when racial issues arise in class.

218

They noted that "white professors and students can construct social situations where Black students are placed in awkward or painful situations" (p. 91). One characteristic experience of students in their study at historically White institutions was feeling the burden placed on them by Whites to be the voice and defenders of their group.

11. McGee and Martin (2012) used "stereotype management" to explain high achievement and resilience among 23 Black mathematics and engineering college students. They describe this coping strategy as a "tactical response to the ongoing presence of stereotype threat" (p. 1354). The authors explained that hiding one's true feelings as "*necessary and strategic responses* to frequently unacknowledged and structurally organized barriers and systemic challenges" (p. 1354, emphasis in original).

12. Solórzano, Yosso, and Ceja's (2000) research approach provides a critical framework that can be used to study how micro-level forms of race and racism are weaved within and throughout the collegiate environment (p. 63). Using focus group interviews, the authors found that many students spoke of feeling "invisible" within the classroom setting. They provided concrete examples of racial denigrations in faculty-student interactions, and articulated nonverbal slights perpetuated by their White counterparts. The compounding impact of the microaggressions experienced by students includes lowered expectations and possible fatigue (also see research by Franklin, 1997, 1999; Pierce et al., 1978; Smith et al., 2011; Sue et al., 2007).

13. Smith and colleagues (2007) used focus group interviews to examine the experiences of 36 Black male students at five universities. The authors identified the three domains in the following ways: campus-academic spaces were on-campus areas traditionally designated for academic or administrative buildings; campus-social spaces were areas where students traditionally socialize or participate in recreational activities (such as dorms, fraternity houses, recreation areas); and, campus-public spaces were areas adjacent to campus (p. 562). The two major findings were that the students experienced anti-Black male stereotyping and marginality along with hypersurveillance and control.

14. Harper (2013) defines niggering as, "the process by which stereotypes about Black boys and men shape people's low expectations for their success in schools and society" (p. 191). He contends that microaggressions along with hearing only negative statistics and pathological narratives about oneself is a way through which Black males are niggered.

15. Jackson (2006) argued that the label of "thug" allows contemporary brute images of Black males to remain intact. As a recent example, National Football League player Richard Sherman of the Seattle Seahawks was referred to as a "thug" during a post-game interview in January 2014. According to Wagner (2014), the word "thug" is used as a shorthand to denote the discomfort experienced by Whites in the presence of Black males. One day following the

game, the word "thug" was used 625 times across all national media markets; this marked the most in the past few years (Wagner, 2014).

16. Ralph Ellison's invisibility theory suggests that African-American men have to cope with the simultaneity of being both present and unseen, which ultimately impacts the ways that they are able to engage in various settings. See *Invisible Man* (New York, NY: Vintage, 2nd ed., 1995). Anderson (1990, 2011) and Staples (1986) are leading authorities on the experiences of Black men in public spaces. Anderson argued that for Black men "master status" often overpowers other positive qualities (1990, p. 163). Similarly, in their focus group interviews with 36 Black males, Smith et al. (2007) demonstrated the complexity and breadth of racial microaggressions by identifying two main factors evident in each space. "One is the understanding that each respondent perceived the encounter in a raced and gendered context. Second, and yet equally critical to note, is that law enforcement personnel were common factors in every case" (pp. 562–63).

17. Stereotyping of Black men is replete in the literature and continues to reveal some of the gendered racism that they experience (Collins, 2004; Ferguson, 2000; McCabe, 2009; Smith et al., 2007).

18. Cooper (2006) contended that popular representations of heterosexual Black men vacillate between a "Bad Black Man" and a "Good Black Man." He argued that these representations create a bipolar Black masculinity. The "Bad Black Man" trope is used to identify Black men as crime-prone and hypersexual while the "Good Black Man" trope references Black men who distance themselves from Blackness and associate with White norms. According to Cooper, "the threat of the Bad Black Man label provides heterosexual black men with an assimilationist incentive to perform our identities consistent with the Good Black male image" (p. 853).

19. In his study, *The Condemnation of Blackness: Race, Crime, and the Making of Modern Urban America*, Khalil Muhammad (2011) delivers a penetrating historical analysis of the contemporary crisis in criminal justice. He begins by examining the "Negro Problem" and how such racialized ideologies crafted Blacks as the "menace" to society. In tracing the connections of the enslavement and the post-enslavement periods, Muhammad shows continuities in how Blacks were criminalized. He argues that slave patrols of the antebellum years were replaced, almost immediately, by modern police departments. He argues that the meaning of Blackness changed in the decades after slavery in ways that opened the door for Black to be correlated with the inclination for criminal behavior.

20. John Hope Franklin and Evelyn Brooks Higginbotham note that the Fugitive Slave Law of 1850 demanded the return of all escaped slaves caught anywhere in the United States. This Law was part of the Compromise of 1850, which favored slaveholders' interests. Franklin and Higginbotham also assert that southerners were completely supportive and "considered enforcement of the

new fugitive slave act in 1850 essential for maintaining the Union" (p. 204). See *From Slavery to Freedom: A History of African Americans* (New York, NY: McGraw-Hill, 9th ed., 2011).

21. Michelle Alexander argues that we can no longer ignore the realities of race and racial stigma in our society. More specifically, she argues that mass incarceration is, metaphorically, the New Jim Crow. She contends that within American society a racial caste system continues to be perpetuated that ultimately assigns People of Color to a permanently inferior status. Further, she argues that drug-war rhetoric has been employed to oppress People of Color in the same ways as Jim Crow laws once did. And, she illustrates how social control continues even after "offenders" are released from prison, through a web of laws that prohibit them from basic needs such as public assistance and citizenship rights such as voting; also, their movements and associations are monitored closely as well. Thus, she argues that the current system of control permanently locks a significant percentage of the African-American community out of the mainstream society and economy. See *The New Jim Crow: Mass Incarceration in the Age of Colorblindness* (New York, NY: New Press, 2010).

22. The history of intentional racial exclusion fits the description of what James W. Loewen describes as "sundown towns." Loewen asserts that throughout the United States these towns were created in waves of violence in the early decades of the twentieth century and then maintained well into the contemporary era. See *Sundown Towns: A Hidden Dimension of American Racism* (New York, NY: Touchstone Press, 2006).

23. The incident and resultant court case reached national prominence as Martin's murder led to protests in Sanford and to a "hoody campaign" where individuals, professional athletes and entertainers, elected officials like Bobby Rush, and even the Miami Heat basketball team of the National Basketball Association donned hoodies to stand in support of Trayvon Martin and as a symbol of injustice. Grinberg (2012) asserts that the hoody leads a dual life. In one sense, it has been a wardrobe staple adorned by a wide array of individuals; yet, at the same time, it still carries a social stigma that has made it the object of legislative bans and political speeches. Additionally, even before the killing of Trayvon Martin, hoodies had been embroiled in negative racial connotations for Black and Latino youth.

24. In recounting his own experiences as a Black man in public spaces and tying these to the killing of Trayvon Martin, George Yancy (2013) posits that the "White gaze" is used often to delineate and discern Black subjectivity. In his essay, "Walking While Black in the 'White Gaze,'" he describes how the Black male body is assumed and projected as different, deviant, and ersatz. All too often, he notes, "Black bodies in America continue to be reduced to their surfaces and to stereotypes that are constricting and false, that often force those black bodies to move through social spaces in ways that put White people at

ease." Additionally, Yancy argues that White gaze is hegemonic and historically grounded in material relations of White power (also see Anderson 2012; Armour, 2000; Oliver, 2006).

25. Solórzano, Ceja, and Yosso (2000) used Critical Race Theory to examine campus racial climate and identified racial microaggressions as part of the predominant narrative for students of color. They defined campus racial climate in broad terms and argued that understanding and analyzing the overall racial climate on college campuses as an important part of examining college access, persistence, and graduation. Similarly, in examining raced- and gendered microaggressions, McCabe (2009) found views of Black men as threatening on a predominantly White campus. The compounding impact of microaggressions and discriminatory treatment is that Black males feel devalued, suffer invisibilities, and may become less engaged on college campuses.

26. Feagin's (1992) research on the continuing significance of racism in higher education is informative. He argued that Black students at predominantly White institutions experienced cumulative discrimination. These experiences translate into a compounding effect of a "college career or lifetime series of blatant and subtle acts of differential treatment by Whites which often cumulates to a severely oppressive impact" (p. 575).

Chapter 5

1. Davis (1999) explored the higher education contexts for Black males and noted that they struggled to become socially integrated in a community of peers and hostile schooling environments that marginalize their presence on campus (p. 135).

2. Numerous researchers have investigated the pathological constructions, deficit framing, and marginalization that Black men face across a range of institutions and spaces (e.g., see Brown, 2011; Dancy, 2014; Franklin, 2004; Harper, 2009, 2013; hooks, 2004; Howard, 2013; Neal, 2013; Smith et al., 2007).

3. Harper (2009) asserted the need for counter-narratives that problematize deficit rhetoric. He offers that critical race counter-narratives are necessary since published insights that reveal Black male student successes and achievement are largely missing from scholarly literature.

4. The unnamed narrator of Ralph Ellison's novel provides a context for the ways in which he was rendered invisible within larger society. Ellison's notion of invisibility is not a self-endorsement, but rather a result of creations by others who both misunderstand and refuse to see. The main point of contention is that his invisibility is imposed on him by others. See *Invisible Man* (New York, NY: Vintage Press, 1952/1995).

5. Franklin and Boyd-Franklin (2000) proposed that adaptive behavior and psychological well-being of African Americans can be affected by personal experiences of perceived prejudice and discrimination. They theorized "invisibility syndrome" as a conceptual model for understanding the marginal social status of African-American men in society. They assert that an enduring climate of prejudice and discrimination allows stereotypes to thrive and racial slights to be carriers of a societal disposition toward African Americans. They identified a variety of ways to manage the stress of invisibility; being in places and circumstances that provide a greater sense of acceptance and legitimacy reduces feelings of invisibility; defying invisibility through self-empowerment; sanity checks as psychic stabilizers; racial identity development; and therapeutic support groups (pp. 39–40). Additionally, Brooms and Perry's (2016) study found that Black men used a variety of self-policing strategies to manage and negotiate being stereotyped and profiled. Several of these elements are endorsed and enacted by the men in the current study.

6. As noted by previous researchers, microaggressions are systemic, especially given the types of ways that race was experienced and how it seems embedded within the environment (e.g., see McCabe, 2009; Mincey et al., 2015; Smith, 2010).

7. In Feagin's study, he developed a typology of discriminatory practices that included three dimensions: (1) the location of the discriminatory action; (2) the type of actor doing the discrimination; and, (3) the type of hostile or discriminatory action directed against Blacks (1992, pp. 573–574). He identified faculty members as barriers to this student population; he documented examples of exclusion and ostracism by treating Black students as typecasts and dismissing them in various ways.

8. Here, I employ "scripts" as a strategy of navigating race relations as described by Lacy (2007) and Dancy (2012). Lacy theorized "strategic assimilation" to demonstrate how Blacks use distinct spaces and places for identity construction among the Black middle classes. She shows various scripts that members of the Black middle class deploy in navigating Black and White worlds. See *Blue-Chip Black: Race, Class, and Gender in the New Black Middle Class* (Berkeley, CA: University of California Press, 2007). Also, Dancy conceptualized the "brother code" and investigated various scripts deployed by Black males as they speak about the intersection of manhood and the college experience. See *The Brother Code*.

9. In addition to survival, Majors and Billson argue that cool pose "propels black males on a collision course with each other and with whites" (p. 2). They argue that Black masculinity is enamored with dilemmas (such as crime and violence) and posing cool—where Black males repress their emotions—is both unhealthy and destructive. See *Cool Pose: The Dilemmas of Black Manhood in America* (New York, NY: Touchstone Press, 1992).

10. Dancy (2012) found that most participants in his study did not feel that Black men were treated, valued, engaged, or embraced equally in their institutions. The students cited college athletes as the most valued at their respective institutions along with White students and international students (p. 106). Thus, as Davis (2012) contends, it is critical that research on Black males be attuned to how Black males negotiate their masculinity in their academic engagement.

11. Dancy (2012) argues that staying true to an authentic self is a prominent self-expectation among many Black males. His respondents described ways in which they both conceptualized and shaped an authentic manhood on campus; the importance of this process, according to Dancy, is that it released the men from "the imprisonment of functioning in a world defined in the expectations of others" (p. 80).

12. Cross (1971) notes that not all individuals will have the same level of salience in the Internalization stage. In his revised model (1991), he collapsed stages 4 (Internalization) and 5 (Internalization-Commitment) together and focused on Multiple Internalization Identities, which included Black Nationalist, Biculturalist, and Multiculturalist (a matrix of three or more cultural frames of reference such as gender or sexual orientation).

13. Bridges (2011) used focus group interviews to examine the relationship of Black males' ethnic identity and their psychological coping at a predominantly White university. He grounded his study in Cross' (1971) model of Nigrescence and used the Cross Racial Identity Scale as an assessment measure. The most common coping strategies that his participants used were distancing themselves from Whites, physically or psychologically, in addition to withdrawal and assertion. Physically distancing oneself from Whites on a majority White campus can be fraught with challenges. Bridges's study is informative and sheds light on a much-needed area of research (pp. 163–64).

14. Utsey and Payne (2000) examined the differential impacts of racism on the psychological well-being on a sample of African-American men. The authors discussed how the current status of African-American men has been impacted by the compounding effect of centuries of unrelenting assaults on their representations and projections, psyche, spirit, humanity, and personhood. They noted, "In viewing racism as a chronic source of stress that permeates many aspects of African American life, we could anticipate a host of psychological stress responses (e.g., depression, anxiety, anger, intense feelings of subjective distress, lowered levels of life-satisfaction, and lowered self-esteem)" (pp. 60–61). The authors examined a total of 126 men, 56 of whom were recruited as a control group and found no differential levels of race-related stress.

15. Davis and colleagues (2004) interviewed 11 Black undergraduate students and, among the five themes identified, offer critical insight and reaffirm prior research about student experiences within a White-dominated space.

In particular, they found that students felt "invisible/supervisible" on campus and some students narrated their experiences within the theme of "unfairness/sabotage/condescension." These types of experiences have a "potentially adverse effect on academic performance." Importantly, "the pervasive nature of unfairness/sabotage/condescension mandates a coordinated institutional and faculty response if efforts to increase success of Black students are effective" (p. 437).

16. Fleming cited a range of literature concerned with the problems of interpersonal relationships, identity, and Black consciousness for students in predominantly White institutions. Fleming found that Black males felt unhappy on White campuses; they displayed academic demotivation, felt that they were treated unfairly, and had lower academic self-concept. See *Blacks in College: A Comparative Study of Students' Success in Black and White Institutions* (San Francisco, CA: Jossey-Bass, 1984).

17. As researchers have shown, many student organizations, especially those of ethnic origin, provide Students of Color with invaluable cultural, social, and academic support systems (Guiffrida, 2003; Museus, 2008) and some gender-centered programming like BMI-type programs have been identified for providing similar strengths through community building and increasing students access to sociocultural capital (Brooms, 2016a, 2016b; Brooms et al., 2015; Zell, 2011).

18. According to Franklin (1997, 1999), "invisibility syndrome" refers to the onslaught of psychic assaults resulting from their ongoing, and often daily, encounters with racism and discrimination. Two critical elements of invisibility include (1) lack of recognition and acknowledgment, and (2) results in feelings of self-doubt (e.g., do I belong here?). Ellison (1995) also explores these themes in his work as well. See *Invisible Man*.

19. Collins (2000, 2004) argued that, "The dominant ideology of the slave era fostered the creation of four interrelated, socially constructed controlling images of Black womanhood, each reflecting the dominant group's interest in maintaining Black women's subordination" (2000, p. 72). These "controlling images" were Mammy, Matriarch, Welfare Mother, and Jezebel. She argues that stereotypical images serve two primary functions: first, they can serve to hide or to normalize oppression by making it seem something that the oppressed person wants to do or something that comes from the oppressed person's nature; second, they can serve to *coerce* people into acting in certain ways.

20. Wingfield (2007) argued that the controlling image of "the angry Black man" suggests that Black male rage at racism is inopportune and unfounded, and simultaneously reinforces the perception of Black men as a threat and a danger to the social order (p. 210).

21. Wilkins (2012) used in-depth interviews with 43 Black university men to investigate race, gender, and emotions. The author found that the men developed emotion strategies to help them cope in taxing environments and

linked their strategies to a "moderate Blackness" identity. According to Wilkins, the moderate Blackness identity strategy works to "facilitate membership in institutions in which the White middle class establishes the emotional rules" (p. 58). Importantly, moderate Blackness is a strategy of emotional restraint whereby Black men control their emotions by learning to ignore, trivialize, and reinterpret everyday racism.

22. In writing about Black men and public spaces, Staples (1986) offered that a "vast, unnerving gulf" lay between Black men and other nighttime pedestrians. He recounts a variety of experiences where his mere presence in public was perceived as dangerous. The experiences and analysis he shares connects with Ellison's unnamed narrator in *Invisible Man* and helps shed light on the ways that Black men often lose their individual identity in public spaces. Also Ralph and Chance (2014) assert that to be Black, in America, "is to perpetually feel foreign, and at the very same time, to recognize that you are feared" (p. 138). In speaking about the White gaze, Yancy (2013) asserts that Black bodies in America "continue to be reduced to their surfaces and to stereotypes that are constricting and false, that often force those black bodies to move through social spaces in ways that put white people at ease."

23. In her study, Wilkins (2012) encoded these strategies as "moderate Blackness." She offered that moderate Blackness has three components: restrained, positive emotional standards; a temperate approach to Black politics; and the ability to get along with White people. Additionally, this strategy "moderates racial discord, distancing itself from stereotypes of blacks as angry and/or dangerous" (p. 43). Ford's (2011) research explored Black masculinity among 29 Black male college students. She focused on *doing Black masculinity* to "signify the process that black college men actively engage in to physically, behaviorally, and materially claim and reclaim a socially constructed, racialized sense of masculinity in black public social spaces, or highly visible sites in which social interactions are likely influenced by societal expectations or group norms (e.g., intraracial social events, organizational meetings, community gatherings)" (p. 41).

24. Moore, Madison-Colmore, and Smith's (2003) study is part of a larger project that investigated the persistence of Black males in engineering programs. This qualitative study used both individual and group interviews to examine the experiences of 24 Black male junior and senior college students. They asserted that the fundamental basis of the prove-them-wrong syndrome is to work harder in reaching one's goals, which simultaneously proves one's critics wrong when they doubt the ability to perform. The authors concluded that more research is needed to further examine how hostile and unwelcoming environments trigger the prove-them-wrong syndrome in Black males.

25. Using multivariate statistics and hierarchical regression techniques, Strayhorn (2014) found that grit, alone, added incremental predictive validity

for Black male collegians over and beyond traditional measures of academic success such as high school grade point average and ACT scores. Thus, he surmised that grit may prove to be an effective lever for raising Black male academic success. Strayhorn concluded that the study provided evidence that sticking with long-range goals and engendering hard work and perseverance seems to pay off in terms of Black males' college grades.

26. Dancy's (2010) qualitative study sought to illustrate how constructions of manhood and masculinity among African-American men may influence their academic, social, and developmental experiences in college. Among the four themes that emerged, most salient to the current study is how Black men constructed manhood through self-expectations—comprised of statements of self-determinism and answerability (i.e., being resilient, being responsible/accountable, being "real" or authentic to a self-constructed manhood) (p. 25). Similarly, in his qualitative study of 32 Black males, Harper's (2004) participants were convinced that their high-achieving activities—such as leadership positions, academic honors, and maintaining a high profile on campus—"would not have made it into the African American undergraduate male portfolio of masculinity" (p. 97). Instead, they asserted that their peers held more heteronormative, patriarchal conceptions.

27. Du Bois (1903/2005) uses the veil throughout *The Souls of Black Folk*, primarily referring to the ways that the true humanity of Blacks is constrained by racism in the United States.

28. Here, I am specifically referring to Zimmerman and West's (1987) conception of "doing gender." These authors contend that gender is a social construction and therefore propose an ethnomethodologically informed understanding of gender "as a routine, methodical, and recurring accomplishment" (p. 126).

29. Whiting's (2006) "Black Male Scholar Identity Framework" is grounded in various achievement-based theories and identifies nine characteristics that Black males can employ to bolster their academic achievement and enhance their sense of belonging in school settings. The characteristics include self-efficacy, future orientation, willing to make sacrifices, internal locus of control, self-awareness, need for achievement/need for affiliation, academic self-confidence, racial identity, and masculinity.

30. Ellison's (1995) notion of invisibility is useful for understanding how Black men are rendered invisible through the social interactions of others. In one of the novel's iconic lines, the unnamed narrator declares, "I am invisible, understand, simply because people refuse to see me" (p. 8). See *Invisible Man*.

31. Steele (1999) analyzed how the threats of stereotypes impact students and asserted that what leads to decreased academic performance is the fear of doing something that would inadvertently confirm that stereotype. Addi-

tionally, Schmader, Major, and Gramzow (2001) found that beliefs about ethnic injustice stereotypes predicted greater discounting and devaluing for both African-American and Latino students in their study regardless of their actual performance in school.

32. Brooms (2016b) found that student learning experiences in BMI were critical in helping to empower students, providing them opportunities for self-discovery, and enhancing their identities. In particular, students reported that the support they received was described as being "lifted up" or "built up" through BMI.

33. See Whiting's (2006) "Black Male Scholar Identity Framework" for further exploration of these topics.

34. Dancy (2011a) identified self-expectations as a predominant theme in his research on the impact of gendered perspectives on African-American males. His participants used statements of self-determinism and answerability to construct their manhood and expressed them in statements such as "achieving goals," "being authentic," and "being responsible" (p. 486; also see Du Bois, 2005; hooks, 2004; Whiting, 2006).

35. Feagin and O'Brien (2003) used a qualitative study to investigate African-American experiences with racism. The study's findings suggest that the response to racism that African Americans used was influenced by the context in which it occurred. The authors found that in many of these situations, acquiescence, or withdrawal, was the preferred response because confrontation was viewed as being too costly in time and energy. Moreover, due to the often subtle nature of racism, many African Americans responded to racist events with a careful evaluation of the situation.

Chapter 6

1. Astin's (1999) theory of student engagement and Tinto's (1993) theory of departure both focused primarily on students. Astin maintained that the quantity and quality of student involvement were paramount to students' persistence while Tinto maintained that students' integration experiences are important predictors of their satisfaction with college. However, neither of these theories accounted for how institutions act upon students. For instance, Tinto asserted that Black students face unique challenges to their academic and social integration at HWIs because their norms and values might not be aligned with the White-centric culture on campus.

2. Barker and Avery (2012) assert that more work is needed in understanding and appreciating what Black males experience in institutional-based Black male programs (see p. 74).

3. Bonner and Bailey (2006) note that although the myriad issues Black males face span the educational continuum, the confluence of six factors have been found to promote a climate of success: peer group influence, family influence and support, faculty relationships, identity development and self-perception, and institutional environment (p. 25). Several of the authors' conclusions are relevant to the current exploration of their experiences in the BMI program. First, they suggest that more attention must be dedicated to the special functions that peer groups serve in the lives of Black male college students. Second, student affairs officials need to make direct contact and a personal request for student involvement in programming efforts. Third, identifying and connecting Black males with faculty (and staff and administrators) provides them with knowledgeable liaisons who might provide academic, social, and personal assistance. And, finally, there is a critical need for Black male collegians to establish a sense of agency within the institutional setting.

4. Here, I adopt Strayhorn's definition for sense of belonging as students' perceived social support on campus, a feeling of connectedness, or that one is important to others. See *College Students' Sense of Belonging: A Key to Educational Success* (New York, NY: Routledge, 2012).

5. Cuyjet's (2006) edited volume includes nine chapters that profile some successful programs across various colleges and universities. Cuyjet notes that these profiles are intended to be descriptive of the program's structure and function and to explain any measurable results that have been observed (p. 251). Therefore, the profiles are not intended to be comprehensive but rather add depth to the focus of Cuyjet's work and help to illuminate a sampling of ideas and strategies that have been beneficial to Black college men. Much of the work of the two BMI programs in the current study used several strategies outlined within these profiles. See *African American Men in College* (San Francisco, CA: Jossey-Bass, 2006).

6. Strayhorn (2012) identified seven core elements of college students' sense of belonging; connected to what Donald and many other students offer, the model situates belonging as a fundamental need, alongside self-actualization, esteem, safety and physiological needs. Importantly, Strayhorn professes that sense of belonging takes on heightened importance in certain spaces and contexts, at certain times, and under certain conditions for particular populations, such as Black men.

7. Bonner and Bailey (2006) also contend that resilient students are found to engage in behaviors that correlate with higher levels of self-esteem than those students who do not exhibit engaging behaviors (pp. 33–34).

8. Guiffrida (2003) interviewed 88 students to explore African-American student organizations as "agents of social integration." He found that involvement in African-American student organizations provided students with con-

nections to Black faculty outside the classroom and an environment in which they could comfortably associate with other African Americans.

9. Yosso (2005) conceptualized six forms of cultural wealth that draws on the knowledge that Students of Color bring with them from their homes and communities into the classroom: aspirational, linguistic, familial, social, navigational, and resistant. Importantly, Yosso asserted that, "These various forms of capital are not mutually exclusive or static, but rather are dynamic processes that build on one another as part of community cultural wealth" (p. 77). Additionally, in a related study (Brooms, 2016b), I show how the men's experiences in BMI increases their sociocultural capital. In particular, the men relate how BMI enhances their sociocultural capital helps them establish a "home space" on campus, gain access to critical support, feel motivated academically, and heighten their sense of self.

10. A range of researchers have argued for and discussed the importance of critical pedagogy (see Alexander-Floyd, 2008; Brooms, 2014b; Giroux, 1985; hooks, 1994; Lynn, 1999) and culturally relevant pedagogy (see Gay, 2000; Ladson-Billings, 1995). Importantly, these efforts have been found to enhance engagement and performance of marginalized students.

11. Branch (2014) developed the four dimensions of Ethnic Identity Exploration in Education: making connections with students' families about ethnic identity; engaging students in ethnic identity discourse; exploration of ethnic histories, traditions, and customs; and, facilitating meaningful relationships between students and role-models in their ethnic groups. Branch contends that exploring students' ethnicity within the school context can enhance student achievement.

12. Several researchers note the importance of Black student organizations and Black support groups in bolstering the college experiences of Black students (Flowers, 2004a; Guiffrida, 2003; Guiffrida & Douthit, 2003; Strayhorn & DeVita, 2010). Guiffrida (2003) surmised that the potential exists for the groups to significantly impact their social integration and racial identity development once integrated into the majority culture of the university (p. 316). Guiffrida and Douthit (2010) also accentuate this point. In reviewing the literature on Black college student academic achievement and persistence at PWIs, they identified involvement in Black student organizations as a key factor. Finally, Patton's (2006) research on Black Cultural Centers also provides fertile ground for understanding how space is a critical element of student support groups and ethnic-based student organizations. These spaces offer students a designated counter-space on campus by recognizing Black culture, people, and history and provide ample opportunities for positive interactions—among both users and visitors to the center. Flowers (2004b) asserted that retaining students remains an important goal in higher education institutions. He encouraged that future

studies investigate the effects of certain policy initiatives, campus services, and organizational constraints on Black student retention.

13. See Strayhorn, 2008a; Tinto, 1993.

14. Research that focuses on Black students and motivation have identified both internal and external factors that contribute to their academic performance. In his study of 15 college-aged Black males, Brooms (2013) found that his participants described intangible and tangible dynamics that motivated them to succeed including the peer group, relationships with faculty and staff, and positive connections with mentors. Other researchers provide critical insight on motivation as well (see Cokley, 2003; Griffin, 2006)

15. Warde's (2008) study is informative here, as he examined the persistence factors of recent Black male college graduates. A key finding among his participants was having an epiphany, or realization, about the importance of obtaining a bachelor's degree as the only way forward for them (p. 64).

16. For instance, Daley and colleagues (1995) framed their study within an Afrocentric worldview, which acknowledges affective reality as well as rationality, strives for system maintenance rather than individual material gain, and views humanity collectively through shared concern for others' well-being. They argue that the African-American community has developed effective problem-solving strategies in response to its needs when the dominant culture excluded it from services and has developed creative responses to new challenges.

17. Although Carter's (2007) research examined the clustering of Black students at a predominantly White high school, given that Black students were in the demographic minority and they faced various modes of hostility similar to the students in the current study, her utility of counter-spaces is useful here. Carter argued that when faced with hostility in predominantly White learning environments, some Black achievers coped by creating and using formal and informal, social and academic identity-affirming counter-spaces as a resistance strategy to buffer experiences with racism and other forms of discrimination. Additionally, she found that the counter-spaces used by students in her study "represent institutionalized mechanisms that serve as protective forces for these students and allow them to maintain a strong racial sense of self, while maintaining school success in a racially hostile environment" (p. 543).

18. Jackson's (2012) ethnographic study of Uplift and Progress (UP), a national organization for Black male undergraduate students, helps in framing BMI as a counter-space as well. Jackson argued that UP functioned as a counter-space in which "group members use the concept of brotherhood to cope with the alienation and discrimination they encounter . . . The men of UP valued caring and emotional openness and sought to reframe giving and receiving social and emotional support as a necessary aspect of brotherhood" (p. 63). He identified three ways in which UP attempted to build brotherhood among new recruits across the initiation process. First, brotherhood was promoted through

formal conversations and relationship building. Second, brotherhood was ritu-
alized through various bonding activities. Finally, brotherhood was policed by
UP leaders as they scrutinized and questioned the behaviors, presence, and
timeliness of recruits.

19. Harper (2013) discusses the critical role that "peer pedagogy" plays
for Students of Color at predominantly White campuses. His study aims to
provide "insights into the role Black students play in teaching their same-race
peers about responding productively to onlyness, racism, and racial stereotypes
on campus" (p. 199). He identified ethnic student organizations as a key site
where Black students deployed their pedagogies and racial socialization methods
to inform their peers about campus culture and academic life at their respective
institutions. In focusing on organizations specifically designed for Black undergraduate men, he asserted that these groups and spaces served more than social
purposes; in fact, they proved quite instrumental for teaching and learning about
the racial realities of the PWIs in his study (p. 204).

20. Lester (2006) confirmed the benefits of a Black Male Rap Session
(B-MRS), a discussion format to exchange dialogue and ideas, on campus. He
offered that the primary goal of B-MRS is to provide a supportive environment,
specifically at majority White institutions, for the discussion of issues and concerns related to Black men.

21. For discussions that highlight the impact of connections to students'
schooling efforts, see Brooms 2016a, 2016b; Guiffrida, 2003; Pascarella & Terenzini, 1991; Tinto, 1993.

Chapter 7

1. Harper examined trends in the 15-year movement to improve Black
male student success, from 1997 to 2012, and charged that one key area of error
has been focusing on the deficit rhetoric and positing Black male students as
those in need of fixing. This view allowed for shortcomings of Black male retention and graduation to be the focus of manifold stories as opposed to identifying
high-achieving students and inquiring about their successes. In many ways, the
current study contributes to this call and others that focus on Black males'
success in higher education and how their engagement and identities matter.

References

Adams, T. A. (2005). Establishing intellectual space for Black students in predominantly White universities through Black Studies. *Negro Educational Review, 56*(1), 285–299.

Aguirre, A. (2010). Diversity as interest-convergence in academia: A critical race theory story. *Social Identities, 16*(6), 763–774.

Akom, A. A. (2003). Reexamining resistance as oppositional behavior: The Nation of Islam and the creation of a Black achievement ideology. *Sociology of Education, 76*(1), 305–325.

Alexander, M. (2010). *The new Jim Crow: Mass incarceration in the age of colorblindness*. New York, NY: New Press.

Alexander-Floyd, N. (2008). Critical race pedagogy: Teaching about race and racism through legal learning writings. *PS: Political Science & Politics, 1*(1), 183–188.

Allen, Q. (2015). "I'm trying to get my A": Black male achievers talk about race, school and achievement. *Urban Review, 47*(1), 209–231.

Allen, W. R. (1985). Black student, white campus: Structural, interpersonal and psychological correlates of success. *Journal of Negro Education, 54*(2), 134–147.

Allen, W. R. (1992). The color of success: African-American college student outcomes at predominantly White and historically Black public colleges and universities. *Harvard Educational Review, 62*(1), 26–44.

Allen, W. R., Bonous-Hammarth, M., & Suh, S. A. (2004). Who goes to college? High school context, academic preparation, the college choice process, and college attendance. In E. P. St. John (Ed.), *Readings on equal education. Vol. 20: Improving access and college success for diverse students: Studies of the Gates Millennium Scholars Program* (pp. 71–113). New York, NY: AMS Press.

American College Testing Program. (2006). *Ready to succeed: All students prepared for college and work*. Ames, IA: ACT.

Anderson, E. (1990). *Streetwise: Race, class, and change in an urban community*. Chicago, IL: University of Chicago Press.

Anderson, E. (2004). The cosmopolitan canopy. *Annals of the American Academy of Political and Social Science*, 595(1), 14–31.

Anderson, E. (2011). *The cosmopolitan canopy: Race and civility in everyday life.* New York, NY: W. W. Norton.

Anderson, E. (2012). Toward knowing the iconic ghetto. In R. Hutchinson and B. Haynes (eds), *The ghetto: Contemporary global issues and controversies* (pp. 67–82). Boulder, CO: Westview.

Armour, J. (2000). *Negrophobia and reasonable racism: The hidden costs of being Black in America.* New York, NY: New York University Press.

Astin, A. W. (1993). *What matters in college? Four critical years revisited.* San Francisco, CA: Jossey-Bass.

Astin, A. W. (1999). Student involvement: A developmental theory for higher education. *Journal of College Student Development*, 40(5), 518–529.

Astin, A. W. (2003). Studying how college affects students: A personal history of the CIRP. *About Campus*, 8(3), 21–28.

Baldridge, B. J. (2014). Relocating the deficit: Reimagining Black youth in neoliberal times. *American Educational Research Journal*, 51(3), 440–472.

Baldridge, B. J., Hill, M. L., & Davis, J. E. (2011). New possibilities: (Re)Engaging Black male youth within community-based educational spaces. *Race, Ethnicity and Education*, 14(1), 121–136.

Baldwin, J. (1961). *Nobody knows my name.* New York, NY: Delta.

Barker, M. J., & Avery, J. C. (2012). The impact of an institutional Black male leadership initiative on engagement and persistence. *College Student Affairs Journal*, 30(2), 73–87.

Beamon, K. K. (2009). Are sports overemphasized in the socialization process of African American males? A qualitative analysis of former collegiate athletes' perception of sport socialization. *Journal of Black Studies*, 41(2), 281–300.

Bell, D. A. (1987). *And we are not saved: The elusive quest for racial justice.* New York, NY: Basic Books.

Bell, D. A. (1992). *Faces at the bottom of the well: The permanence of racism.* New York, NY: Basic Books.

Bell, D. A. (1996). *Gospel choirs: Psalms of survival for an alien land called home.* New York, NY: Basic Books.

Bell, D. A. (2004). *Silent covenants: Brown v. Board of Education and the unfulfilled hopes for racial reform.* New York, NY: Oxford University Press.

Bonner, F. A., & Bailey, K. W. (2006). Enhancing the academic climate for African American college men. In M. J. Cuyjet and Associates (Eds.), *African American men in college* (pp. 24–46). San Francisco, CA: Jossey-Bass.

Bonilla-Silva, E. (2010). *Racism without racists: Color-blind racism and the persistence of racial inequality in the United States* (3rd ed.). Lanham, MD: Roman & Littlefield.

Bourdieu, P. (1986). The forms of capital. In J. G. Richardson (Ed.), *Handbook of theory and research for the sociology of education* (pp. 241–258). New York, NY: Greenwood Press.

Bowman, N. A., Park, J. J., & Denson, N. (2015). Student involvement in ethnic student organizations: Examining civic outcomes 6 years after graduation. *Research in Higher Education, 56*, 127–145.

Branch, A. J. (2014). Ethnic identity exploration in education promotes African American male student achievement. *Journal of African American Males in Education, 5*(1), 97–103.

Braxton, J. M., Milen, J. F., & Sullivan, A. S. (2000). Faculty teaching skills and their influences on the college student departure process. *Journal of College Student Development, 41*(2), 215–227.

Bridges, E. M. (2011). Racial identity development and psychological coping strategies of undergraduate and graduate African American males. *Journal of African American Males in Education, 2*(2), 151–167.

Brooms, D. R. (2013). "I need drive and determination": A qualitative analysis of inner-city Black males' educational experiences. *Issues in Race & Society: An International Global Journal, 1*, 65–87.

Brooms, D. R. (2014a). "Trying to find self": Promoting excellence and building community among African American males. In J. L. Moore III & C. W. Lewis (eds.), *African American male students in PreK–12 schools: Informing research, policy, and practice* (Advances in race and ethnicity in education) (pp. 61–86). United Kingdom: Emerald Group Publishing.

Brooms, D. R. (2014b). Mapping pathways to affirmative identities among Black males: Instilling the value and importance of education in K–12 and college classrooms. *Journal of African American Males in Education, 5*, 196–214.

Brooms, D. R. (2016a). Encouraging success for Black male collegians: Support, brotherhood and bonding on campus. *Issues in Race & Society: An International Global Journal, 4*(1), 35–60.

Brooms, D. R. (2016b). "Building us up": Supporting Black male college students in a Black Male Initiative program." *Critical Sociology*, published online August 2016, DOI: 10.1177/0896920516658940.

Brooms, D. R. & Perry, A. R. (2016). "It's simply because we're Black men": Black men's experiences and responses to the killing of Black men." *Journal of Men's Studies, 24*(2), 166–184.

Brooms, D. R., Goodman, J., & Clark, J. (2015). "We need more of this": Engaging Black men on college campuses. *College Student Affairs Journal, 33*(1), 105–123.

Brown, A. L. (2011). "Same old stories": The Black male in social science and educational literature, 1930s to the present. *Teachers College Record, 113*(9), 2047–2079.

Campbell, R. T. (1983). Status attainment research: End of the beginning or beginning of the end? *Sociology of Education, 56*(1), 47–62.

Carter, P. L. (2003). "Black" cultural capital, status positioning, and schooling conflicts for low-income African American youth. *Social Problems, 50*(1), 136–155.

Carter, D. J. (2007). Why the Black kids sit together at the stairs: The role of identity-affirming counter-spaces in a predominantly White high school. *The Journal of Negro Education, 76*(4), 542–554.

Chavous, T. M., Harris, A., Rivas, D., Helaire, L., & Green, L. (2004). Racial stereotypes and gender in context: An examination of African American college student adjustment. *Sex Roles, 51*(1/2), 1–16.

Cokley, K. (2000). An investigation of academic self-concept and its relationship to academic achievement in African American college students. *Journal of Black Psychology, 26*(2), 148–162.

Cokley, K. O. (2003). What do we know about the motivation of African American students? Challenging the 'anti-intellectual' myth. *Harvard Educational Review, 73*(4), 524–558.

Coleman, J. S. (1988). Social capital in the creation of human capital. *American Journal of Sociology, 94*, S95–S121.

Collins, P. H. (1990). *Black feminist thought: Knowledge, consciousness, and the politics of empowerment*. Boston, MA: Unwin Hyman.

Collins, P. H. (2000). *Black feminist thought: Knowledge, consciousness, and the politics of empowerment* (Revised 10th Anniversary 2nd ed.). New York, NY: Routledge.

Collins, P. H. (2004). *Black sexual politics: African Americans, gender and the new racism*. New York, NY: Routledge.

Cooper, R. (2006). Against bipolar Black masculinity: Intersectionality, assimilation, identity performance, and hierarchy. *University of California at Davis Law Review, 39*, 853–906.

Crenshaw, K. (1991). Mapping the margins: Intersectionality, identity politics, and the violence against women of color. *Stanford Law Review, 43*(6), 1241–1299.

Cross, W. E., Jr. (1971). The Negro to Black conversion experience: Toward a psychology of Black liberation. *Black World, 20*, 13–27.

Cross, W. E., Jr. (1991). *Shades of Black: Diversity in African-American identity*. Philadelphia, PA: Temple University Press.

Cuyjet, M. J. (1997). African American men on college campuses: Their needs and their perceptions. *New Directions for Student Services, 80*(Winter), 5–16.

Cuyjet, M. J. (2006). *African American men in college*. San Francisco, CA: Jossey-Bass.

Daley, A., Jennings, J., Beckett, J. O., & Leashore, B. R. (1995). Effective coping strategies of African Americans. *Social Work, 40*(2), 240–248.

Dancy. T. E. (2010). African American males, manhood, and college life: Learning from the intersections. *College Student Affairs Journal, 29*(1), 17–32.

Dancy, T. E. (2011a). Colleges in the making of manhood and masculinity: Gendered perspectives on African American males. *Gender & Education*, 23(4), 477–495.

Dancy, T. E. (2011b). Becoming men in burning sands: Student identity, masculinity, and image construction in Black Greek-lettered fraternities. In M. Hughey & G. Parks (Eds.), *Empirical studies of Black Greek-lettered organizations* (pp. 95–111). Oxford, MS: University of Mississippi Press.

Dancy, T. E. (2012). *The Brother Code: Manhood and Masculinity among African American males in college.* Charlotte, NC: Information Age Publishing.

Dancy, T. E. (2014). Theorizing manhood: Black male identity constructions in the education pipeline. In F. A. Bonner (Ed.), *Building on resilience: Models and frameworks of Black male success across the P-20 pipeline* (pp. 140–158). Sterling, VA: Stylus.

Davis, A. R. (2013). The stories of resiliency: A study of African American men persisting to higher education degree attainment. Unpublished dissertation, Benedictine University.

Davis, J. E. (1994). College in Black and White: Campus environment and academic achievement of African American males. *The Journal of Negro Education*, 63(4), 620–633.

Davis, J. E. (1998). Campus climate, gender, and achievement of African American college students. *African American Research Perspectives*, 4, 40–46.

Davis, J. E. (1999). What does gender have to do with the experiences of African American college men? In V. C. Polite & J. E. Davis (Eds.), *African American males in school and society: Practices and policies for effective education* (pp. 134–148). New York: Teachers College Press.

Davis, J. E. (2003). Early schooling and academic achievement of African-American males. *Urban Education*, 38(5), 515–537.

Davis, J. E. (2012). Negotiating masculinity in college: African American males and academic engagement. In M. C. Brown, T. E. Dancy, & J. E. Davis (Eds.), *Educating African American males: Contexts for consideration, possibilities for practice* (pp. 53–66). New York: Peter Lang.

Davis, M., Dias-Mitzi, Y., Greenberg, K., Klukken, G., Pollio, H. R., Thomas, S. P., & Thompson, C. L. (2004). "A Fly in the buttermilk": Descriptions of university life by successful Black undergraduate students at a predominately White southeastern university. *Journal of Higher Education*, 75(4), 420–426.

Delgado, R. (1989). Storytelling for oppositionists and others: A plea for narrative. *Michigan Law Review*, 87(8), 2411–2441.

Delgado, R. (Ed.). (1995). *Critical race theory: The cutting edge.* Philadelphia, PA: Temple University Press.

Delgado Bernal, D. (2002). Critical race theory, LatCrit theory, and critical raced-gendered epistemologies: Recognizing students of color as holders and creators of knowledge. *Qualitative Inquiry*, 8(1), 105–126.

Denzin, N. K., & Lincoln, Y. S. (2005). *The Sage handbook of qualitative research* (3rd ed.). Thousand Oaks, CA: Sage.

Diamond, J., & Lewis, A. (2015). *Despite the best intentions: How racial inequality thrives in good schools.* Cambridge, MA: Oxford University Press.

Douglas, K. B. (1998). Impressions: African American first-year students' perceptions of a predominantly White university. *Journal of Negro Education, 67*(4), 416–431.

Du Bois, W. E. B. (1903). "The Talented Tenth," from *The Negro problem: A series of articles by representative Negroes of to-day.* (New York, 1903). Retrieved from http://www.yale.edu/glc/archive/1148.htm.

Du Bois, W. E. B. (2005). *The souls of Black folk.* New York, NY: Dover. (Original work published in 1903).

Educational Testing Service. (2013). Black male teens: Moving to success in the high school years (A statistical profile). Princeton, NJ: Author.

Ellison, R. (1995). *Invisible man.* New York, NY: Vintage. (Original work published in 1952)

Epps, E. G. (1972). *Black students in White schools.* Worthington, OH: Charles A. Jones.

Fashola, O. S. (2003). Developing the talents of African-American male students during non-school hours. *Urban Education, 38*(4), 398–430.

Feagin, J. R. (1992). The continuing significance of race: Discrimination against Black students in White colleges. *Journal of Black Studies, 22*(4), 546–578.

Feagin, J. R. (2014). *Racist America: Roots, current realities, and future reparations.* New York, NY: Routledge.

Feagin, J. R., Vera, H., & Imani, N. (1996). *The agony of education: Black students at White colleges and universities.* New York, NY: Routledge.

Fergus, E., & Noguera, P. (2010). Doing what it takes to prepare Black and Latino males in college. In C. Edley and J. Ruiz (eds), *Changing places: How communities will improve the health of boys of color* (pp. 97–139). Berkeley, CA: University of California Press.

Ferguson, A. A. (2000). *Bad boys: Public schools in the making of Black masculinity.* Ann Arbor, MI: University of Michigan Press.

Fisher, B. J., & Hartmann, D. J. (1995). The impact of race on the social experience of college students at a predominantly White university. *Journal of Black Studies, 26*(2), 117–133.

Fitzgerald, T. D. (2014). *Black males and racism: Improving the schooling and life chances of African Americans.* New York, NY: Routledge.

Fleming, J. (1984). *Blacks in college: A comparative study of students' success in Black and White institutions.* San Francisco, CA: Jossey-Bass.

Flowers, L. A. (2004a). Examining the effects of student involvement on African American college student development. *Journal of College Student Development, 45*(6), 633–654.

Flowers, L. A. (2004b). Retaining African-American students in higher education: An integrative review. *Journal of College Student Retention, 61*(1), 23–35.

Ford, K. A. (2011). Doing fake masculinity, being real men: Present and future constructions of self among Black college men. *Symbolic Interaction, 34*(1), 38–62.

Fordham, S., & Ogbu, J. U. (1986). Black students' school success: Coping with the "burden of 'acting white.'" *Urban Review, 18*(3), 176–208.

Franklin, A. J. (1997). Invisibility syndrome in psychotherapy with African American males. In R. L. Jones (Ed.), *African American mental health*. Hampton, VA: Cobb & Henry Publishers.

Franklin, A. J. (1999). Invisibility syndrome and racial identity development in psychotherapy and counseling men. *The Counseling Psychologist, 27*(6), 761–793.

Franklin, A. J. (2004). *From brotherhood to manhood: How Black men rescue their relationships and dreams from the invisibility syndrome*. Indianapolis, IN: John Wiley & Sons.

Franklin, A. J., & Boyd-Franklin, N. (2000). Invisibility syndrome: A clinical model of the effects of racism on African-American males. *American Journal of Orthopsychiatry, 70*(1), 33–41.

Franklin, J. H., & Higginbotham E. B. (2011). *From slavery to freedom: A history of African Americans*. New York, NY: McGraw-Hill.

Freeman, K. (2005). *African Americans and college choice: The influence of family and school*. Albany, NY: SUNY Press.

Frier Britt, S. L. (2002). High-achieving Black collegians. *About Campus, 7*(3), 2–8.

Garibaldi, A. M. (1992). Educating and motivating African American males to succeed. *The Journal of Negro Education, 61*(1), 4–11.

Garibaldi, A. M. (2007). The educational status of African-American males in the 21st century. *Journal of Negro Education, 76*(3), 324–333.

Gay, G. (2000). *Culturally responsive teaching: Theory, research, and practice*. New York, NY: Teachers College Press.

Giroux, H. A. (1985). Teachers as transformative intellectuals. *Social Education, 49*(5), 376–379.

Griffin, K. (2006). Striving for success: A qualitative exploration of competing theories of high-achieving Black college students' academic motivation. *Journal of College Student Development, 47*(4), 384–400.

Grinberg, E. (2012). Hoodie's evolution from fashion mainstay to symbol of injustice. *CNN* (March 27, 2012). Retrieved from: http://www.cnn.com/2012/03/27/living/history-hoodie-trayvon-martin/.

Guiffrida, D. A. (2003). African American student organizations as agents of social integration. *Journal of College Student Development, 44*(3), 304–319.

Guiffrida, D. A., & Douthit, K. Z. (2010). The Black student experience at predominantly White colleges: Implications for school and college counselors. *Journal of Counseling and Development, 88*(3), 311–318.

Hammond, W. P., & Mattis, J. S. (2005). Being a man about it: Manhood meaning among African American men. *Psychology of Men & Masculinity, 6*(2), 114–126.

Harper, S. R. (2004). The measure of a man: Conceptualizations of masculinity among high-achieving African American male college students. *Berkeley Journal of Sociology, 48*, 89–107.

Harper, S. R. (2006). Peer support for African American male college achievement: Beyond internalized racism and the burden of acting white. *The Journal of Men's Studies, 14*(3), 337–358.

Harper, S. R. (2008). The effects of sorority and fraternity membership on class participation and African American student engagement in predominantly White classroom environments. *College Student Affairs Journal, 27*(1), 94–115.

Harper, S. R. (2009). Niggers no more: A critical race counternarrative on Black male student achievement at predominantly White colleges and universities. *International Journal of Qualitative Studies in Education, 22*(6), 697–712.

Harper, S. R. (2012). *Black male student success in higher education: A report from the national Black male college achievement study.* Philadelphia: University of Pennsylvania, Center for the Study of Race and Equity in Education.

Harper, S. R. (2013). Am I my brother's teacher?: Black undergraduates, racial socialization, and peer pedagogies in predominantly White postsecondary contexts. *Review of Research in Higher Education, 37*(1), 183–211.

Harper, S. R. (2014). (Re)setting the agenda for college men of color: Lessons learned from a 15-year movement to improve Black male student success. In R. A. Williams (Ed.), *Men of color in higher education: New foundations for developing models for success* (pp. 116–143). Sterling, VA: Stylus.

Harper, S. R., & Harris, F. (2006). The role of Black fraternities in the African American male undergraduate experience. In M. J. Cuyjet (Ed.), *African American men in college* (pp. 129–153). San Francisco, CA: Jossey-Bass.

Harper, S. R., & Kuykendall, J. A. (2012). Institutional efforts to improve Black male student achievement: A standards-based approach. *Change, 44*(2), 23–29.

Harper, S. R., Davis, R. J., Jones, D. E., McGowan, B. L., Ingram, T. N., & Platt, C. S. (2011). Race and racism in the experiences of Black male resident assistants at predominantly White universities. *Journal of College Student Development, 52*(2), 180–200.

Harris, A. L. (2006). I (don't) hate school: Revisiting oppositional culture theory of Blacks' resistance to schooling." *Social Forces, 85*(2), 797–833.

Harris, A. L. (2011). *Kids don't want to fail: Oppositional culture and the Black-White achievement gap*. Cambridge, MA: Harvard University Press.

Harris, F., III, Palmer, R. T., & Struve, L. E. (2011). "Cool posing" on campus: A qualitative study of masculinities and gender expression among Black men at a private research institution. *Journal of Negro Education*, 80(1), 47–62.

Harris, P. C. (2014). The sports participation effect on educational attainment of Black males. *Education and Urban Society*, 46(5), 507–521.

Hausmann, L. R., Schofield, J. W., & Woods, R. L. (2007). Sense of belonging as a predictor of intention to persist among African American and White first-year college students. *Research in Higher Education*, 48(7), 803–839.

Herndon, M. K., & Hirt, J. B. (2004). Black students and their families: What leads to success in college? *Journal of Black Studies*, 34(4), 489–513.

hooks, b. (1994). *Teaching to transgress: Education as the practice of freedom*. Boston, MA: Routledge Kegan Paul.

hooks, b. (2004). *We real cool: Black men and masculinity*. New York, NY: Routledge.

Hotchkins, B. K. (2014). Guess who's coming to the meeting? African American student leadership experiences unpacked. *College Student Affairs Journal*, 32(1), 171–188.

Howard, T. (2003). "A tug of war for our minds": African American high school students' perceptions of their academic identities and college aspirations. *High School Journal*, 87(1), 4–17.

Howard, T. C. (2008). Who really cares? The disenfranchisement of African American males in PreK–12 schools: A Critical Race Theory perspective. *Teachers College Record*, 110(5), 954–985.

Howard, T. C. (2013). *Black male(d): Peril and promise in the education of African American males*. New York, NY: Teachers College Press.

Hunter, A., & Davis, J. (1992). Constructing gender: Afro-American men's conceptualization of manhood. *Gender & Society*, 6(2), 464–479.

Hunter, A., & Davis, J. E. (1994). Hidden voices of Black men: The meaning, structure, and complexity of manhood. *Journal of Black Studies*, 25(1), 20–40.

Jackson, B. A. (2012). Bonds of brotherhood: Emotional and social support among college Black men. *The Annals of the American Academy of Political and Social Science*, 642(1), 61–71.

Jackson, J. F. L., & Moore, J. L. III. (2006). African American males in education: Endangered or ignored? *Teachers College Record*, 108(2), 201–205.

Jackson, R. L. II. (2006). *Scripting the Black masculine body: Identity, discourse, and racial politics in popular media*. Albany, NY: SUNY Press.

James, M., & Lewis, C. W. (2014). Villains or virtuosos: An inquiry into Black-maleness. *Journal of African American Males in Education*, 5(2), 105–109.

Jenkins, T. S. (2006). Mr. Nigger: The challenges of educating Black males within American society. *Journal of Black Studies, 37*(1), 127–155.

Kozol, J. (2012). *Savage inequalities: Children in America's schools* (Reprint edition). New York, NY: Broadway Books.

Kuh, G. D., Cruce, T. M., Shoup, R., & Kinzie, J. (2008). Unmasking the effects of student engagement on first-year college grades and persistence. *Journal of Higher Education, 79*(5), 540–563.

Kuh, G., & Hu, S. (2001). The relationships between computer and information technology and information technology use, selected learning and personal development outcomes and other college experiences. *Journal of College Development, 42*(3), 217–231.

Kunjufu, J. (1995). *Countering the conspiracy to destroy Black boys.* Chicago, IL: African American Images.

Lacy, K. R. (2007). *Blue-chip Black: Race, class, and status in the new Black middle class.* Berkeley, CA: University of California Press.

Ladner, J. (1998). *The ties that bind: Timeless values for African American families.* Somerset, NJ: John Wiley & Sons.

Ladson-Billings, G. (1995). But that's just good teaching! The case for culturally relevant pedagogy. *Theory into Practice, 34*(3), 159–165.

Ladson-Billings, G. (2006). From the achievement gap to the education debt: Understanding achievement in U.S. schools. *Educational Researcher, 35*(7), 3–12.

Lareau, A., & Horvat, E. M. (1999). Moments of social inclusion and exclusion: Race, class, and cultural capital in family-school relationships. *Sociology of Education, 72*(2), 37–53.

Lewis-McCoy, R. L. (2014). *Inequality in the promise land: Race, resources, and suburban schooling.* Stanford, CA: Stanford University Press.

Lester, E. (2006). Black male rap session. In M. J. Cuyjet and Associates (Eds.), *African American men in college* (pp. 288–299). San Francisco, CA: Jossey-Bass.

Loewen, J. W. (2006). *Sundown towns: A hidden dimension of American racism.* Champaign, IL: University of Illinois Press.

Lorde, A. (2007). *Sister outsider: essays and speeches.* Berkeley, CA: Crossing Press.

Lynn, M. (1999). Toward a critical race pedagogy: A research note. *Urban Education, 33*(5), 606–626.

Majors, R., & Billson, M. (1992). *Cool pose: Dilemmas of Black manhood in America.* New York, NY: Simon & Schuster.

Maslow, A. H. (1943). A theory of human motivation. *Psychological Review, 50*, 370–396.

McCabe, J. (2009). Racial and gender microaggressions on a predominantly-White campus: Experiences of Black, Latina/o, and White undergraduates. *Race, Gender & Class, 16*(1–2), 133–151.

McClure, S. (2006). Improvising masculinity: African American fraternity membership in the construction of a Black masculinity. *Journal of African American Studies*, 10(1), 57–73.

McGee, E. O., & Martin, D. B. (2011). "You would not believe what I have to go through to prove my intellectual value!" Stereotype management among academically successful Black mathematics and engineering students. *American Educational Research Journal*, 48(6), 1347–1389.

Mincey, K., Alfonso, M., Hackney, A., & Luque, J. (2015). The influence of masculinity on coping in undergraduate Black men. *Journal of Men's Studies*, 23(3), 315–330.

Moore, J. L. III, Madison-Colmore, O., & Smith, D. M. (2003). The prove-them-wrong syndrome: Voices from unheard African-American males in engineering disciplines. *The Journal of Men's Studies*, 12(1), 61–73.

Muhammad, K. G. (2011). *The condemnation of Blackness: Race, crime, and the making of modern urban American.* Cambridge, MA: Harvard University Press.

Museus, S. (2008). The role of ethnic student organizations in fostering African American and Asian American students' cultural adjustment at predominantly White institutions. *Journal of College Student Development*, 49(6), 568–586.

Mutua, A. (2006). *Progressive Black masculinities.* New York, NY: Routledge.

Nagasawa, R. & Wong, P. (1999). A theory of minority students' survival in college. *Sociological Inquiry*, 69(1), 76–90.

Neal, M. A. (2013). *Looking for Leroy: Illegible Black masculinities.* New York, NY: New York University Press.

Ng, J., Wolf-Wendel, L., & Lombardi, K. (2014). Pathways from middle school to college: Examining the impact of an urban, precollege preparatory program. *Education and Urban Society*, 46(6), 672–698.

Noguera, P. A. (2003). The trouble with Black boys: The role and influence of environmental and cultural factors on the academic performance of African American males. *Urban Education*, 38(4), 431–459.

Noguera, P. A. (2008). *The trouble with Black boys: . . . And other reflections on race, equity, and the future of public education.* San Francisco, CA: Jossey-Bass.

Oliver, W. (2006). "The streets": An alternative Black male socialization institution. *Journal of Black Studies*, 36(6), 918–937.

Palmer, R. T., & Young E. M. (2009). Determined to succeed: Salient factors that foster academic success for academically unprepared Black males at a Black college. *Journal of College Student Retention*, 10(4), 465–482.

Palmer, R. T., Davis, R. J., & Hilton, A. A. (2009). Exploring challenges that threaten to impede the academic success of academically underprepared Black males at an HBCU. *Journal of College Student Development*, 50(4), 429–445.

Palmer, R. T., Moore, J. L. III, Davis, R. J., & Hilton, A. A. (2010). A nation at risk: Increasing college participation and persistence among African American males to stimulate U.S. global competitiveness. *Journal of African American Males in Education, 1*(2), 105–124.

Palmer, R. T., Wood, J. L., Dancy, T. E. II, & Strayhorn, T. L. (2014). *Black male collegians: Increasing access, retention, and persistence in higher education.* ASHE Higher Education Report.

Pascarella, E. T., & Terenzini, P. T. (1991). *How college affects students.* San Francisco, CA: Jossey-Bass.

Pascarella, E. T., & Terenzini, P. (2005). *How college affects students: A third decade of research.* San Francisco, CA: John Wiley & Sons.

Patton, L. D. (2006). Black culture centers: Still central to student learning. *About Campus, 11*(2), 2–8.

Patton, L. D. (2006). The voice of reason: A qualitative examination of Black student perceptions of their Black culture center. *Journal of College Student Development, 47*(6), 628–646.

Patton, L. D., & Bonner, F. A. (2001). Advising the historically Black Greek letter organization: A reason for angst or euphoria. *NASAP Journal, 4*(1), 17–29.

Picca, L. H., & Feagin, J. R. (2007). *Two-faced racism: Whites in the backstage and frontstage.* New York, NY: Routledge.

Pierce, C., Carew, J., Pierce-Gonzalez, D., & Willis, D. (1978). An experiment in racism: TV commercials. In C. Pierce (Ed.), *Television and education* (pp. 62–88). Beverly Hills, CA: Sage.

Polite, V. C., & Davis, J. E. (1999). *African American males in school and society: Practices and policies for effective education.* New York, NY: Teachers College Press.

Portes, A. (1998). Social capital: Its origin and applications in modern sociology. *Annual Review of Sociology, 24,* 1–24.

Portes, A. (2000). The two meanings of social capital. *Sociological Forum, 15*(1), 1–12.

Robertson, R. V., Bravo, A., & Chaney, C. (2014). Racism and the experiences of Latina/o college students at a PWI (predominantly White institution). *Critical Sociology, 1–24.* Published online September 30, DOI: 10.1177/0896920514532664.

Schmader, T., Major, B., & Gramzow, R. H. (2001). Coping with ethnic stereotypes in the academic domain: perceived injustice and psychological disengagement. *Journal of Social Issues, 57*(1), 93–111.

Sedlacek, W. E. (1999). Black students on White campuses: Twenty years of research. *Journal of College Student Development, 40*(5), 538–550.

Smith, S. S., & Moore, M. R. (2000). Intraracial diversity and relations among African-Americans: Closeness among Black students at a predominantly White university. *American Journal of Sociology, 106*(1), 1–39.

Smith, W. A. (2004). Black faculty coping with racial battle fatigue: The campus racial climate in a post-Civil Rights era. In D. Cleveland (Ed.), *A long way to go: Conversations about race by African American faculty and graduate students at predominantly White institutions* (pp. 171–190). New York, NY: Peter Lang.

Smith, W. A. (2010). Toward an understanding of Black misandric microaggressions and racial battle fatigue in historically White institutions. In E. M. Zamarni-Gallaer and V. C. Polite, (Eds.), *The state of the African American male in Michigan: A courageous conversation*, (pp. 265–277). East Lansing, MI: Michigan State University Press.

Smith, W. A., Allen, W. R., & Danley, L. L. (2007). "Assume the position . . . you fit the description": Psychosocial experiences and racial battle fatigue among African American male college students. *American Behavioral Scientist, 51*(4), 551–578.

Smith, W. A., Hung, M., & Franklin, J. D. (2011). Racial battle fatigue and the miseducation of Black men: Racial microaggressions, societal problems, and environmental stress. *The Journal of Negro Education, 80*(1), 63–82.

Smith, W. A., Yosso, T. J., & Solórzano, D. G. (2006). Challenging racial battle fatigue on historically White campuses: A critical race examination of race-related stress. In C. A. Stanley (Ed.), *Faculty of color teaching in predominantly White colleges and universities* (pp. 299–327). Bolton, MA: Anker.

Solórzano, D. & O. Villalpando. (1998). Critical Race Theory, marginality, and the experience of Minority students in higher education (pp. 211–224). In C. Torres & T. Mitchell (Eds.), *Emerging issues in the Sociology of Education: Comparative perspectives.* New York, NY: SUNY Press.

Solórzano, D. G., & Yosso, T. J. (2001). Critical race and LatCrit theory and method: Counterstorytelling Chicana and Chicano graduate school experiences. *International Journal of Qualitative Studies in Education, 14*(4), 471–495.

Solórzano, D. G., & Yosso, T. J. (2002). Critical race methodology: Counterstorytelling as an analytical framework for educational research. *Qualitative Inquiry, 8*(1), 23–44.

Solórzano, D., Ceja, M., & Yosso, T. (2000). Critical Race Theory, racial microaggressions, and campus racial climate: The experiences of African American college students. *The Journal of Negro Education, 69*(1/2), 60–73.

Stack, C. (1974). *All our kin: Strategies for survival in a Black community.* New York, NY: Harper & Row.

Stanton-Salazar, R. D. (2011). A social capital framework for the study of institutional agents and their role in the empowerment of low-status students and youth. *Youth & Society, 43*(3), 1066–1109.

Stanton-Salazar, R. D., & Dornbusch, S. M. (1995). Social capital and the social reproduction of inequality: The formation of informational networks among Mexican-origin high school students. *Sociology of Education, 68*(2), 116–135.

Staples, B. (1982). *Black masculinity: The Black males' role in American society*. San Francisco, CA: Black Scholar.

Staples, B. (1986). Black men and public space. *Harpers*, 12/86.

Steele, C. M. (1997). A threat in the air: How stereotype shape intellectual identity and performance. *American Psychologist, 52*(6), 613–629.

Steele, C. M. (1999, August 1). Thin ice: Stereotype threat and Black college students. *The Atlantic*. Retrieved from: http://www.theatlantic.com/magazine/archive/1999/08/thin-ice-stereotype-threat-and-black-college-students/304663/.

Strayhorn, T. L. (2008a). Fittin' in: Do diverse interactions with peers affect sense of belonging for Black men at predominantly White institutions?. *Journal of Student Affairs Research and Practice, 45*(4), 501–527.

Strayhorn, T. L. (2008b). The role of supportive relationships in facilitating African American males' success in college. *NASPA Journal, 45*(1), 26–48.

Strayhorn, T. L. (2012). *College students' sense of belonging: A key to educational success*. New York, NY: Routledge.

Strayhorn, T. L. (2014). What role does grit play in the academic success of Black male collegians at predominantly White institutions? *Journal of African American Studies, 18*(1), 1–10.

Strayhorn, T. L., & DeVita, J. M. (2010). African American males' student engagement: A comparison of good practices by institutional type. *Journal of African American Studies, 14*(1), 87–105.

Sue, D. W., Capodilupo, C. M., Torino, G. C., Bucceri, J. M., Holder, A. B., Nadal, K. L., & Esquilin, M. (2007). Racial microaggressions in everyday life: Implications for clinical practice, *American Psychologist, 62*(4), 271–286.

Tinto, V. (1993). *Leaving college: Rethinking the Causes and Cures of Student Attrition* (2nd ed.). Chicago, IL: University of Chicago Press.

Tinto, V. (1997). Classrooms as communities: Exploring the educational character of student persistence. *The Journal of Higher Education, 68*(6), 599–623.

Tinto, V. (1998). College as communities: Taking the research on student persistence seriously. *Review of Higher Education, 21*(2), 167–178.

Toldson, I. A. (2008). *Breaking barriers: Plotting the path to academic success for school-age African-American males*. Washington, DC: Congressional Black Caucus Foundation, Inc.

Toldson, I. A., Braithwaite, R. L., & Rentie, R. J. (2009). Promoting college aspirations among school-age Black American males. In H. T. Frierson, J. H. Wyche, & W. Pearson Jr. (Eds.), *Black American males in higher education: Research, programs and academe* (pp. 117–137). United Kingdom: Emerald Publishing.

Utsey, S. O., & Payne, Y. (2000). Psychological impacts of racism in a clinical versus normal sample of African American men. *Journal of African American Men, 5*(3), 57–72.

Venezia, A., & Jaeger, L. (2013). Transitions from high school to college. *Future of Children, 23*(1), 117–136.

Wagner, K. (2014, January 12). The word "thug" was uttered 625 times on TV on Monday. That's a lot. *Regressing.* Retrieved from http://regressing.deadspin.com/the-word-thug-was-uttered-625-times-on-tv-yesterday-1506098319.

Warde, B. (2008). Staying the course: Narratives of African American males who have completed a baccalaureate degree. *Journal of African American Studies, 12*(1), 59–72.

Weiss, R. (1994). *Learning from strangers: The art and method of qualitative interview studies.* New York, NY: The Free Press.

West, C. (1993). *Race matters.* Boston, MA: Beacon Press.

West, C., & Zimmerman, D. H. (1987). Doing gender. *Gender & Society, 1*(2), 125–151.

Whiting, G. W. (2006). From at risk to at promise: Developing scholar identities among Black males. *The Journal of Secondary Gifted Education, 17*(4), 222–229.

White House. (2014). *My Brother's Keeper Task Force report to the President.* The White House. Retrieved from https://www.whitehouse.gov/my-brothers-keeper#.

Wilkins, A. (2012). "Not out to start a revolution": Race, gender, and emotional restraint among Black university men. *Journal of Contemporary Ethnography, 41*(1), 34–65.

Wingfield, A. H. (2007). The modern mammy and the angry Black man: African American professionals' experiences with gendered racism in the workplace. *Race, Gender & Class, 14*(1/2), 196–212.

Wood, J. L., & Palmer, R. T. (2015). *Black men in higher education: A guide to ensuring student success.* New York, NY: Routledge.

Wood, J. L., & Williams, R. C. (2013). Persistence factors for Black males in the community college: An examination of background, academic, social, and environmental factors. *Spectrum: A Journal on Black Men, 1*(2), 1–28.

Woodland, M. H. (2008). Watcha' doin' after school? A review of the literature on the influence of after-school programs on young Black males. *Urban Education, 43*(5), 537–560.

Woodland, M. H., Martin, J. F., Hill, R. L., & Worrell, F. C. (2009). The most blessed room in the city: The influence of a youth development program on three young Black males. *The Journal of Negro Education, 78*(3), 233–245.

Woodson, C. G. (2011). *The mis-education of the Negro.* New York, NY: Tribeka Books. (Original work published 1933)

Yancy, G. (2013, September 1). Walking while Black in the "White gaze." *New York Times, Opinionator*. Retrieved from: http://opinionator.blogs.nytimes.com/2013/09/01/walking-while-black-in-the-white-gaze/?_r=0.

Yosso, T. J. (2005). Whose culture has capital? A critical race theory discussion of community cultural wealth. *Race Ethnicity and Education, 8*(1), 69–91.

Yosso, T. J., Smith, W. A., Ceja, C., & Solórzano, D. G. (2009). Critical Race Theory, racial microaggressions, and campus racial climate for Latina/o undergraduates. *Harvard Educational Review, 79*(4), 659–690.

Young, A. A., Jr. (1999). The (non) accumulation of capital: Explicating the relationship of structure and agency in the lives of poor Black men. *Sociological Theory, 17*(2), 201–227.

Young, A. A. (2004). *The minds of marginalized Black men: Making sense of mobility, opportunity, and future life chances.* Princeton, NJ: Princeton University Press.

Zaback, K., Carlson, A., & Crellin, M. (2012). *The economic benefit of postsecondary degrees: A state and national level analysis.* Boston, MA: State Higher Education Executive Officers Association.

Zell, M. (2011). I am my brother's keeper: The impact of a Brother2Brother program on African American men in college. *Journal of African American Males in Education, 2*(2), 214–233.

Index

100 Black Men of America, 6, 204n.

academic achievement, 16, 34, 38, 42, 161, 177, 190, 208n., 226n., 229n.
afterschool programs, 38, 208n., 209n.
American College Testing Program, 43
Anderson, Elijah, 18, 109, 116, 206n., 219n.
angry Black man, 103–104, 127–128, 224n.
Arizona State University, 6, 204n.
Arkansas African American Male Initiative, 6

Baldwin, James, 17–18
Baldridge, Bianca, 12, 38, 205n., 208–209n.
Bell, Derrick, 12–13, 15–16, 205n.
Blackmaleness, 15–16, 19, 52, 62–63, 90, 110, 115–116, 182–185, 191, 194–195, 206n.
Black Cultural Centers, 93, 211n., 215–216n., 229n.
Black Male Initiative (BMI), 5–8, 143–146, 188–193, 204n., 214n., 227n., 229n.
  academic impact, 75–77, 161–162
  college transition, 70–75

  cooperative support, 143–146, 195
  counter-space, 73–75, 143–144, 173–176
  learning environment, 158–161
  getting involved, 151–154
  sense of belonging, 70–72, 144–145, 162–164, 188
  supportive atmosphere, 156–168, 191–193, 198–199, 208
  positioning to matter for student success, 188–193
Black Male Scholar identity, 137–138, 142, 226n., 227n.
bonding, 70–72, 87, 145–146, 150, 154, 156, 166, 176–179, 186–187, 230–231n.
brotherhood, 145–146, 151, 165–167, 173, 178, 183, 187, 204n., 230–231n.
Brothers & Scholars, 8, 70–71, 198

campus climate, 116–118, 127–129, 129–138, 173, 185, 191–192, 205n.
  academic, 103–106
  Black male enrollment, 125–129
  hostilities, 91–95
  interpersonal relationships, 99–103
  racial battles, 102, 104–105, 106–111
  segregation on campus, 95–99

college aspirations, 27–37
  family connections, 32–34
  family support, 28–31
  self-improvement, 34–37
college concerns, 46–52
  academic, 37–41
  belonging, 49–52
  financial, 48–49
  stress, 59–60, 64–66
college life
  joys of, 78–81
  stress, 83–86
college preparation, 37–46
college transition, 56–66, 67–69,
  83–87, 126, 193–194
College Transition Program (CTP),
  70–72, 87
Collins, Patricia Hill, 15, 127, 206n.,
  219n., 224n.
community-based education, 38,
  208n.
cool pose, 123, 213
cooperative masculinity, *see*
  masculinity
coping strategies, 106, 130, 138–143,
  146–147, 173–175, 224n., 229n.,
  230n.
  BMI support, 143–146
  individual focus, 121–125
  focus and determination, 129–132
  prove them wrong, 133–138, 147,
    183–184, 225n.
  self-empowerment, 138–143
counter-spaces, 23, 73–75, 143–148,
  173–179, 187
counter-narratives, 9–11, 14, 221n.
counterstories, 11, 14, 120
Critical race theory, 12–15, 176,
  203n., 205–206n.
cultural capital, 42, 53–54, 70,
  73–76, 176, 210n., 214n.

cultural wealth, 41, 53, 163, 172,
  176, 229n.
Cuyjet, Michael, 2, 6, 11, 203n.,
  204n., 228n.

Dancy, T. Elon, 58, 61, 206n., 212n.,
  222n., 223n., 226n., 227n.
Davis, James Earl, 11, 16, 120, 212n.,
  221n., 223n.
deficit framing, 4–5, 11, 14, 37, 117,
  134, 144, 183–184, 209n., 221n.,
  231n.
Delgado, Richard, 13
determination, 39, 41, 64, 131–135,
  145, 186, 189, 191, 210n.
discrimination, 62, 92, 111–118
Du Bois, W. E. B., 12, 16–17, 136,
  206n., 226n.
  double consciousness, 16–17,
    136–138, 146, 206n., 212n.
  veil, 16–18, 136–137, 226n.

Education Testing Service, 26
Ellison, Ralph, 17–18, 219n., 221n.,
  224n., 225n., 226n.
emotional labor, 114, 128–130, 134,
  147

family and aspirations, 28
  family connections, 32–34
  family support, 28–31
Ferguson, Ann Arnette, 204n.
Fordham, Signithia, 5, 213n.

Griffin, Kimberly, 85, 210n.

Harper, Shaun, 10–11, 18, 188,
  204n., 211n., 218n., 221n.,
  226n., 231n.
Howard, Tyrone, 10–11, 208n., 210n.
hypervisibility, 18–19, 107–108, 110

identity work, 129, 136–138, 148
invisibility, 17–18, 107–111, 115–
    117, 121, 127, 138–139, 218n.,
    219n., 221n., 223–224n., 226n.
  invisibility syndrome, 18, 121,
    206n., 222n., 224n.
integration, 20, 227n.
  social integration, 20, 168–169,
    177–179, 188, 228–229n.
involvement (student), 20–21, 62, 64,
    77–83, 135–137, 143, 150, 214n.,
    215n., 227n., 228n., 229n.

Jackson College, 5

Kunjufu, Jawanza, 207n.

Lorde, Audre, 11–12

manhood, 16, 58–59, 124, 206n.,
    212n., 213n.
  expressiveness, 186, 206n.
  hegemonic, 213n.
  independence, 58–59, 185
  manhood constructs, 33–34, 46,
    58, 61, 182–183
  resilience, 131–132, 134–135
  responsibility, 28, 30, 59–60,
    140–143, 164–165, 185–186
  self-expectations, 58, 62–63, 124,
    142, 160, 223n., 226n., 227n.
  strength, 142–143
Martin, Trayvon, 114, 220n.
masculinity, 16, 46, 58, 88, 135, 143,
    184–185, 206n., 207n., 212n.,
    223n., 225n., 226n.
  bipolar, 109, 219n.
  cool pose (masculinity), 65,
    123–124, 213n., 222n.
  cooperative, 88, 121, 143–148,
    160, 165, 175–179, 187

hegemonic, 16, 61, 160, 186, 187,
    212n.
  masculine identity, 29, 46, 160
  scripts, 121, 123–124, 132, 143,
    147, 185–187, 222n.
Maslow, Abraham, 20–21
master status, 18, 108, 116–117,
    206n., 219n.
microaggression, 8–9, 19, 22, 62,
    105–107, 123–125, 147, 204–
    205n., 218n., 221n., 222n.
  Black misandry, 19–20, 102–108,
    117, 123
  racial, 8–9, 19, 106, 116, 204–
    205n., 206n., 217n., 219n.,
    221n.
Mighty Men Mentoring, 8, 70, 198
motivation, 215n., 230n.
  college aspirations, 34–37
  family, 27–29, 33–34, 45
  peer, 76–77, 170–172
  self-motivation, 40, 56–57, 125,
    141, 188–190, 210n.
Mutua, Athena, 15, 118

Neal, Mark Anthony, 207n.
Nigrescence model, 125, 223n.
Noguera, Pedro, 4, 204n., 209n.
non-cognitive skills, 41, 53, 125,
    131, 189–191

Ogbu, John, 5, 213n.
Ohio State University, 6, 80, 169,
    170
onlyness, 126, 144, 147, 231n.
oppositional behavior/culture, 5, 27,
    65, 208n., 213n.
otherize, 17, 102–103, 128–131,
    216n.

Parkland College, 5

peer pedagogy, 174, 231n.
personal development
    growth and maturity, 81–83
Prairie State College, 5
preparation for college, 37–46, 52–54
prove them wrong, *see* coping strategies

racial battle, 96, 102, 105, 108, 128,
    172–173, 175
    racial battle fatigue, 19–20,
    124–127, 204–205n., 217n.
racism, 12–13, 64, 94–95, 105, 106–
    118, 206n., 216n., 218n., 221n.,
    222n., 223n., 224n., 224–225n.,
    226n., 227n., 230n.
    gendered racism, 15, 115–116,
    216n., 217n., 219n.
    in local community, 111–115
    two-faced racism, 101, 217n.
resilience, 120–121, 124, 128, 152,
    178, 192–194, 218n.
    identity and resilience, 131–132,
    135–137, 143–148
Rutgers University, 6

self-improvement, 34–37
    self-awareness, 33–34, 45–46, 50,
    66, 82, 164–165
    self-determination, 140, 160, 210n.

sense of belonging, 3, 20–21, 47, 49,
    52–53, 56, 193–195, 228n.
social capital, 70, 73, 135, 176–177,
    189, 214n.
sociocultural capital, 70, 74, 186–
    187, 210n., 224n., 229n.
Staples, Robert, 100, 216n., 225n.
Stereotyping (of Black males), 18,
    106–111, 115–118, 139, 218n.,
    219n.
    stereotype management, 106, 218n.
Stack, Carol, 207n.
Strayhorn, Terrell L., 20–21, 49, 150,
    214n., 215n., 225–226n., 228n.
    33, 66, 184
Student African American Brother-
    hood, 6, 204n.
student-athlete, 40, 141
    athletic identity, 40, 48, 52, 210n.

UCLA, 6
University System of Georgia, 6

white gaze, 16, 114, 117, 142,
    220–221n., 225n.

Yancy, George, 114, 117, 220–221n.,
    225n.
Young, Alford, 10, 214n.